ADVANCE PRAISE FOR *THE JESUS CREED*

"This book is a rare treat. A biblical scholar of the first rank offers the fruit of his own personal study, life experience, and prayerful reflections. It is clearly written, eminently practical, and based on a wide range of sage traditions (Protestant, Catholic and Jewish). One does not have to agree with Scot McKnight in all the particulars to see that he has produced a work of real value. No doubt this book will draw many readers closer to Christ, and more deeply into the wisdom of God's Word."

—Scott Hahn, Ph.D., Professor of Scripture and Theology,
Franciscan University of Steubenville

"Spiritual formation is being discussed by Christians everywhere. Finally, someone asks what it meant to Jesus. *The Jesus Creed* explains it for everyone."

—Bill Hybels, Senior Pastor at Willow Creek Community Church

"Scot McKnight gives a compelling invitation to intentional spiritual growth, and presents a clear path to follow. *The Jesus Creed* is both informational and formational. It will lead individuals and groups into a deeper understanding of the heart of Jesus and the meaning of spiritual formation."

—Doreen L. Olson, Executive Minister, Dept. of Christian
Formation, Evangelical Covenant Church

"In a world of pop spirituality and quick fix, self-help guides, Scot McKnight's *The Jesus Creed* offers stimulating research and genuine insight into what the Gospels actually say about Jesus' call to spiritual growth. In addition, the guides that accompany each chapter will help both individuals and groups move beyond information to formation, beyond shallow reading to deep reflection on the Scriptures; in short, beyond half-hearted spiritual discipline to a more biblically oriented discipleship."

—George H. Guthrie, Benjamin Perry Professor of Bible,
Union University

LOVING GOD, LOVING OTHERS

The Jesus Creed

Scot McKnight

PARACLETE PRESS

BREWSTER, MASSACHUSETTS

February 2007   Sixth Printing
December 2005   Fifth Printing
June 2005   Fourth Printing
February 2005   Third Printing
October 2004   Second Printing
September 2004   First Printing

© 2004 by Scot McKnight

ISBN 978-1-55725-400-9

Quotations found on pages 213–217 are taken from *What's So Amazing About Grace?* by Philip D. Yancey. Copyright © 1997 by Philip D. Yancey. Used by permission of the Zondervan Corporation.

Quotations found on pages 260 and 286–288 are taken from *Sing Me to Heaven: The Story of a Marriage* by Margaret Kim Peterson. Copyright © 2003 by Margaret Kim Peterson. Used by permission of Brazos Press, a division of Baker Book House Company.

All Scripture quotations are taken from the *Holy Bible, New International Version. NIV.* © 1973, 1978, 1984 by International Bible society. Used by permission of Zondervan Publishing House. All rights reserved.

Library of Congress Cataloging-in-Publication Data
McKnight, Scot.
   The Jesus creed : loving God, loving others / Scot McKnight.
      p. cm.
   Includes bibliographical references.
   ISBN 1-55725-400-1 (trade paper)
   1. Love–Religious aspects–Christianity.   I. Title.
   BV4639.M39 2004
   241' .4–dc22   2004013729

10 9 8 7 6

Published by Paraclete Press
Brewster, Massachusetts
www.paracletepress.com

Printed in the United States of America.

FOR *Kris*

CONTENTS

PART THREE

The Society of the *Jesus Creed*
A spiritually formed person lives out kingdom values.

PART FOUR

Living the *Jesus Creed*
A spiritually formed person loves Jesus.

PART FIVE

Jesus and the *Jesus Creed*

A spiritually formed person participates in the life of Jesus.

My first exposure to the work of Scot McKnight came through my wife, Nancy. She breezed through the doorway one day and said, "I met a man at church who has a fabulous mind, you absolutely have to meet him." Whenever my wife becomes that interested in another man, it piques my curiosity, so I arranged to have lunch with him.

That first meeting led to a series of conversations and was the beginning of a relationship that continues to this day over a couple of thousand miles.

Scot has the kind of fertile mind that ranges from conversion theory to the debate over the search for the historical Jesus to Los Angeles Lakers coach Phil Jackson's triangle offense, in a single sitting. He relates well to people across every kind of spectrum. I suppose it's a backhanded compliment to refer to a scholar as a normal guy, but I can't think of a better term to describe Scot.

Most of all, Scot has a great love for Jesus, a passionate commitment to discover all that can be learned about Jesus' message and world. He combines this with a deep desire to help make the best of such learning accessible to people who will never earn a degree in Semitic languages or biblical archaeology.

When I was in seminary, David Hubbard (who was both president and Old Testament professor) talked about how the average seminary student today has access to more information than Luther or Calvin did at the height of their learning. The problem, of course, is that in this era of information overload we have more information than we can handle streaming into our consciousness every day, from junk mail to high-definition screens and fiberoptic cables. In this book we find no such informational overload, because Scot keeps his information in the proper perspective.

In *The Jesus Creed,* Scot has given a great gift to any follower of Jesus as he invites us back into the world in which Jesus lived. We learn, a step at a time, what it meant to be a Jewish rabbi in first-century Galilee. In these pages the identities, hopes, and struggles of Joseph and Mary, of John the Baptist, and of Simon Peter are portrayed in ways that are both fresh and deeply illuminating. Scot wears his learning lightly. We discover the significance of what it means to wrestle with being one of the *tsadiqim** or the *Am ha-aretz**—not simply for the sake of information, but because of the light it sheds on our own calling to follow Jesus. Scot, in the words of Garrison Keillor, "puts the hay down where the goats can get it."

I am excited for you as you begin your journey through the pages of this book. I believe two gaps will grow smaller for you as you read it. One is the distance between you and Jesus. His world will draw closer to yours. In discovering the actual identities and struggles of the people around Jesus, you will discover that you are reading your own story. You will find that little gestalt aha! escaping from your lips as time after time you come to understand the essential dynamics at work in the gospel narratives.

The other gap that will shrink is the one between the person you are right now and the person God created you to be. Dallas Willard has noted that all of us are constantly being spiritually formed for better or for worse—our wills and hearts are being shaped whether we want them to be or not. Jesus is, among other things, the maestro of spiritual formation. *The Jesus Creed* is both an invitation and a resource to put your spirit into his hands, to dine at the Master's table. Enough with the preliminaries: time to get on with the main course.

John Ortberg
Pastor, Menlo Park Presbyterian Church

I didn't confess a creed until I discovered Jesus' personal creed. Occasionally, of course, I'd find myself speaking at a church where we all confessed the Apostles' Creed or the Nicene Creed. Still, confessing a creed wasn't routine for me. Now I begin each day in a quiet recitation of the one used and taught by Jesus. When it comes to mind throughout the day, I recite it again. It is, for me, his gentle reminder of what life is all about.

All around the world, young and old, people are asking about spiritual formation. What does it mean, they are asking, to live before God in our world? For direction, they turn to modern writers as diverse as Thomas Merton and Richard Foster and Dallas Willard. As well, they turn to classical spiritual masters who have taught the church for the ages, masters like St. Augustine and Teresa of Avila and Brother Lawrence. I have turned to both the modern and classical myself, and I will turn to them again.

But sometimes we forget the source of these spiritual masters. Sometimes we forget to turn to the source of their ideas, to Jesus and to his words about what it means to be spiritually formed. I ask you to turn to him in this book, to discover his answer to the great question about the center of spiritual growth.

A Jewish expert on the *Torah** (the Law) once asked Jesus what was the most important thing for spiritual formation. Jesus' answer turned history upside down for those who followed him. This book is an invitation for you to explore Jesus' answer to that man. I call it the *Jesus Creed,* and what he said should shape everything we say about Christian spirituality. Everything.

Note for the reader: In the following text many words in italics are explained in the *Glossary of Terms* at the back of this book. (The first time these words appear in the text they are marked with an asterisk.) The sources for quotations, including references to the Bible, can be found in *References* at the back of the book. Each chapter can be understood without reading the Gospel passages listed at the beginning of the chapters, but it is recommended that each reading begin with those biblical passages.

PART ONE

The *Jesus Creed*

When asked by an expert in the law where to begin with spiritual
formation, Jesus answered by giving the *Jesus Creed*.
The *Jesus Creed* defines what spiritual formation is.

THE *JESUS CREED*
"Hear, O Israel, the Lord our God, the Lord is one.
Love the Lord your God with all your heart,
with all your soul,
with all your mind, and with all your strength."
The second is this: "Love your neighbor as yourself."
There is no commandment greater than these.

Jesus thereby amends the *Shema* of Judaism (Deuteronomy 6:4–9)
by adding Leviticus 19:18, revealing that spiritual formation is
about the love of God *and others.*

The first principle of spiritual formation is this:
A spirituallly formed person loves God and others.

In the next six chapters we will explore how
spiritual formation begins with loving God and loving others.
Spiritual formation is about relationship—with God and with others.

CHAPTER 1

The *Jesus Creed*

GOSPEL READINGS
Mark 12:28–33; Luke 9:57–62

Jesus knows what life is all about.

Thomas à Kempis knows: he wants to be in complete union with God. Brother Lawrence knows: he desires to converse with God constantly. John Woolman knows: he strives to do what was right in every situation. J. I. Packer knows: he longs to be fired with holy zeal for God. Richard Foster knows: he craves the grace of inner spiritual transformation through the spiritual disciplines. Dallas Willard knows: he hungers, in this physical existence of ours, to be like Christ. John Ortberg knows: he pines to morph into the image of Christ. Rick Warren knows: he thirsts for a life driven by God's purposes.

What makes these spiritual masters so attractive to us today is this: *They know what they mean when they discuss "spiritual formation."* They know what a spiritually formed person looks like, and they yearn to see it happen in each of their lives and in the lives of others. I learn from them on a daily basis, and so I am deeply aware that my attempts even to summarize their "aim" don't do them justice.

But behind these influential masters is Jesus, and he also knows.

So, the big questions are these: What does Jesus know (and say) about spiritual formation? What, according to Jesus, does a spiritually formed person look like? These questions are different than to ask which spiritual disciplines Jesus practices and teaches. These questions stand quietly behind the disciplines and ask: What are they for?

Did Jesus ever express his view of spiritual formation? Yes. And he does so by transforming a creed. I call it the *Jesus Creed* and the *Jesus Creed* becomes clear (on nearly every page of the four Gospels) when we recall the Jewish context of Jesus. So, we begin there (To highlight the importance of this creed for Jesus, I will refer to his amendment of the *Shema* as the *Jesus Creed* throughout the book.).

THE CREED OF JUDAISM

Daily, when awaking and when retiring, the observant Jew recites aloud a creed. This creed is lifted from the Bible, from one of the books of Moses, Deuteronomy 6:4–9, along with two other texts. (It is completely presented in the *Glossary of Terms* section at the end of the book.) This sacred Jewish creed is called the *Shema** (pronounced, Skē-mə or Sh'ma). Anyone who wants to understand what Jesus means by spiritual formation needs to meditate on the *Shema* of Judaism. It is the Jewish creed of spiritual formation, and Jesus liked it and, as we will see, transformed it for his followers:

> Hear *(shema)*, O Israel: The Lord our God, the Lord is one. Love the LORD your God with all your heart and with all your soul and

with all your strength. These commandments that I give you today are to be upon your hearts. Impress them on your children. Talk about them when you sit at home and when you walk along the road, when you lie down and when you get up. Tie them as symbols on your hands and bind them on your foreheads. Write them on the doorframes of your houses and on your gates.

According to a specialist of modern Jewish devotion, the *Shema* "is the first 'prayer' that [Jewish] children are taught to say," and it is the "quintessential expression of the most fundamental belief and commitment of Judaism."[1]

The *Shema* expresses what is most important for spiritual formation: *YHWH** (the sacred Hebrew name for God) alone is Israel's God, Israel is chosen by God, and Israel is to love God—with heart, soul, and strength. The *Shema* outlines a *Torah** lifestyle for spiritual formation: memorize, recite, instruct, and write out the *Torah*, and wear *tzitzit* (fringes) to remind themselves of *Torah*. There is promise attached to living life according to the *Shema*: when Jews lived by the *Shema* they would be "blessed" beyond imagination.

One can say, then, that the creed of Judaism is this: Love God by living the *Torah*. So where does Jesus stand in a world of Judaism that affirms a *Shema* of loving God by living the *Torah*?

---

1 All references and notes can be found at the back of the book. Many of the *italicized* words (these words are marked with an asterisk the first time they appear in the text) have an entry in the *Glossary of Terms* at the back of the book.

THE *JESUS CREED* AS THE FIRST AMENDMENT

As a good Jew, Jesus devotionally recites the *Shema* daily. Later in his life, he encounters an expert in the law who asks him, "Of all the commandments, which is the most important?" For a Jew this man's question is the ultimate question about spiritual formation. He is asking for the spiritual center of Judaism. He thinks Jesus might know. He does.

Jesus answers the man by reciting the *Shema* but adds to it, and in so doing, transforms a creed so he can shape the spiritual center of his followers. I call it the *Jesus Creed*.

THE *JESUS CREED*

"Hear, O Israel, the Lord our God, the Lord is one.
Love the Lord your God with all your heart, with all your soul,
with all your mind, and with all your strength." [So far, so good;
this is Deuteronomy. 6:4-5.]
[And now Jesus adds a verse from Leviticus. 19:18.]
The second is this: "Love your neighbor as yourself."
There is no commandment greater than these.

Right here we discover the *Jesus Creed* for spiritual formation. As Thomas à Kempis puts it, in the *Jesus Creed* Jesus has "put a whole dictionary into just one dictum." Everything about spiritual formation for Jesus is shaped by his version of the *Shema*. For Jesus, love of God and love of others is the core. Love, a term almost indefinable, is unconditional regard for a person that prompts and shapes behaviors in order to help that person to become what God desires. Love, when working properly, is both emotion and will, affection and action.

We cannot overemphasize the importance of the *Shema* for Jewish spiritual formation. So when Jesus amended the *Shema,* we need to take note. To be sure, Jesus accepted the *Shema,* but he also added to it. The question we then ask is this: Is Jesus suggesting only a subtle amendment? No. It takes real pluck (or chutzpah) to add to the sacred *Shema,* but this addition reveals the heart of the *Jesus Creed.*

Most of my readers will know the Apostles' Creed and will know if I were to add a few lines after "and life everlasting"—such as, "and in supporting your local church by giving a tithe of income, before taxes!"—that even in a civilized church I would get sucker-punched. "You don't mess with creeds, sugar," the attendant would say to me in the ambulance as she carted me away.

But, adding is just exactly what Jesus does. Instead of a Love-God *Shema,* it is a Love-God-and-Others *Shema.* What Jesus adds is not unknown to Judaism, and he is not criticizing Judaism. Jesus is setting up his very own shop within Judaism. Loving others is central to Judaism, but it is not central to the creed of Judaism, to the *Shema.* So, what Jesus says is Jewish. But the emphasis on loving others is not found in Judaism's creed the way it is found in the *Jesus Creed.* Making the love of others part of his own version of the *Shema* shows that he sees love of others as central to spiritual formation.

It is not enough just to observe that Jesus amends the *Shema* of Judaism. There is more here than first meets the eye. When the *Shema* becomes the *Jesus Creed,* it becomes personal. To see this we need to look at the Gospel of Luke to see how Jesus explains what it means to love God, because for Jesus loving God now means following him.

THE *SHEMA* GETS PERSONAL IN THE *JESUS CREED*

Jesus regularly invites others to join his small band of disciples. When one man hears about this, he volunteers to join and, in so doing, he thinks he will love God more deeply. The man comes to Jesus with a simple request, "Lord," I want to love God and follow you, but "first let me go and bury my father." Jesus abruptly states: "Let the dead bury their own dead." Ouch! All this man is asking for is an opportunity, with perhaps a little delay, but still an opportunity to love God with all his heart. Jesus, however, is redefining what it means to love God.

Surely, it is a stretch to understand Jesus' telling a man not to attend his father's funeral. So important is it in Judaism to bury one's father, an exception is made: "One whose dead is lying before him [awaiting burial] is exempt from the recitation of the *Shema*." Even the sacred *Shema* is suspended to bury one's father. Still, how could Jesus ask a man to skip his father's funeral? A little understanding of burial customs sheds light on how the *Jesus Creed* worked itself out in real life. These customs show how loving God becomes personal for Jesus.

At the time of Jesus, burials took place in two stages. First, immediately after the death of a father, the family (led by the oldest son) placed the body in a casket and then into a tomb so the body could decompose. The family sat *shiva** (mourned) for seven days. The body decayed for approximately one year in the tomb. Then, second, the bones were removed from the tomb and casket, placed in an *ossuary* (a box for bones), and then reburied, this time for good. This is how good Jews showed respect for a father, how they applied the commandment to honor one's parents, how they loved God by following the *Torah.*

Many today think the proper context of Jesus' encounter with this man is between the first burial and the second burial. To begin with, it is unlikely that a family member sitting *shiva** (after first burial) would be out and about anyway, and it is hard to imagine Jesus' refusing this most sacred obligation. *If* the encounter with Jesus occurs between the first and second burial, then as much as a year's lag could occur before he would begin to follow Jesus.

The man is caught in the dilemma that the *Jesus Creed* creates: Should he follow Jesus or should he follow (how he understands) the *Torah?* Jesus calls the man to follow him and, *in so doing, equates loving God to having a personal relationship with Jesus.* To use other terms, the *Shema* of Judaism becomes the *Jesus Creed: One loves God by following Jesus.* This is a revolutionary understanding of the *Shema,* and it is what the spiritual life is all about for Jesus.

Let's put this all together now: As a normal Jew, spiritual formation for Jesus begins with the *Shema* of Judaism. But Jesus revises the *Shema* in two ways: loving others is added to loving God, and loving God is understood as following Jesus.

This is the *Jesus Creed,* and it is the foundation of everything Jesus teaches about spiritual formation. Jesus, too, knows what life is all about, and that life is about love—for God and for others. As Rick Warren states, "Life minus love equals zero." And: "The best use of life is love. The best expression of love is time. The best time to love is now."

It is also time to put that love into practice by learning the *Jesus Creed.*

THE *JESUS CREED* TODAY

After teaching about Jesus for twenty years, I have come to the conviction that the most historically accurate way of presenting what Jesus teaches about spiritual formation is the *Jesus Creed*. Jesus learned to recite the *Shema* as a child, and his own followers, as Jews, would have recited it as a matter of course. I have every reason to believe that his followers would have continued this practice after they met Jesus, but they would have recited it in a slightly amended form: they would have recited a "love God and love others" creed, what I call the *Jesus Creed*.

Put in its simplest form, Jesus gave to his followers a creed in order to shape their spiritual formation. That creed has been given to us as well.

It is my recommendation that each of us, in an experiment of ordering our lives around the spiritual-formation principle of Jesus, memorize and then repeat the *Jesus Creed* daily—to remind ourselves of what our Lord asks of us. The *Jesus Creed* has become a silent partner in my life: Sometimes when I sit, sometimes when I walk, sometimes when I lie down, but always when I rise in the morning, I simply and quietly recite to myself, and before God, the *Jesus Creed*.

It punctuates my morning; it sets a rhythm to my day and settles my day into a comfortable spot. It constantly reminds me, not as a command but as a confession, that whatever I do throughout the day is to be shaped by loving God and loving others. I need that reminder.

Whatever our vocations, spiritual formation, for Jesus, begins with the *Jesus Creed*. Jesus calls each of us to offer our vocations to him so that we might, in the words of Parker Palmer, "let our life speak." What you become and what I become will be different, but it will be the life we have been given to speak to others—and that life is to be shaped by the *Jesus Creed.*

A scribe asks Jesus about the essence of spiritual formation, and Jesus gives him an old answer with a revolutionary twist: Love God *and* love others, and love God by following me. The scribe realizes that he will need to recenter everything.

CHAPTER 2

Praying the *Jesus Creed*

GOSPEL READINGS
Luke 11:1–4; Matthew 6:9–13

Sometimes prayer is like dry lima beans in a dry mouth on a dry day.

Other times, in the words of Richard Foster, prayer "catapults us onto the frontier of the spiritual life" and "is the central avenue God uses to transform us." Maybe so, but it doesn't always feel that way. In fact, each year scads of new strategies and routines become available so we can get more from our prayer lives.

Why? Prayer is hard, it gnaws into our schedule, and it can be as much a source of frustration as satisfaction. Brother Lawrence, who has probably encouraged more people in prayer than anyone in the history of the Church, found routines in prayer dry and dull. He was bluntly honest about his own perplexity with prayer. Such honesty about prayer by a champion of prayer encourages us all in our own struggle to pray.

At the bottom, prayer is simple. It is *loving communication with God*. All we need for prayer is an open heart. But this doesn't mean there aren't prayer sessions that drag, times when our lips are uttering graceful words while our minds are murmuring clumsy thoughts. "Struggle" is the true news about prayer.

The good news for us is that it was struggle with prayer that gave rise to the Lord's Prayer. The disciples were struggling with their own prayer lives. After observing Jesus pray, one of his disciples said, "Lord, teach us to pray." To help them with prayer, he gave them a prayer; Christians call it the "Our Father" or the "Lord's Prayer."

When the disciples heard Jesus give this to them the first time, they recognized it—but there was something different. To see this, we need to look at that ancient Jewish prayer and then observe how Jesus amended it in light of the *Jesus Creed.*

THE *KADDISH* OF JUDAISM AND THE *KADDISH* OF JESUS

At the time of Jesus there was a Jewish prayer called the *Kaddish* ("The Sanctification"):

> Magnified and sanctified be his great name in the world He created according to His will.
> May He establish His kingdom during your life and during your days, and during the life of all the house of Israel, speedily and in the near future.
> And say Amen.

This liturgical prayer, with some striking similarities to the Lord's Prayer, is one of Jesus' favorite prayers. So favorite he makes it his own.

When the disciples ask Jesus for a prayer, he takes this *Kaddish* and amends it.

The *Kaddish* of Judaism	The *Kaddish* of Jesus (Lord's Prayer)
	Father
Name magnified and sanctified	Name sanctified [not *magnified*]
Kingdom established soon	Kingdom established [not *soon*]
	Bread
	Forgiveness
	Temptation
Amen	[no *Amen*, no big deal, they said it anyway]

We observed earlier that Jesus amended the *Shema* of Judaism to form his own *Shema*. Now Jesus revises a sacred prayer. If what Jesus does to the *Shema* is the "first amendment," what he does to the *Kaddish* is the "second amendment."

There are three basic changes: First, the Lord's Prayer begins with "Father" (*Abba**). Second, Jesus adds three lines (italics above). Third, the additional lines shift from "your" to "us." As a result of these changes, the Lord's Prayer has two parts: the "You" petitions and the "We/Us" petitions.

You petitions	We/Us petitions
May *your* Name be hallowed	Give *us* our daily bread
May *your* kingdom come	Forgive *us* our sins as we for give those . . .
May *your* will be done on earth . . .	Lead *us* not into temptation but deliver . . .

Why amend a sacred prayer? Recall that Jesus amends the sacred love God-only *Shema* to a (just as sacred) love God-*and-others Shema*. Something similar happens to the *Kaddish*. In the *Kaddish* of Judaism there is a concern for God, but in the *Kaddish* of Jesus there is a concern *both* for God *and* for others. So, we have this:

Shema of Judaism:	Love God (by following *Torah*)	
Shema of Jesus:	Love God (by following *Jesus*)	*and love others.*
Kaddish of Judaism:	Petition for God's glory	
Kaddish of Jesus:	Petition for *Abba's* glory	*and petition for others*

These last few paragraphs show us that the Lord's Prayer has two sections: one on love of God and one on love of others. The proof of one's theology is in prayer. Jesus' creed of loving God and loving others (the *Jesus Creed*) morphs into a prayer of love of God and love of others (the Lord's Prayer). Thus:

Love-of-God petitions	Love-of-others petitions
May *your* Name be hallowed	Give *us* our daily bread
May *your* kingdom come	Forgive *us* our sins as we . . .
May *your* will be done on earth . . .	Lead *us* not into temptation but . . .

THE LORD'S PRAYER AS A GIFT FOR LITURGY

When the disciples asked Jesus for a prayer, he said "When you pray, *say*." Literally, "say" means "repeat." Some Christians (including me) are wary of liturgical prayers because they may turn into mindless, heartless repetition, to mere rote memory, and to external ritual.

But surely Jesus was aware of these problems when he gave this prayer to his disciples. From experience in his Jewish world (where liturgical prayers had a long history), Jesus knows that his liturgical prayer will *provide a framework* for prayer, some hooks on which his disciples can hang their own praises and requests, their own complaints and queries. Also, the Lord's Prayer provides for each of us a *structured conversation with God*. Dallas Willard relates how using the Lord's Prayer as a framework strengthened his prayer life and how he began to "live" in the prayer.

Jesus also knows this prayer will *remind his followers of his priorities*—priorities like God's Name, kingdom and will, priorities physical, spiritual, and moral. As Richard Foster puts it, "In prayer, real prayer, we begin to think God's thoughts after Him: to desire the things He desires, to love the things He loves." As Thomas à Kempis puts it: "O Lord, You know what's good and bad, what's better and worse, what's best and worst—may my prayer be as You wish it to be."

Jesus also knows that his own prayer will prevent his disciples from *lapsing into self-saturated prayers*. Lauren Winner, a convert from liturgical Judaism to liturgical Christianity, observes: "Liturgy is not, in the end, open to our emotional whims." And Jesus knows that giving them this prayer gift will *establish a new tradition* to inform and inspire all his followers—world without end.

There you have it, a brief defense of the personal, liturgical use of the Lord's Prayer. Again, Richard Foster tells how one of the most liberating experiences of his life was when he learned to pray "so that my experience conformed to the words of Jesus rather than trying to make his words conform to my impoverished experience."

Two years ago, as a result of pondering the Lord's Prayer, I became convinced of its centrality for understanding Jesus. The Lord impressed upon me that if I thought this way, I needed to make it more real in my teaching. Now, when each of my Jesus classes is over, we all recite the Lord's Prayer. I am daily amazed at the truth of what Tertullian, an early Christian leader, observed: "In the [Lord's] Prayer is comprised an epitome [summary] of the whole Gospel." (Not only do we end each class with the Lord's Prayer, but we begin each class by reciting the *Jesus Creed*.)

The Lord's Prayer is a gift to guide our prayers, and when we use the Lord's Prayer to nurture our prayers, we rub the oil of the *Jesus Creed* into the chambers of our heart. We learn at least four things when we permit the Lord's Prayer to mentor our prayer life.

We learn to approach God as Abba

The first distinctive feature of the Lord's Prayer is its emphasis on addressing God as *Abba*. We begin right here: confident, eye-to-eye love with our *Abba*. To love God means, in prayer, to call him *Abba*. This is the signature term of Jesus, and it marks the center of his teaching about God.

We learn what God really wants

If we love someone, we love what they love. God's love plan is for his glorious Name to be honored and his will to become concrete reality on earth. Earth is *Abba*'s frontier; heaven is already his. In pondering God's Name, kingdom and will, we are prompted (daily) to *yearn* for what God yearns for. Love always prompts yearning.

When our daughter, Laura, first went off to school, we noticed that she loved her teachers and yearned to become a teacher. As parents, we joined in her yearning to teach, which she was already "doing." In her first year of school, in Nottingham (England), she came home from class, wrapped her chair and herself behind the long curtains of our living room, and taught her class behind the curtains. When we moved back to the United States, our attic became a classroom with a desk, chalkboard, table, and bookshelf. When she went off to college, her little classroom went silent, but it was no surprise to us when, in her senior year of college, she returned to sort through her things for a "real" classroom.

Weekends at home meant endless conversations with her about how to draw up a résumé, how to write a cover letter, which schools to contact and which references to include. Her life was prompted by her love: a yearning to teach. We were all grateful when the opportunity came; she signed the contract, and (now five years later) she loves what she yearned to be: a teacher.

How do we learn to yearn for what Jesus taught? The wisdom of our fathers teaches us to use the Lord's Prayer as a framework for how our love for God is to be expressed in prayer. Each day we can repeat the Lord's Prayer and "hang our own words" on its hooks. We repeat "Hallowed be your name," and we ponder it; then we repeat "your kingdom come," and we do the same; and then the same for "your will be done on earth as it is in heaven." The prayer provides structure; its content is rock solid; it helps us avoid selfishness; and these simple words quietly create a little miracle of transformation.

We learn to think of others

The most conspicuous amendment to the *Kaddish*? Petitions about others. As Jesus didn't leave the *Shema* to be a God-only thing, so he didn't leave the *Kaddish* to be a God-only thing. And he doesn't want it to be an I-only thing either. If we learn to hang our prayers on the framework of the Lord's Prayer, we will learn to pray for others. We do this, not to observe a routine, but because this is what happens to love for others when it morphs into prayer.

We learn what everyone needs

Hanging our prayers on the framework of the Lord's Prayer will lead us to yearn that all will have provision, be granted forgiveness, and be spared temptation. What do these mean? We need to think our way back into Jesus' world by recalling that we have just petitioned the *Abba* about his Name, kingdom, and will. Our concern is with God's breaking into history to make this world right *for all of us*. And that means praying for others so that they will have adequate provisions, spiritual purity*, and moral stability.

I don't know about you, but I tend to begin my prayers for others with what I know about them and what they need. Jesus offers another path: We can begin with what he wants for them. By using the Lord's Prayer, we join his loving prayer for them.

THE LORD'S PRAYER AS
GIFT FOR ACTION

Prayer does not stop with the "Amen." It rises to its feet and walks off, with our built-up yearning turned into action. For years I have taught that the Lord's Prayer is a commitment of the pray-er to the values of the Lord's Prayer, but no one has said this better than Frank Laubach:

> It [the Lord's Prayer] is the prayer most used and least under-stood. People think they are asking God for something. They are not—they are offering God something.
>
> . . . the Lord's Prayer is not a prayer to God to do something we want done. It is more nearly God's prayer to us, to help Him do what He wants done. . . . He wanted that entire prayer answered before we prayed it. . . . The Lord's Prayer is not intercession. It is enlistment.

Again, the Lord's Prayer is what happens to the *Jesus Creed* when it turns into prayer. But it is the *Jesus Creed* ultimately that is the design of God for our lives. We are made to love God by following Jesus and to love others.

Mike Breaux, formerly pastor at Southland Christian Church in Lexington, Kentucky, realized that Jesus' words in Luke 14:13-14 about inviting the poor and the disabled to banquets were intended to be practiced as well as prayed. High school proms are the extravagant event of the year where students divide up into social classes, display privilege, and dance the night into their dreams. Mike noticed that the disabled students in the community found the traditional prom to be disprivileging and nightmarish.

Acting on what the Bible says about loving others enough to do something about it, he and his team devised what they call the "Jesus Prom: Night of the Stars." If Jesus invited all to his table, so the church could and would—to the tune of about 500 disabled (and not just disabled) promgoers! Donors in the church provided tuxes and dresses and limousine services, as well as a lavish banquet and the dance. These kids might not be graceful dancers or have the quickest feet, but the joy on their faces when they experienced the Jesus Prom thrilled the hearts of Southland Christian Church and brought a little of the kingdom to Lexington.

What Breaux and his team did is exactly what Jesus meant when he amended the *Kaddish* in light of the *Jesus Creed*. Pray for what your *Abba* wants; pray for what others need; and when done praying, live out the *Jesus Creed*.

CHAPTER 3

The *Abba* of the *Jesus Creed*

GOSPEL READINGS
Matthew 6:9–15; Luke 15:11–32

As a nine-year-old I took up the game of golf, much to my mother's delight. At a minimum, she reasoned, my hyperactivity would vanish from the house for five hours—or, with any luck at all, for six or seven hours. My father's joy, so I think now, was a response to my mother's relief.

My father golfed only occasionally, but one time he told me this golfing truth: "If you hit the ball straight, you will have better scores." The problem with truths, of course, is *absorbing them* into the core of our being so that they can shape our lives. Even today, when traipsing through weeds off the fairway or poking my club into some pond to retrieve a ball, I recall that little golfing truth my father told me. He was, and is, right.

The most important divine truth ever given is far truer and even more difficult for us to absorb than a simple golfing truth. From Moses to Malachi and from Jesus to John, the Bible witnesses to this elemental truth: *God loves us*. He loves you, and he loves me— as individuals. This big truth needs to be absorbed into our beings.

God's love is an easy creed to confess but difficult to absorb.

The *Jesus Creed* works like this: Because God loves us, because he knows what is best for us and wants what is best for us, he invites us to find that "what is best" by loving him back. When this happens, the windows are thrown open to the breezes of his healing love. If the content of the *Jesus Creed* is loving God and loving others, the premise of the *Jesus Creed* is that God loves us. That love is expressed in the Lord's Prayer, the distinctive prayer of Jesus that begins with a name for God. When uttered by humans, this name opens the window to God's very loving presence.

A B B A , FATHER

The Lord's Prayer begins with "*Abba*, Father." Jesus is decidedly lopsided when it comes to names for God: *every prayer* of Jesus recorded in the Gospels begins with "*Abba*, Father" except the famous "My God, my God, why have you forsaken me?" utterance from the cross. Jesus' contemporaries had plenty of "names" for God—the most notable of which (*YHWH*) was never pronounced. Other names were used, like Lord and God and God Almighty. Rarely did they address God as "Father" in prayer.

So why does Jesus focus so narrowly on *Abba* as the name for God? God may be *YHWH,* but that sacred name evokes mystery; *YHWH* may be King, but that term evokes distance. From a long list of names, Jesus chooses *Abba*. What Jesus wants to evoke with the name *Abba* is God's unconditional, unlimited, and unwavering love for his people. In this name for God we are standing face-to-face with the very premise of spiritual formation: God loves us and we are his children.

In *Abba* Jesus chooses a term from home because love originates in the home where an *Abba* dwells. Not only does love begin there, but our first understandings of God begin at home and are *transfers* from both parents to God. We are wired this way. This is not something we do rationally and intentionally. It is something we do instinctually.

Grant me this point, and I'll give you one back: since none of us has perfect parents, none of us has a perfect sense of love to transfer to God. In fact, some of us—and I say this with the empathy of someone who has heard students' stories for two decades—had awful childhoods, and just thinking about God's love is confusing, bewildering, and nearly incomprehensible.

Some of our heart openings are rusted shut because of the way our parents loved (or didn't love) us. Those of us with this past need the reeducation of our hearts and a new vision of the beauty of God's love taught by Jesus. What we need is the oil of *Abba*'s love to penetrate through our rusty heart openings, as it did to the heart of Wesley Nelson.

Wesley was an emotional, sensitive child, and a self-confessed crybaby. When family members teased him in good fun, it wounded him. He describes the crucial moment.

> One day we were out in front of our farmhouse when I suddenly realized that my mother had left. She probably just went into the house, but as soon as I missed her I began, as usual, to scream for her. My father had grown weary of this endless crying and had begun to chide me for it. This time he said, "Mother is gone. She's tired of your yelling. She's left for good. She'll never come back." With that, of course, I only screamed louder. . . . I am sure that my mind would have told me that it was not true, but all I

could do was feel the weight of his words and the yearning for
my mother.

At the simplest of physical levels, of course, he did find her.
But hear these life-shaping words of his:

> The fact is that my mother did not come back to me. I am sure
> that she must have come back and taken me in her arms and com-
> forted me as she always had done before, but that act was blot-
> ted from my memory. What my father had said made such an
> impression on me that *I had to make it come true.* I know, of
> course, that she continued to care for me, *but for me the emo-
> tional ties were broken, and her love and care were no longer
> even a memory to me.* . . . For fifty years I cried for her.

This story takes a psychologist to unravel, but this much I can
understand: Wesley's perception of God as a loving *Abba* was
distorted by some cruel words from his father and some insensitive
moments from his mother. It would take fifty years of heart work
for Wesley to come to terms with *Abba*'s love for him. This is what
I mean when I say that God's love for us originates in our homes
with our mothers and our fathers. If being spiritually formed means
we are to love God, that formation can begin only if we are open to
receive *Abba*'s unconditional love for us.

To compensate for his emotional pain, Wesley Nelson transferred
his love to the unwavering consistency of machines and science
and rational formulas. Internally, he rusted shut. Time with the
gospel of *Abba's* love, however, worked like a solvent and shifted
his trust from love of machines to love of God, and then to love of
others.

Fifty years later, Wesley records the day when God's gracious solvent penetrated into his heart to release God's love:

> One warm afternoon . . . I drove to the top of the Berkeley hills, to a spot overlooking the Golden Gate. I sat on the ground and read awhile; and then I just sat and meditated. Suddenly it was as though I heard a voice saying, "I love you."
>
> . . . What made this moment unique was that it was the God of steadfast love himself who was inviting me to apprehend the gospel. . . . Relaxed and released, I drove home, just in time for the evening meal. As we sat chatting together around the table, Margaret [his wife] said, "It's nice to have you home again."

Wesley Nelson's life was never the same again: The solvent of *Abba's* love dissolved the rust clogging his heart. As he says it, "The difference was that I had for once really heard with my soul the word that God loved me just as I was, with all my anxieties, defeats, frustrations, and problems."

God's love is the premise of the *Jesus Creed*, and there is no better place to see this premise than in the oft-told Parable of the Prodigal Son.

ABBA WELCOMES A SON BACK HOME

If the center of Jesus' heart is the *Jesus Creed,* and the Lord's Prayer is what the *Jesus Creed* looks like in prayer, the Parable of the Prodigal Son is what the *Jesus Creed* looks like as a story. Jesus is surrounded by a crowd, and accusations are being made about his association with sinners with a sort of "What on earth is he up to now?" air hanging over everyone's heads. So, Jesus tells a story and tells his audience what God is up to on earth—and what he is up to is surprising.

A father has two sons, and the younger one wants his share of the estate early so he can venture off into a remote corner of the Roman Empire to goof off. Surprisingly, the father grants him his wish and cashes in some property, and the son abandons the Holy Land to waste the cash in wild living. The kid, bless his heart, runs out of money and works for a Gentile pig farmer (not your typical Jewish vocation). Reduced to yearning for pig slop, he comes to his senses and returns home. He confesses his selfish sinfulness for taking his father's money and for disgracing his father's name. Surprisingly, this *Abba* blows *Torah*-honoring social gaskets by throwing a party for the filthy son. To complete the picture, Jesus also tells of a not-all-that-surprising older son who pouts at his *Abba*'s love for his brother and who (again not surprisingly) pleads for special attention because of his own traditional good behavior.

Remember, Jesus is surrounded and is being asked why he eats with sinners. Jesus tells this story to justify his behavior. He justifies *his love for others* (the second part of the *Jesus Creed*) by appealing to an *Abba* who is the focus of the parable. And when we look at this parable carefully, we see that this *Abba* is surprisingly loving and gracious.

Another surprising feature of this parable is that the *Abba* is the first to notice his son's return. Some Bible scholars observe a Jewish custom between the lines: when a son disgraces his father through sinful behaviors, runs away from him, and then later returns, the elders of the city take the young man to the village center and break a pot at his feet. The broken pot is a legal act of banishment. These scholars also think, in this parable, the *Abba* runs to his son so that he can prevent the really awful event he fears: others banning him from the community if they reach him first. So, the *Abba* sprints to the son and announces, "Quick! Bring the best robe."

The parable also tells us that the *Abba* celebrates reunion with his children. No public rebuke here when the son returns, and no need to drag the kid through the mud in front of everyone. His son's return was clear proof of a softened heart. The *Abba* who justifies Jesus' eating with sinners throws a party for his repentant children and grants them the clothing of elevated acceptance: they wear *his* robe, *his* ring, and *his* sandals. They roast the best calf and celebrate! This, Jesus says, is why I eat with sinners: I'm like the *Abba* who celebrates reunions with returning sons.

The premise of the *Jesus Creed* is that God loves us. And that premise is all found in the term *Abba*.

ABSORBING THE TRUTH

Even better, the premise that God loves us is also a promise. God takes the first step toward us. It all begins with his gracious love for us, regardless of who we are and what we have done. He promises this much: he will love us.

Jesus gives to each of us the name *Abba* to remind us daily, as we pray the Lord's Prayer, that God loves us. But this truth is hard to absorb, partly because our wiring has been distorted by wounds in our pasts. So what can we do to absorb the truth of his love more completely? What can we do to make a living reality of what Jesus meant when he said his creed was to *love* God?

Knowing God's love begins when we *open our hearts to Abba's love*. Opening here is a metaphor for vulnerability to God in the quiet of our hearts; it is trusting God's love the way we relax on a doctor's table, knowing he or she can heal us. Healing can't happen until we relax in trust. We trust or become "open" to *Abba*'s love by sitting in his presence until we are inwardly still, clearing our minds of clutter, focusing on God, and consciously opening our hearts to *Abba*'s love. We trust him; we abide in his presence; we surrender to his love. The key to opening the heart is that we have hearts that have been keyed to open: God made our hearts, and he put in them openings for his key of love.

Another way to open up to *Abba*'s love is to repeat throughout the day a short prayer reminder: "Father, thank you for loving me." The wisdom of short—sometimes called breath—prayers has been planted in the church, in the pages of the Bible, and in the lives of spiritual advisors.

Third, we can practice one faith action of God's love a day. Most obvious is the act of faith we may call self-talk: telling ourselves that God loves us. We can say: "God loves me. He loves me, especially me. He knows me, especially me. I am loved by God." I can shrug off a wounding comment by telling myself that even though some person (the jerk) might not like me, God loves me. We can turn the assault of a painful memory into a glancing blow by reminding ourselves that, like the prodigal son, God welcomes the sinful home. Or, when we are tempted to think God loves only the (apparently) lovable people—who've got it all together, who are successful, who look great and are popular, who speak well in public, who've got big houses and cute kids and nice cars—we can remind ourselves of the sin-infested, pig-smelling, and years-wasting son who returned to the *Abba*. It was for him that the *Abba* threw a party. We can tell ourselves: A seat at *Abba*'s feast is better than anything, even if we arrive a bit late in dirty clothes.

The *Jesus Creed* is to love God, and the premise under the *Jesus Creed* is a promise of truth: *Abba* loves us.

CHAPTER 4

The *Jesus Creed* as a Table

GOSPEL READINGS
Matthew 11:16–19; Mark 2:14–17; Luke 19:1–10

Tables create societies.

A few years ago my son, Lukas, and some of his high school friends created their own holiday meal. However they came up with the name—and I'm told it was from a TV show—they now celebrate Festivus between Thanksgiving and Christmas. "Festivus," they say, "for the rest of us and the best of us."

A better name would be "Crude-idicus Man-icus." They've combined a medieval menu with medieval table manners. (We have a "don't ask" arrangement.) When Festivus began, the young men were all single and women weren't invited—unless they were willing to cook (in crude medieval fashion). Festivus is nothing but meat, potatoes, dessert, and libations. They eat with their hands—scooping potatoes with slabs of meat and spooning pie out of a plate with their fingers. Sleeves do quite well as napkins. For libation, they have a common bucket—they downed a small oak tree, cut out a small section, carved out its center, and each year they line it with a small plastic bag—for hygiene, they say. But, mostly, because it leaks like a politician's office.

Good, clean fun. Mostly. What interests me is the choice of a table to express their "fellowship" and "values." Tired of the frills of holiday-season meals, put off by the choice of dishes at family holiday meals, wearied by the hours spent preparing such meals, annoyed by the need to wear uncomfortable clothing, and knowing that the mother of all holidays (Christmas) was now officially inching into their lives—they hopped off the rails that take us from Thanksgiving to Christmas and created a "man's kind of meal." Festivus: for the rest of us and the best of us. Their table created a society.

THE TABLE: A THICK WALL OR AN OPEN DOOR?

Tables can create societies; they can also divide societies.

Jesus used the table to create an inclusive society, but some of his contemporaries understood his table to create a dangerous society. Jesus used the table to declare the *Jesus Creed,* while some of his critics wanted the table to speak tradition. He wanted to include people, while his opponents wanted to uphold purity customs.

At the time of Jesus, table customs could be used to measure one's commitment to the *Torah.* That is, fellow Jews were to eat with those who were pure; they were to eat what was kosher. Some who were careful about observing the *Torah* frowned on Jesus' table customs. Frowned is a gentle description. "Denounced" would be a better term. An overlooked accusation against Jesus is this: "Here is a *glutton and a drunkard.*" The accusation is more than it first appears. It is a precise quotation of an ancient Israelite law book, which we'll look at soon, and it is pinned to Jesus' lapel because of his table customs. They saw in Jesus' table customs, a table that was creating a society that was not the society they wanted.

So what was Jesus doing? The apostle Matthew, to celebrate his newfound faith in Jesus, once hosted an evening dinner for Jesus. He invited his friends, who happened to be a group of raw reformed sinners, but some Pharisees raised their eyebrows and winced and then whined over the presence of such people at table. For the Pharisees, the table was supposed to talk, but it was to say "kosher" and "purity." For them, the table became a wall between the observant and nonobservant—not because they were mean, but because they were zealous in their commitment to how they thought the *Torah* should be applied.

But for Jesus the table was to be a place of fellowship and inclusion and acceptance. For Jesus the table was to embody the *Jesus Creed*: To love God and to love others means to invite all to the table. Jesus' attitude gave him a bad name.

For his custom of including all at the table, Jesus was called a "glutton and drunkard." This expression points to a legal charge against Jesus. The accusers of Jesus use the specific language from a passage regulating how parents are to make legal charges against a rebellious son. Parents are to take the son to the elders and say, "This son of ours is stubborn and rebellious. He will not obey us. He is a *glutton and a drunkard*." Then they are to stone the rebellious son to death in order to purge evil from the community. Yikes!

All because of what Jesus is doing at the table. Tables can create a society. Jesus was trying to communicate something powerful in his table practice; they took his practice as awful. Why? Because they thought the table was to create a society of

"*Torah* and tradition." Jesus wanted his table to create a society shaped by the *Jesus Creed.*

We can now put together our first few chapters. Jesus teaches that the center of life before God is the *Jesus Creed.* When the *Jesus Creed* turns into prayer, it becomes the Lord's Prayer; when it becomes a story, it becomes the Parable of the Prodigal Son. And when it becomes a society, it becomes the table of welcome around Jesus.

So when Jesus gets into trouble with the Pharisees about his table customs, it is the *Jesus Creed* that is being called into question. What Jesus wants his table customs to reveal is that the table is an open door for others to enter and not a thick wall between people.

When Jesus opens the table to all, the table begins to tell a new story. But it is a story unlike the story of his contemporaries.

THE *JESUS CREED* AS A TABLE

The observant person's table story: You can eat with me if you are clean. If you are unclean, take a bath and come back tomorrow evening. Jesus' table story: clean or unclean, you can eat with me, and I will make you clean. Instead of his table *requiring* purity, his table *creates* purity. Jesus chooses the table to be a place of grace. When the table becomes a place of grace, it begins to act. What does it do?

It heals, it envisions, and it hopes.

The table heals

Jesus invites to his table those who are (spiritually and socially) sick, because Jesus can heal. When chided by the Pharisees for eating at Matthew's table, Jesus says, "It is not the healthy who need a doctor, but the sick." He heals them by inviting them to the table and dispensing grace through his presence and his words. In other words, at the table of Jesus other human beings found *Abba*'s love, and they find love of others—a fellowship of the *Jesus Creed.*

I am often amazed at what a physical object can do to create space for the invasion of grace. Sometimes the object is a park where people can find quiet and wander about in wonder. Sometimes it is a church into which people can slip away from the bustle of a city to find a tranquil place to hear God speak. At other times it is a chair in a home, or a back screened porch, or a table at the local diner. These are physical objects that bring us into contact with *Abba*, objects that by themselves create for us a story—and tell a story of healing.

My favorite story of a physical object's leading to the onset of healing is about Alec Guinness (known to most of us as Obi-Wan Kenobi in the megahit *Star Wars*). While acting the role and wearing the garb of the priest Father Brown in Burgundy, France, he tells of a late-evening shoot that attracts a fair number of local folk, including children. He walks to his room that evening still wearing his priestly "costume" with no thought of what is to happen. He writes in his autobiography, *Blessings in Disguise*:

> A room had been put at my disposal in the little station hotel three kilometers away [from location]. By the time dusk fell I was bored and, dressed in my priestly black, I climbed the gritty winding road to the village. In the square children were squealing, having mock battles with sticks for swords and dustbin lids for shields. . . . Discovering I wouldn't be needed for at least four hours [I] turned back towards the station. By now it was dark. I hadn't gone far when I heard scampering footsteps and a piping

voice calling, "Mon père!" [French for "my Father"]. My hand was seized by a boy of seven or eight, who clutched it tightly, swung it and kept up a non-stop prattle. He was full of excitement, hops, skips and jumps, but never let go of me. . . . Although I was a total stranger he obviously took me for a priest and so to be trusted. Suddenly with a "Bonsoir, mon père," and a hurried sideways sort of bow, he disappeared through a hole in a hedge.

Guinness continues with a reflection about the little boy that stood time still for him and created a story of healing:

He had had a happy, reassuring walk home, and I was left with an odd calm sense of elation. Continuing my walk I reflected that a Church which could inspire such confidence in a child, making its priests, even when unknown, so easily approachable could not be as scheming and creepy as so often made out. I began to shake off my long-taught, long-absorbed prejudices.

As the physical garment Guinness wears evokes the onset of healing for this movie star, so the table Jesus establishes evokes healing for the many who gather around it. That table does more than just heal people; it creates an alternative reality for them.

The table envisions

Jesus' table fellowship actually *creates a new vision of what Israel means and is to become*. When people sit at the table with Jesus, they are seeing and living a new society—the kingdom society of Jesus. Jesus' kingdom society is the society in which the *Jesus Creed* transforms life. "Israel" now refers to those who love God by following *Jesus*. "Israel" describes those who are *spiritually* attached to Jesus.

For Jesus, the table envisions a new society, and that means that the table is a boundary breaker and grace giver—a place where we can see what God can do when people are restored to fellowship with *Abba*. The table envisions because it is a door that opens and invites and includes. As such, the table creates a society.

We should never lose touch with the power of sight, with the power that physical objects contain. Jesus uses a physical object, a table, to embody his vision for a kingdom society, those who are living out the *Jesus Creed*. The table of Jesus talks by envisioning a new society, a society of grace, of inclusion, of restoration, and of transformation. We need to ask what, at the physical level, our churches are saying.

The table hopes

Jesus' table customs anticipate the Age to Come. This is a bit of a claim, so notice how Jesus talks about his table fellowship. He states very clearly that his table anticipates eternity. He tells his followers that Gentiles can respond to him because in the Age to Come Gentiles will sit at his table. In that Day, Jesus says, ethnic boundaries will no longer matter. At the Last Supper, Jesus tells his disciples that he will not eat with them again until he sits at the table with them again in the kingdom.

These two statements by Jesus lead to this perception: sharing table with Jesus is a foretaste of the kingdom of God for each of us. Take time, Jesus is saying to those who sit with him at the table, for a little taste of paradise.

WHEN THE *JESUS CREED* BECOMES A TABLE IN OUR WORLD

Abba loves us. Therefore, we are to love *Abba* and share *Abba* love with others. This will mean inviting people to our "table," or our church, fellowship, home, or office, regardless of who they are or what they have been. What they will discover at the table is healing, envisioning, and hoping.

My family and I attend Willow Creek, a "local" fellowship where doors have been thrown open to one and all, where healing occurs, where envisioning excites the imagination, and where hope settles in. Willow Creek, under the direction of its pastor, Bill Hybels, reaches into its community to invite all to the "table of fellowship," and in reaching that community, it has set an example to churches across the globe. It tries to answer the question, "Is there room at your table for me?" with a resounding "Yes!" No church is perfect; Willow is not either. But as a local expression of the table of Jesus, it is doing its part to live out the vision Jesus created at his table.

It welcomes to the table with loving, ministering arms those with sexual problems, those with cancer and their families, those who need career guidance, those with addictions, those who need simple supplies and food, those with marriage and family problems, and those with developmental challenges. It helps families with financial advice, it has a special ministry for motorcyclists (called "Cruisin' Creekers!), it has a shop that "heals" broken-down cars and donates them to those who need cars. Also, it has a special knack at encouraging those with gifts in the arts; and it has a flourishing ministry for single adults (the most-neglected group in many churches). And among evangelical churches, no church has done more for embracing and ennobling women in ministry. It has a developing ministry for Latin Americans, and the ministry team is working hard for greater integration of African Americans.

Nothing creates a society like a table, especially the table that turns the *Jesus Creed* into concrete realities.

CHAPTER 5

A *Creed* of Sacred Love

GOSPEL READINGS
Matthew 6:9–15; Luke 7:36–50; 19:1–10

Our love for God is sacred.

Followers of Jesus daily confess in the *Jesus Creed* that they love God with all their heart, soul, mind, and strength. It is the word *all* that reveals the nature of our love for God: It is a sacred love.

Love is sacred because genuine love is total in its commitment. Love asks from us either "everything" or it asks for "nothing." It asks for "all." As Lewis Smedes says: In making a commitment of love to another "we surrender our freedom and we surrender our individuality." God's love for us is sacred. In Smedes's memorable language, "Yahweh is the sort who sticks with what he is stuck with."

Any love that does not "stick with what it is stuck with" is not sacred, and it soon surrenders its splendor. And because love is sacred, compromises of love can crush the heart, darken the day, and harden the arteries of trust, as the following story reveals.

THE NIGHTMARE

Surely one of the most honest, penetrating, and heart-wrenching stories about the sacredness of love is Laurie Hall's *An Affair of the Mind*. In this book Laurie painfully and carefully details how her husband, Jack, offered not his "all" but only "some" of his love to Laurie. Jack spiraled into sexual addictions, Laurie was nearly destroyed by his shallow love, and they are struggling to regain the sacredness of their former love. After enduring disappointments, dinners alone, excuses about Jack to the children, and then discovering what Jack was really doing, Laurie separates from him. She then begins to write him letters.

> Here I am, three weeks into our separation. I didn't sleep much last night. The bed seemed so cold without you in it. Finally, somewhere in the wee hours, I dozed off fitfully. When I woke up this morning, I thought back to that first morning when I awakened in your arms, so happy, so hopeful of all the bright tomorrows we were going to have. Yet, here I am 20 years later, thinking about how I might never again lie in your arms.
>
> Besides loneliness, I feel sick—like I'm going to throw up—and I tell myself I have to be strong for the children. But that's not all I feel. What I feel mostly is anger. I'm mad. I don't understand why you won't let go of the pornography and the hookers. How could you choose them over the children? How could you choose them over me? You were all I ever wanted. How come I wasn't enough for you?

Why does she ask this series of questions? Because love is sacred and survives only when it is held in honor.

We know our love must be sacred because God's love is sacred.

One of Israel's great prophets, back in the eighth century BC, discovered this secret about God's love.

HOSEA'S OPEN SECRET: GOD IS A LOVER

The prophet Hosea openly revealed his secret to Israel by announcing that an entire nation needed to revise its understanding of its God. Prior to Hosea the relationship of God with Israel went something like this: "I am your God" and "you are my people." After Hosea the relationship of God with Israel was: "I am your Lover and I want you, Israel, for myself." Prior to Hosea no one dared to speak of God as a Lover.

YHWH loves Israel the way a husband is to love his wife. Israel is to love *YHWH* with the same kind of love. Shockingly, Hosea then has the temerity to compare Israel's love to the "love" of a wife who walks out the door one day and turns herself into a prostitute. It may be a little cheeky on Hosea's part, but you've got to give him this: "prostitute" is an image that sticks in the mind, and his message doesn't vaporize like a bland sermon.

Incredibly, Hosea next suggests that God is so heartsick over his people's unfaithfulness to him that he pleads with Israel to come back to him. *YHWH*, the spurned Lover of Israel, sounds like someone singing on an FM station. Speaking about his unfaithful wife, he announces:

> I am now going to allure [or, romance] her;
>> I will lead her into the desert
>> and speak tenderly to her.

> There I will give her back her vineyards,
>> and will make the Valley of Achor a door of hope.
> There she will sing as in the days of her youth,
>> as in the day she came up out of Egypt (Hos. 2:14-15).

Hosea says God will *romance* Israel into exile, into the wilderness, into a honeymoon experience. There Israel will recollect herself, and begin to respond to him as she originally did. There she will, like Celine Dion, sing "it's all coming back to me now." Then, Hosea says, Israel will repeat her wedding vows to *YHWH*, saying "My husband."

This is Hosea's open secret: God is the Lover of Israel. God loves his people with a sacred love. He won't let go. Israel's love is to be sacred.

So, when the *Jesus Creed* calls us to love God with all our heart, soul, mind, and strength, we are called to form a love relationship with God that is utterly sacred.

JESUS' OPEN SECRET: GOD IS AN *ABBA* LOVER

According to Jesus, Hosea doesn't go far enough when he reveals his open secret that God is a Lover. Jesus wants his disciples to know that God is a Lover whose sacred name is *Abba*. Jesus' open secret, that God is to be loved as a human loves her or his own father, makes discipleship a relationship of sacred love to a loving *Abba*. Over and over, as we saw in chapter 3, Jesus calls God *Abba*.

By revealing this secret, Jesus is not being disrespectful to, or overly familiar with, God. Indeed, Jesus urges his followers to speak of God's special *Abba*hood uniquely: "Do not call anyone on earth 'father,' for you have one Father, and he is in heaven." That is sacred love, written into the fabric of a name.

That Jesus chooses *Abba* as the Name of God intensifies the significance of "love" in the *Jesus Creed*. When we comprehend our love of God as a sacred love for an *Abba* who loves us with a sacred love, we will learn to honor that love in heart, soul, mind, and strength. That is, our love for God is only truly sacred when we surrender to him totally, when it is our "all," as the *Jesus Creed* emphasizes.

A LIFE OF SACRED LOVE

John Woolman, an early American Quaker*, was a sensitive soul who demonstrates what it means to live out the *Jesus Creed* with a sacred love. One of America's finest writers on spiritual formation, Richard Foster, says that "no book outside the Bible has influenced me more than *The Journal of John Woolman*."

Converted to obedient faith in Jesus Christ as a young man, Woolman's creed is the *Jesus Creed*: "True religion consisted in an inward life, wherein the heart doth love and reverence God the Creator and learn to exercise true justice and goodness [toward others]." What makes Woolman's love sacred is that this creed shaped his entire life. Woolman's focus in life was to call the world to equal treatment of all (especially African Americans and Native Americans) because *Abba*'s sacred love is for all. This means that we are to love others—all others.

Nothing better illustrates Woolman's response to *Abba* than a series of events in his last year. In 1772, as a result of the typical

Quaker openness to God's leading, Woolman was drawn to England to declare in that country that slavery was contrary to the gospel of a God who loves all and the gospel call for Christians to love others. So sensitive was he of disturbing his wife, whom he deeply loved, that he vanished from his bed before daybreak without even saying good-bye. Instead of traveling in the nicer cabins on the ship, he bunked with the sailors in their sloppy, musty, cramped quarters—to minister to them and so he could empathize with the squalor of slave trade.

What struck person after person after Woolman's arrival in England was his plain-clothing witness to a simplicity that was fired by his sacred love of God as well as by his love of all creation. Instead of riding from London to the north of England, he walked, believing that the coach business abused animals and overworked its drivers. When Woolman made his trip, he was in weak health and tragically died in York, England, of smallpox. The family attending him was humbled (as we are) by his desire not to be a burden to them.

What we see in Woolman, in fact, is what Jesus expects of anyone who comprehends what happens when one surrenders completely to, and in, the sacred love of *Abba*. This *Creed* of a sacred love transforms our lives; it calls for our "all." When we genuinely love God with *all* of our hearts, *all* of our souls, *all* of our minds, and *all* of our strength, this sacred love will transform our speech, convert our actions, and inspire our worship.

Sacred love transforms our speech

Jews at the time of Jesus *speak of God with reserve*. In so doing, they give us a little lesson on how speech can be transformed by sacred love. "Verbal" reserve begins with the command not to take the Name (*YHWH*) in vain. The logic of Jesus' contemporaries is this: if we never pronounce *YHWH*, we will never use *YHWH* in vain. So, they figure out ways to avoid using the Name. Here's a good illustration of Jesus' own reserve: when on trial, he tells the authorities that they "will see the Son of Man sitting at the right hand of the Mighty One." Instead of using the Name of God, Jesus says "The Mighty One" out of reverence. Jesus follows the Jewish custom of verbal reverence in the Lord's Prayer: "Our Father, hallowed be *your name*."

Messianic Jews today seek to retain the piety of this sort of Judaism. Some of them apply "verbal reserve" in how they *write* "God": they write "G—d" so "God" can't be pronounced. While I am not in favor of getting nutty here, it wouldn't hurt modern Christians to develop some reserve in their "God talk." But this reserve does not arise because God is a judge who, like Zeus, threatens the world with death-dealing thunderbolts if humans get out of hand. No, reserve in speech is what happens to a Christian's speech when that speech is shaped by a sacred love for God, when the Christian loves God with "all the mind."

Sacred love not only transforms speech; it quickly makes an impact on our actions.

Sacred love converts our acts

If the *Jesus Creed* expresses the essence of what God asks of us, then what he asks of us is to love him and to love others. Sin is any action that violates that love. Repentance is what happens when we realize in our deepest selves that we have violated the sacred trust of love with *Abba* and seek to renew our commitment. Repentance needs to be removed from the legal desk of "divine scorekeeping" where one line is balanced by another. Instead, it needs to be placed in Hosea's divine bedroom of love.

What animates this repentance is the utter awe of seeing what the sacred love of God is really all about. *Abba* is impeccably pure, majestically marvelous, and embarrassingly faithful in his love for us. It is this good sense of embarrassment that evokes repentance from us, and helps us to see our violations of love against God and others as sin.

From the story Luke tells us about Zacchaeus, we learn that he is a "wee little man." More important, he is a tax collector. What he collects above the taxes owed to the Roman Empire is his to keep. That is how the system works. Tax collectors at the time of Jesus were notorious for fraud, and that is why the gospel writers list them with sinners. In acting the part, though, Zacchaeus violates the sacred trust of living with a sacred love for a loving God. And he violates a proper love for others by treating them and their property without integrity and respect.

Sacred love once learned, however, converts acts of sin to acts of love.

Jesus finds Zacchaeus in a tree and invites himself to eat at his house. Normally, Jews would not enter the home of a tax collector because the home would not be kosher. Jesus vindicates his socially unacceptable behavior of eating in a nonkosher home by drawing from the heart of Zacchaeus a sacred love—cleansing repentance. Zacchaeus stands tall, renews his love for others, and gives half his possessions to the poor and repays those he has poached fourfold.

This is what happens when humans permit the sacred love of God to enter their lives. Soon that sacred love for God inspires worship, as can be seen in the life of a woman who lives out the prophecy of Hosea's prostitute.

Sacred love inspires our worship

Luke tells us of Jesus' dining in the home of a Pharisee named Simon. A woman who "earns her oil" as a courtesan (a female prostitute reserved for wealthy Roman leaders) discovers the sacredness of loving God in Jesus. Assuming a place at the feet of Jesus, she weeps buckets of tears, kisses his feet, and then dries them with her hair. Then she pours expensive oil on his feet.

The *Torah*-observant and tradition-conscious host pitches a fit, informing Jesus that this woman is a "sinner"—a nice euphemism for "hooker." Jesus responds by reminding the host that this woman has loads of sins in her memory, a memory that reminds her constantly of how she has violated love of God and herself. She now adores Jesus because he leads her to the sacred love of *Abba* and his forgiveness.

I can think of no better illustration of what genuine Christian worship is all about: Worship happens when I comprehend (1) who I really am before God—a love-violating sinner, (2) how faithful and gracious God is to his sacred commitment of love for me, and (3) how incredibly good God is to open the floodgates of that love to me.

When I comprehend this, I anoint his feet with oil and wipe dry his feet of grace.

CHAPTER 6

A *Creed* for Others

GOSPEL READINGS
Luke 10:25–37; Mark 12:28–34

Sometimes we need to get caught in order to learn.

One time I got caught. My father was a driver's-education instructor. One of his lectures taught that it was unsafe to drive in the winter before we had completely (and he meant completely) cleaned the windshield of all ice and snow.

One night it rained hard, then it got cold, and then the rain froze. My junky station wagon's windshield was covered with about a half inch of ice. I scraped for what seemed an eternity and was able only to clear a circle about the size of a basketball on the windshield. Running late to pick up my girlfriend (now wife), I took a chance that I would be able to see well enough. I could see well what was ahead, and what I saw was that I was heading into the side of a new Buick Electra. I smashed into a nice lady's car and did some serious damage to it. She escaped unhurt. My car showed no signs of damage, with only some ice cracked off in a few places. My station wagon had the bulk and strength of a Hummer.

I got caught driving contrary to good sense, and I learned my lesson. I gave the same lecture to my children and still do to unsuspecting students.

GETTING CAUGHT BY JESUS

Jesus tells parables that catch his readers in the web of a moral dilemma so they can learn. A good example is the Parable of the Good Samaritan.*

An "expert in the *Torah*" asks Jesus how to inherit eternal life. Jesus says, "What does the *Torah* say?" The expert answers, probably because he has heard the *Jesus Creed* from others: "Love your God . . . and love your neighbor as yourself." Jesus says, "A+!"

Riding a little wave of Jesus' approval, he gets a little chesty like a first-year theology student: "Well then, who is my neighbor?" What the scribe is really asking is not just "who is my neighbor?" but "who is pure and who is not?" He's asking about a classification system. The "who is pure?" question is also a "who is to be loved?" question. Knowing that the question masks a larger concern, Jesus tells a story to catch this expert in the web of a moral dilemma so we can all learn.

On a trip from Jerusalem to Jericho a man is attacked by a gang of robbers, leaving him nearly dead. A priest and a temple assistant (a Levite) come upon him separately, but fearing *impurity** from contact with a corpse, they skirt to the other side of the road. They are following the *Torah*, mind you. One of Moses' books spells it out: Dead bodies spread impurity.* In another of his books, priests are told not to contract corpse impurity unless from the body of a "close relative." If close enough to a corpse to cast one's shadow over the corpse, the person casting the shadow becomes impure. So, they shuffle to the other side of the road. This is not heartlessness so much as it is obedience. Therein lies the learning.

There is not a Jew who hears Jesus' parable who thinks the priest (or the Levite) is doing anything but what the *Torah* regulates. The irony of his little plot is that in "obeying" the *Torah* the priest and Levite are disobeying what is at the bottom of the *Torah*: loving others. Ironically, it is a stereotyped character that does what is right: a *Samaritan*. *Samaritan* in this parable stands for social hostility and religious heresy. The priest and Levite get caught while the Samaritan gets the teacher's thumbs up.

If we are to love God and love others, Jesus is asking his audience, what happens when love-of-God-as-obeying-*Torah* (the *Shema* of Judaism) comes into conflict with love-of-God-as-following-Jesus (the *Shema* of Jesus)? That's a tough one, for all of us. But for Jesus the answer is clear: Loving God properly always means that we will tend to those in need.

A plot within a plot. Jesus catches anyone who attends to the *Torah* (like avoiding impurity) but fails to attend to a person in need.

LOVE OF TORAH OR TORAH OF LOVE?

The *Torah*, so says Jesus, is a love-God-and-love-others *Torah*. Jesus is not against the *Torah*. He is against understanding it in such a way that its fundamental teachings about loving God and others are missed. The priest and Levite followed the *letter* of the *Torah* but failed in the *spirit* of the *Torah*.

The experts question is "Who is my neighbor?" By catching the *Torah*-down-to-the-letter followers in an unloving act, Jesus reshapes that *Torah*-like question about classification into another question: "To *whom* can you be neighborly?" First-class plotting, I'd say, and few there are who are not caught on the rough side of this plot.

Put differently, we are not called to the love of *Torah* but to the *Torah* of love. It is easy for us, in our twenty-first-century catbird seat, to look down our noses at the priest and Levite and toss on hot coals of criticism. It is easy but misguided because it shows that we, too, are caught in love of *Torah* instead of a *Torah* of love. "Love doesn't sound so dangerous until you've tried it," says Paul Wadell. Jesus calls us to surrender our "safe neighbor love," which the priest and Levite were doing when they looked straight ahead; Jesus calls us instead *to look to the side* to see our neighbor who is in need, which is what the Samaritan did. Neighborly loves looks to the side. When he walked on that path, he looked to the side and saw a wounded man in need.

There are many Christians today doing all they can to look to the side and show compassion to those in need.

LOOKING TO THE SIDE TO SEE OUR NEIGHBOR

Southeast Asia's Singapore Anglican churches are looking to the side. When they do, they see the mangled lives of the wounded in their communities. Instead of skirting around the wounded out of devotion to their own piety, they are dirtying their hands in help. Their work can inspire a new vision for ministries elsewhere.

To avoid the so-frequent "division of labor" into evangelism or social action, they have developed an integrated ministry of reaching into the community called SHOW: Softening Hearts and Opening

Windows. This work is not just for individuals "with the gift" of social action. All are learning that a broad and integrated ministry is the heart of following Jesus. Leaders lead in this effort, and families serve as families. Perhaps most significantly, the budget of the local churches is constructed in such a manner that as much as 50 percent is spent on (what Americans would call) social work for the community.

To keep this vision for an integrated ministry fresh, the leaders of these churches have a strategy of intentionally looking to the side so they can find new needs: *praying* for the community corporately and privately, *profiling* their local community so they can discover the real needs, *pursuing* projects of both kindness and penetration, and *partnering* with other Christians to enhance their impact.

Perhaps like the Samaritan and like these Singapore Christians, we need to spend more of our time looking to the side by profiling our communities in neighborly love. When we do, I suggest the following is what our love for others will look like.

Neighborly love begins in the home

Surely one of the most touching scenes in the life of Jesus is when, on the cross, he issues the request to John to take responsibility for his mother, by saying, "Dear woman, here is your son," and to his disciple, "Here is your mother." Jesus clearly affirms here the duty of loving one's family. Sadly, far too many Christians love others with abandon while their own families are starving for their love. Let this be clear: *Our home is also in our neighborhood.*

It is attention-grabbing to love the poor, to show compassion to AIDS sufferers, and to show mercy to victims. But it is attention-deflecting to wake up in the morning and ask, "What does my wife or husband, my daughter or son need?" and then attend to those needs. It is easier to see love in the public square than to show love in the home.

The Parable of the Good Samaritan is often misused here: as if love is shown only in the most extravagant of places, at the most unusual of times, and to the most needy of all persons. Not so, Jesus suggests: neighborly love begins in the home. In fact, if it is not shown in the home, it is a sham in public. How can we show such love?

A suggestion: In our morning prayers for our families, we could perhaps ponder each person in the family with this question: "What can I *do* for [name] today?" In so doing, our prayers for our families will become both private prayers of love and plans of neighborly love for the day.

Neighborly love is *whenever love and wherever love*

In the Parable of the Good Samaritan, Jesus is calling his listeners to act with compassion whenever and wherever a need arises. It was normal to travel from Jerusalem to Jericho. It was not normal to defile oneself in order to show compassion. But neither is it normal to come upon a man hovering near death. What the priest and Levite manage to circumnavigate (an unclean corpse) is a person whom the Samaritan manages to surround with compassion. We can't calculate when the call of the second part of the *Jesus Creed* will be heard. We are to be ready whenever needed, as some friends were with us when I was studying in England.

I teach today (in part, or even more) because of some "whenever" neighborly love by people who were like the good Samaritan: By "looking to the side," they saw someone in need. One day a neighbor, Claire, asked Kris what we were going to do the following year. Kris said in passing that we were not sure how long our funds would last. Claire made it a concern of hers. When John (our pastor) and Elisabeth Corrie heard this, they prayed over the matter—all unknown to us. One Sunday, John asked if he could come by some evening for a chat. The knock came, we asked him in, and after the exchange of pleasantries that the British are so good at, he said, "Elisabeth and I have heard you may have a financial need if you are to continue your research. Some years ago we received some funds, and we have dedicated them to helping people like you. We will pay for your tuition bills next year. If the Lord blesses you, we'd like you to replenish the funds." We gasped in gratitude, but inwardly our hearts were leaping in the joy of knowing *Abba*'s provision. It was their act of "whenever" neighborly love that set off a series of good events for us: it permitted me to finish the degree, which permitted me to get a teaching position, which permitted us to replenish their fund for others—and it is still going on.

The *Jesus Creed* is a creed to love others, whenever and wherever.

And as the *Jesus Creed* calls us to a sacred love for God, so it calls us to a sacred love for others.

Neighborly love is moral love

Because our society has elevated tolerance to the highest of virtues, our society remains confused about what "love" means. Christians are not called to tolerance; Christians are called to love. Toleration condescends; love honors.

But for many, love-as-toleration implies not exercising moral judgment about another's choices and actions. We all hear about Christian love a plenty—and what we hear is that Jesus says, "Do not judge, or you too will be judged." Thus, they infer, Jesus teaches love that means we are not to make moral judgments about others. *Eau contraire*: Jesus' love is always moral, because love is always sacred. Love is the human response to others in light of the *Abba*'s sacred love and our sacred love for *Abba*.

Jesus' amendment of loving God is revealing: He adds to the sacred *Shema* of Israel a verse from Leviticus 19:18: "Love your neighbor as yourself." Jesus hereby *endorses* the authority and meaning of "love" in Leviticus at some level. Jesus never defines what he means by love, but by quoting Leviticus he doesn't have to: That chapter defines it for him.

Love in that book of Moses means respecting parents, providing for the poor, protecting private property, honoring one's word, caring for the physically challenged, seeking justice for the powerless, living in sexual purity, showing love for one's enemies—and lots more! This is the source for the amendment in the *Jesus Creed*. And that source reveals that love is morally sound, or sacred.

The *Jesus Creed* is a call for each of us to become channels of God's love to others in need. James Bryan Smith, in his *Embracing the Love of God*, succinctly sums up the second part of the *Jesus Creed*: "God has created a world in which we are the ones who care for one another. To put it another way, God cares for us *through* one another."

No book was more influential in the heady days of the late 1960s and early 1970s among evangelicals than Francis Schaeffer's *The Mark of a Christian*. His final words are profound because they reflect a sacred love in search of others:

Love—and the unity it attests to—is the mark Christ gave Christians to wear before the world. Only with this mark may the world know that Christians are indeed Christians and that Jesus was sent by the Father.

PART TWO

Stories of the *Jesus Creed*

THE *JESUS CREED*
"Hear, O Israel, the Lord our God, the Lord is one.
Love the Lord your God with all your heart,
with all your soul,
with all your mind, and with all your strength."
The second is this: "Love your neighbor as yourself."
There is no commandment greater than these.

A spiritually formed person loves God by following Jesus and loving others.

As an expression of loving God and loving others,
a spiritually formed person embraces the stories of others who love Jesus.

In later creeds, Christians will confess that
they believe in the "communion of saints."
This communion was under way during the lifetime of Jesus.
Already, those who were associated with Jesus
were sharing their stories and their lives.
Already during the lifetime of Jesus,
the disciples were living out the second table of
the *Jesus Creed* by loving one another.

At the table in the community of Jesus,
we listen to the stories of a number of people:
the predecessor of Jesus, John the Baptist;
the family of Jesus, especially Joseph and Mary;
the special followers of Jesus, including Peter and John;
and the growing number of women who find joy
in the community of Jesus.

Each has a story to tell.

In the community of Jesus, each story is embraced.

CHAPTER 7

John the Baptist: The Story of New Beginnings

GOSPEL READINGS
Luke 3:1–20; John 1:6–9, 15, 19–34

Yellow is not my favorite color.

But now that I know the story of Vincent van Gogh, I have come to value yellow differently. This famous Dutch painter, sadly, tossed away the truth imparted to him in his Christian home and sank into depression and destruction. By the grace of God, as he later began to embrace that truth again, his life took on hope, and he gave that hope color.

The best-kept secret of van Gogh's life is that the truth he was discovering is seen in the gradual increase of the presence of the color yellow in his paintings. Yellow evoked (for him) the hope and warmth of the truth of God's love. In one of his depressive periods, seen in his famous *The Starry Night*, one finds a yellow *sun* and yellow swirling *stars*, because van Gogh thought truth was present only in nature. Tragically, the church, which stands tall in this painting and should be the house of truth, is about the only item in the painting showing no traces of yellow. But by the time he painted *The Raising of Lazarus*, his life was on the mend as he began to face the truth about himself. The entire picture is (blindingly) bathed in yellow. In fact, van Gogh put his own face on Lazarus to express his own hope in the Resurrection.

Yellow tells the whole story: life can begin all over again because of the truth of God's love. Each of us, whether with actual yellows or metaphorical yellows, can begin to paint our lives with the fresh hope of a new beginning.

Some, like van Gogh, may need to start opening their hearts to God, some need to hop back on the tracks after failures have derailed them, some simply need a time of retreat to discover once again God's restoring Spirit. Some are suffering through divorce and are struggling to glue together the remaining chunks of life. Others are enduring a particularly stressful time at work and need to settle into a more balanced life. Some have recently lost their jobs and need to hear from God that he is with them. Some are swirling in an internal vertigo as a result of an illness, while others are struggling with their children packing off to college. (Others holler a hoot of joy!) Some are grieving the death of a best friend, or a spouse, a parent, or a child. Each of us sometimes needs to begin life all over again, all the time.

If the promise is that we can begin all over again, the question for us is "How?"

The first thing we need to do is return to the Jordan River, where the prophet John the Baptist urges his listeners to begin again.

A PROPHET AT THE JORDAN

The Jordan River calls to mind two crucial moments in history. Each is about new beginnings. First, when the children of Israel finally crossed that river they began a new life in the Land of Israel. Second, those who were baptized by John began life all over again—and they, too, crossed back over the Jordan to live in the Land of Israel.

To understand how John offered his audience the opportunity of beginning life all over again, it is important to grasp how prophets in Israel operated in their day. Three items shape what we can learn from John.

We can begin by *comparing priests and prophets*, a good comparison because John's father was a priest and John was a prophet. A priest speaks for humans to God in the privacy of the temple. A prophet speaks for God to humans in the publicity of the town square. Priests wiped sins from the people; prophets wiped sins in their faces. Most importantly, priests summoned people to tell the truth so they could make restitution, but prophets summoned people to tell the truth so they could start all over again.

But prophets didn't always use words. Occasionally, they *acted things out*. Readers of the Bible know that the ancient prophets often acted out their messages. Consider, from the Old Testament, the following prophetic dramas:

- Jeremiah burying his "underwear" (Jer. 13:1–7)
- Ezekiel acting out a "trip to Babylon" (Ezek. 12)
- Isaiah walking around naked for three years (no kidding, look it up in Isa. 20)

John the Baptist, the son of a priest, digs in his feet at the edge of the Jordan River and acts out his drama. For his act, he baptizes people in the famous River Jordan.

Location also matters. John sets up his baptismal stage *on the far side of the Jordan*. It is here that the children of Israel entered the water to cross the Jordan to enter the Land. John is saying that if Israel wants to enjoy the blessings of God, they need to go back to the Jordan and begin again. Amazingly, John's prophetic drama is a *reenactment of the entry into the Land.*

This is the only way to make sense of John in his world: He wants his audience to see that life can begin all over again. At the Jordan, John gives us the opportunity to start over. How? John has a word for it.

LIFE BEGINS ALL OVER AGAIN WITH TRUTHTELLING

The first word out of John's mouth is "*Repent!*" This is repentance with an edge—a sharp one. As Frederick Buechner puts it so memorably: "No one ever invited a prophet home for dinner more than once." John maybe not even once.

John explains that repentance means they must *confess their sins.* Herein lies the secret to a new beginning, a secret van Gogh began to discover only late in his life. To confess means that we *tell God the truth.* Nothing simpler, nothing harder. Why? As America's essayist Joseph Epstein says,

> We all exist on at least three levels: there is the person as he or she appears in public; the person as he or she is known to intimates, which include family and dear friends; and that person, deepest of all, who is only known to him- or herself, where all the aspirations, resentments, fantasies, desires, and much else that is not ready for public knowledge reside.

Facing reality is telling the truth about each of our levels to God: our public persona (not so hard), our family image (that's meddling), and our inner self (the hard part).

The *Jesus Creed* begins with loving God. Love, for it to work at all, *requires* truthtelling. Telling this truth to God is how we genuinely love *Abba*, and it creates a new beginning in life. Our "Yes" to God is, in the words of theologian Dietrich von Hildebrand, "the primal word" and "cannot be spoken too clearly, too wakefully, too explicitly."

Ever since Eve and Adam, we have been trying to hide from God, to no avail, for the Creator of Eden continues to summon us in our own gardens, asking "Where are you?" Because we have learned to hide, we need new beginnings to set us free, and the new beginnings begin at our own Jordans when we tell the truth. As John Paul II has put it:

> To acknowledge one's misery in the sight of God is not to abase oneself, but to live the truth of one's own condition. . . . The truth thus lived is the only thing in the human condition that makes us free.

It takes *utter honesty* to tell the (real) truth to God, and we are *inclined to blame* others. Mark Twain gave some advice to "good little boys" that included this line: "You should never do anything wicked and then lay it on your brother . . . "—and, had he stopped there, it would be sound advice. But, Twain being Twain, he continues, ". . . when it is just as convenient to lay it on some other boy." This won't do. We need to take responsibility for our lives. In the words of Henri Nouwen, who was not a Twain, we have to "drink our own cup." Drinking our own cup permits truth to penetrate and awaken us at the deepest levels of the heart.

TRUTHTELLING AWAKENS FORGIVENESS

Telling God the truth awakens forgiveness. Sometimes one gets the impression from misguided experts that God is holding a club over our heads, and the moment we tell the truth he cracks us a good one and then says, "You ugly little sinner!"

But *Abba* is not like that. The promise of the *Jesus Creed* is that *Abba* loves us. He creates us to love him; he desires our fellowship. So, truthtelling is not an opportunity for head bashing, but an opportunity for the heart of *Abba* to be thrilled by reconciling forgiveness.

Henri Nouwen once confessed the following about truthtelling:

> I am beginning now to see how radically the character of my spiritual journey will change when I no longer think of God as hiding out and making it difficult as possible for me to find him, but, instead, as the one who is looking for me while I am doing the hiding.

Truthtelling reunites us with God because it unleashes his forgiveness. Prior to telling the truth, we hide and are in what Philip Yancey calls the cycle of ungrace. By failing to tell the truth, we face God with our heads cocked sidewise. Lewis Smedes, who has poured grace all over the discussion of forgiveness, tells us, "without truthfulness, your reunion [with God] is humbug."

About what are we to tell the truth? Our whole self, of course. But let's look at what sins John trots out on his stage at the Jordan. He makes repentance real.

TRUTHTELLING GETS REAL

He calls us to tell the truth about a number of things:

1. Our spirituality: Luke 3:7–9

Some religious experts in John's audience think they can appeal to their heritage, clinging to their faith line with Abraham. John stands on the shoulders of other prophets who gave the same warning: "Your ethnic background won't save you," he tells his audience. John is no doubt proud to be a Jew, but he knows that spirituality is more than good spiritual genes.

We need to hear the same: we may live in the spirituality of our fathers and mothers, but our father's and mother's faith won't live in us (until we tell the truth to God about ourselves). If we transcend our backgrounds by telling the truth, life can begin all over again.

We need to tell the truth about our spirituality: where is it anchored?

John faces another set of people gathered at the Jordan, and in so doing faces us as well.

2. Our possessions: Luke 3:10-11

The Bible speaks often of money because it is with money that we exercise the freedoms of choice. This is hard for many Western Christians, because so many of us are soaking in what J. I. Packer calls "hot tub religion." The unquenching human desire for more— bigger houses, spiffier cars, trendier clothes—is what led St. Francis to renounce possessions, what led the Mennonites to a simple lifestyle, and what leads some to urge all Westerners to live more with less.

"The man with two tunics," John says, "should share with him who has none." This warning about accumulating things only for ourselves John barks out on the banks of the Jordan. Jesus soon will echo John's message about economic justice on the hills of Galilee. Their warnings still await a Church that will listen. Heeding the call of John leads to a new beginning.

If we love God and love others, we will find the truth about how close our hearts are to our possessions.

We need to tell the truth about our possessions: How important are they?

John turns to two more groups. In facing them, he also sees our faces.

3. Our power: Luke 3:12–14

John sees the faces of tax collectors who've gathered to listen to him at the Jordan. John knows they are freelance experts in theft. He then faces the soldiers, who are known for extortion and injustice. The two groups stand together in the name of abusing power.

But power is not just in their hands. Abusive power is seen when fathers wrench the hearts out of their daughters with despicable acts, bosses break the spirits of employees with unrealistic or uncommunicated demands, and pastors devastate their congregations when they carry on behind closed doors. Power is also wielded destructively when brutal words brand themselves on the memories of those we love or with whom we work. If we love God and love others, we will use our power for the good of others. When we do, we are offered a new beginning in life.

We need to tell the truth about power: how do we use it?

For those who learn to tell the truth, John implies, there will be a story to tell. And a spiritually formed person embraces the stories of those who love God and others, who embrace the *Jesus Creed*. In the next few chapters we will focus on some of those stories, but we conclude this chapter by looking at a man who changed the world because his story was one of truthtelling.

A TRUTHTELLER

Every Christmas many of us encounter men and women standing in public places ringing bells near suspended red buckets. They are members of the Salvation Army. They collect funds to relieve the spiritual and social suffering of a quarter of a million persons a year. These efforts began with William Booth, who is a good example of truthtelling. Here Booth faces the truth eye-to-eye:

> The entrance to the Heavenly Kingdom was closed against me by an evil act of the past which required restitution. [He had deceived his friends and received a silver pencil-case as a reward. He knew it was wrong and should give it back.] . . . to confess the deception I had practiced upon them was a humiliation to which for some days I could not bring myself.
>
> I remember, as if it were but yesterday, . . . the resolution to end the matter, the rising up and rushing forth, the finding of the young fellow I had chiefly wronged, the acknowledgement of my sin, the return of the pencil-case—the instant rolling away from my heart of the guilty burden, the peace that came in its place, and the going forth to serve my God and my generation from that hour.

Booth told the truth to God and to others, and because he did, his life began all over again.

When we tell God the truth and accept responsibility for who we are and what we've done, we find the Jordan to be a stream of living and forgiving and empowering water, a river that washes us so we can begin all over again. This river, so I suggest, is awash in van Gogh's yellow.

CHAPTER 8

Joseph: The Story of Reputation

G O S P E L   R E A D I N G
Matthew 1:18–25

I was converted in high school.

My pride suffered because my reputation was so important to me. I was an athlete, and that was my identity. I ran cross country, played basketball, and competed for the track team. A three-sports kind of guy. That was my reputation, and I liked it. I wasn't Bo Jackson or anything, but I wasn't a wimp either. I was somebody, and I had a reputation because, so I thought, I was an athlete.

When I wasn't looking over my shoulder, and when I was least expecting it, the Lord invaded my life, worked the miracle we call "conversion," and simply "ruined" my reputation. It happened early in the month of August, and by the time school started up, I had a whole new set of friends and habits, including a voracious appetite to read the Bible, pray, and spend time in group Bible studies. We quickly organized a high school Bible study at our church at seven o'clock on Friday mornings, and as that word got around, word also got around that "McKnight had religion."

I remember entering the locker room the first time my senior year. I had a Bible on top of my books and one of my friends grabbed it, held it up for all to see, and said something rather insulting about my manhood—as only athletes can do. It hurt, but I held my tongue. When I explained to a teacher that I had decided to go to a Christian college instead of somewhere else, he told me (in front of my classmates) that I was "wasting my life." That hurt too. But deep inside, I was so contented I was able to deflect the wounding words.

I reached a point where I didn't mind the hassle, but I also discovered that I had to learn to think of myself in different terms. I was no longer "Mr. Athlete" but an ordinary Christian like any other Christian. I learned in the low-heat crucible of high school interaction that what someone else thinks of me (my reputation) is not the final answer: I know what I "think" of me and I know what God thinks of me (my identity), and it is what God thinks that really matters.

Our reputation (what others think of us) is not as important as our identity (who we really are). Spiritual formation begins when we untangle reputation and identity, and when what God thinks of us is more important than what we think of ourselves or what others think of us.

Around the table of Jesus sit people who tell stories of their newfound identities. One of those is Jesus' own father, and the story he has to tell us about his life—his autobiography—is a story about his losing a hard-earned reputation and gaining an identity.

The story of Joseph begins with his Jewish religious context. Joseph's story is one of the great ones of the New Testament, though few know it. But to understand what Joseph went through, we have to explain Joseph's religious and social dilemma.

1. I AM A TSADIQ*

What is Joseph's reputation? The Gospel of Matthew tells us that Joseph is "righteous." That is, in the Hebrew word of his day, he is a *tsadiq*. Sounds like tsa-DEEK. This label, this reputation, is given to anyone who studies, learns, and observes the *Torah* scrupulously. In Joseph's world, that means he recites and lives the *Shema* daily, that he follows the food laws, that he supports the synagogue, and that he regularly celebrates the high holy days in Jerusalem. Joseph is proud of his reputation. In Joseph's world there are no reputations more desirable than *tsadiq*— unless you are a priest (unusual), a prophet (rare), or the Messiah (very rare).

Joseph's reputation as a *tsadiq* is about to be challenged because things are being said in the "locker rooms" of Nazareth about his fiancée.

2. MY REPUTATION IS CHALLENGED

Before their marriage, word is out that Mary is pregnant. Neighbors are saying, to use that clever term of the American South, that Mary is "common."

Transfer "common" to the world of Joseph, who follows the *Torah*, and get another reputation for Joseph. If Joseph continues in his relationship with Mary, he will be called what Jews called the religiously common, or *Torah*-tacky people of their day. They will call him a member of the *Am ha-aretz*.* Such people don't observe the *Torah*: they eat ham sandwiches, pass on tithing, and idle on street corners with Gentiles. Young women who dabble in sexual

relations before marriage are not much different—for that is what
the neighbors are thinking Mary has done.

And Joseph is about to marry such a woman. If he does, he will
lose his reputation as a *tsadiq*, and reputation matters to Joseph.
Joseph will be no better than the *Am ha-aretz*, common people who
think the *Torah* is hooey. So, what is Joseph to do?

3. I APPEAL TO *TORAH*

Joseph knows what to do if he wants to maintain his reputation.
He is a *tsadiq*, a Bible believer, so he consults the Books of Moses
to see what he is to do. We need to slow down here to explain a few
complex "legal" matters, because these are going through Joseph's
head as he struggles to maintain his reputation.

In the *Torah* he learns what to do with Mary: She has either
been seduced or raped. If she has been seduced, the *Torah* says that
both Mary and her seducer are to be stoned to death. If she has been
raped, the rapist is to be put to death. But, if no one confesses, the
Torah says that Mary is to drink the "waters of bitterness." If she
dies from the water, she is guilty; if she doesn't die, she is innocent.
Or, from yet another part of the *Torah* Joseph could have consulted,
her parents could produce "tokens of virginity," which needs no
explanation.

With these options swirling in Joseph's head, he hears Mary's
story: she claims that she was neither seduced nor raped. Instead,
she claims the pregnancy is the result of a miracle: God has done
this.

Here is where Joseph finds himself: he is a *tsadiq* who will do
anything to follow the *Torah*. Mary, the woman he loves and wants
to marry, is pregnant. She claims her pregnancy is from God. If

Joseph marries her, he loses his reputation. But, he asks himself, what if Mary is right? What if the baby is a miracle baby? Joseph is struggling with God. Would God do something like this?

4. I STRUGGLE WITH GOD

Joseph wants to know what to do. He is caught on the horns of a dilemma: will he love God by obeying the *Torah* (as understood in his circle), or will he love Mary and take her as his wife? Unknown to Joseph, he is caught on the horns of the dilemma created by what will become the *Jesus Creed*.

With his reputation grasping for control, he chooses a "private" divorce to avoid a public spectacle . . . until an angel tells him *not to fear*. Not to "fear"—why? Because if he marries Mary, he will destroy his reputation.

The angel explains to him that the baby has been conceived virginally. Joseph is acutely aware that few of his friends will believe his story about the angelic visitation, and (surely) no one will buy the report of a conception* through the Holy Spirit. Joseph, they will be thinking, is attempting to cover up Mary's big fat miracle story with a kosher Jewish wedding!

Sometimes the implication of listening to the voice of God is that we ruin our reputation in the public square. Loving God, as the *Jesus Creed* teaches, involves surrendering ourselves to God in heart, soul, mind, strength—and reputation. The minute we turn exclusively to the Lord to find our true identity is *the day reputation dies*. We learn, as Thomas à Kempis puts it, that when you surrender your reputation, "you won't care a fig for the wagglings of ten thousand tongues." This is what Joseph and Mary learn. It is also what John Stott had to learn.

John Stott, the Church of England pastor who may be the most influential evangelical leader of the twentieth century, faced Joseph's dilemma between identity and reputation while in college. When he became convinced that the Lord was calling him into the ministry, John informed his father, Arnold, a physician. John knew that his father would think his gospel calling "would bring to nothing, in his [father's] eyes, the high hopes he cherishe[s] for his son."

If Arnold Stott sees in John's decision to go into the ministry a destruction of reputation, it is no wonder that John later defined spiritual formation in terms of identity: "When the Christian loses himself, he finds himself, *he discovers his true identity*." Hinting at his own personal struggle, Stott says that Christ's Lordship "includes our career. . . . God's plan may be different from our parents' or our own."

We don't know what Joseph's parents thought, but we do know what his heavenly Father thought. Joseph turns to God.

5. I AM MARY'S HUSBAND AND JESUS' (LEGAL) FATHER

The decisive act of Joseph is found in a simple expression: "He did as he was told." Soon Joseph gives Mary's little boy a name, and so makes the relationship to the child legal.

Joseph's reputation was getting worse as his identity was getting better. Legally, now, Joseph is tied to two persons with sullied reputations: Mary is perceived as an adulteress (a *na'ap*) and Jesus is considered an illegitimate child (a *mamzer**). The decision to take Mary home and legally adopt Jesus is unbecoming for a *tsadiq*. For Joseph it is a decision of obedience for he now finds his identity in God. Joseph is no longer a *tsadiq*. Instead, he is husband of Mary and the (legal) father of Jesus.

JOSEPH AND THE *JESUS CREED*

Joseph, while Jesus is but an "embed" in Mary, is already learning the *Jesus Creed*: Joseph is to love God by following Jesus (not by following the *Torah* and its interpretation), and he is to love others—both Mary and the baby. In fact, we can be forgiven if we wonder if maybe Jesus learned the *Jesus Creed* at the feet of his father and mother.

The first story heard around the table of Jesus is that identity is more important than reputation. Joseph learns that who he is before God (his identity) is more important than who he is in the circle of his pious friends (his reputation).

Another who followed the example of Joseph is St. Augustine, Bishop of Hippo (North Africa), the telling of whose story set new standards of honesty. His autobiography charts a journey from reputation to identity. He says of his preconversion days: "For in those my notion of a good life was to win the approval of these people" (reputation). And of his postconversion days: "I find no safe place for my soul except in you [God]" (identity).

God, too, "loses his reputation" when he chooses for his Son to be born to parents with bad reputations—Mary as an adulteress and Joseph as a disgraced *tsadiq*. God also chooses to reveal himself most dramatically in the reputation-losing death of his very Son on a cross. Ironically, it is in the reputation-losing death of that Son where an identity-forming life is discovered for those who live out the *Jesus Creed*. Joseph is one of the first to pull his story up to the table.

Joseph becomes like the *Am ha-aretz* in the eyes of the *tsadiqim* to provide room for a baby boy who gives the *Am ha-aretz* an even better reputation than *tsadiq*. So, what God asks of Joseph he himself has already done: "Whatever game He is playing with His creation," Dorothy Sayers observes, "He has kept His own rules and played fair. He can exact nothing from man that He has not exacted from Himself."

On one evening, Joseph, Mary, and the child Jesus step out the front door of their humble dwelling, face the wind, and somehow know that this was just the beginning. Just the three of them. Three who would change the world, but who would have to do it climbing uphill.

CHAPTER 9

Mary:
The Story of
Vocation

GOSPEL READING
Luke 1:46–55 (the Magnificat)
(extra reading: Psalm 149)

Each of us has a vocation.

This great term *vocation* has two meanings. In a *general* sense, vocation is what all Christians are to do as Christians (live out the *Jesus Creed*). But *specifically*, vocation is the *special assignment that only you can do* (parenting your kids, exercising your spiritual gifts, working at the office). In the potent words of Dorothy Sayers, our vocation

> is not, primarily, a thing one does to live, but the thing one lives to do. It is, or it should be, the full expression of the worker's faculties, the thing in which he finds spiritual, mental, and bodily satisfaction, and the medium in which he offers himself to God.

> It is the business of the Church to recognize that the secular vocation, as such, is sacred.

> Let the Church remember this: that every maker and worker is called to serve God in his profession or trade—not outside it.

Whatever we are called to "do" is not a "job" but a sacred vocation.

A VOCATION FOR EACH OF US

Our vocation is to be what God made us to be, as many have learned only after considerable struggle. Parker Palmer, after decades of wrestling to please others, came to a shady oasis when he absorbed some Quaker wisdom on vocation: "Let your life speak." His spark of insight: "Before you tell your life what you intend to do with it, listen for what it intends to do with you."

What Palmer is asking us to learn is this: God will not ask us, "Were you (like) Mother Theresa or the prophet Daniel or Peter or your father or mother?" Instead, God will ask us, "Were you the 'you' I made you to be?" Os Guinness echoes this wisdom: "The truth is not that God is finding us a place for our gifts but that God has created us and our gifts for a place of his choosing—and we will only be ourselves when we are finally there."

You are to be who God meant you to be, as the wise of the Church have always known. One who learned this lesson so well is the mother of Jesus, Mary, who also pulls her story up to the table of Jesus. It is the story of her past being swallowed up in the goodness of God.

1. I HAVE A REPUTATION

God's special work, Mary tells us, is to turn difficult pasts into a vocation.

Mary's difficult past is this: Well before Joseph knows that Mary is pregnant, Mary is told by the angel Gabriel that she is to conceive supernaturally. Mary instantaneously grasps what this means: She will be labeled in her community as a *na'ap* (adulteress). The label is inaccurate, but it sticks. She also grasps that this revelation is from an angel, and angels come from God. And that means God must have chosen something special for her. It was this label that was most difficult for Mary to live with.

But God sends this Mary "on vocation" to be *Mother of Messiah,* and her response is a glorious song of joy. One of the Bible's highlighted passages is the Song of Mary, often given its Latin name, the *Magnificat.* As Tom Wright describes it, Mary's Song is the "gospel before the gospel" and it "goes with a swing and a clap and a stamp." Mary's Song is an expression of gratitude for God morphing her bad reputation into a messianic vocation. But her past is even more than this unfortunate label.

2. I AM POOR, BUT I HOPE FOR LIBERATION

Joseph is a *tsadiq,* a man totally observant of the *Torah.* But, Mary pokes her head out of a different nest, the *Anawim** (the pious poor). Historians agree on three characteristics of Mary's people, the *Anawim.* These people suffer because they are poor, but they express their hope by gathering at the temple in Jerusalem. There they express to God their yearning for justice, for the end of oppression, and for the coming of the Messiah. Each of these characteristics of the *Anawim* finds expression in the life of Mary and especially in the *Magnificat.*

For instance, Mary is poor. At Jesus' dedication, his parents present to the temple assistants *two birds* for their offering. Why? The real question is, "Why did they not offer a lamb?" Back in the days when Israel's neighbors were sacrificing babies to nonexistent gods, Israelites instead sacrificed a lamb. But the offering of Mary and Joseph is two birds, the offering prescribed in the *Torah for those who could not afford the lamb*. Their offering is that of a poor family.

Mary may have been poor, but she was not hopeless—which is another characteristic of the *Anawim*. Notice these lines in Mary's Song that express yearning for liberation from injustices that she knows by experience:

> [God] has scattered those who are proud in their inmost
> thoughts.
> He has brought down rulers from their thrones
> but has lifted up the humble.
> He has filled the hungry with good things
> but has sent the rich away empty.

When Mary and Joseph take Jesus home after his temple dedication, they place that little baby in *a bed prayed over in the hope* that justice will come to God'sr people.

Mary's Song is actually announcing a social revolution. The King at the time is Herod the Great, and he is a power-tossing and death-dealing tyrant. Mary is announcing that he will be dealt his own due and have his power tossed to the winds. In his place, Mary declares, God will establish her very own son. Unlike Herod, he will rule with mercy and justice.

Now here's the story Mary pulls up to the table of Jesus: Mary has a sullied reputation, and she is poor, but God accepts her past, creates it anew, and sends her "on vocation" to announce the Good News that the Messiah is ready to appear.

If spiritual formation is about learning to love God with our "all," then one dimension of loving God is surrendering the "all" of our past to God. We dare not make light of our past—whether it was wondrous or abusive, reckless or righteous. All we can do, like Mary, is offer to the Lord who we are and what we've been. He accepts us—past and all.

Roberta Bondi, in her account of learning to love God in *Memories of God*, expresses the importance of coming to terms with her own identity when she reflects on a breakthrough encounter: "Never before, I think, had I actually been glad that I was me and not somebody else." This is not easy to achieve: to dig deep enough to discover who we are, to accept who we are, and to look into the mirror with our eyes open and be grateful for what we see. Roberta learns she can accept who she is because "it is only God who can look with compassion on the depth and variety of our individual experience and our suffering, and know us as we really are." Our vocation, whatever that might mean for each of us, sweeps up our entire past for, as Roberta says so memorably, "even Jesus was resurrected with his wounds."

I like that: we, too, are raised to a vocation with the wounds of our past intact, visible, and a witness to what God can do. Mary knew her own wounds, but knew also that God was about to heal those wounds with a vocation.

3. I HAVE A VOCATION: TO NURTURE THE CHILDREN

In the history of the Church, Christian traditions have differed on the physical relations of Joseph and Mary after the birth of Jesus. Some think they never engaged in marital relations, while others think they did. Some think the "siblings" of Jesus are merely cousins, others that they are children of Joseph from a previous marriage, and others that Mary actually gave birth to them. What is important here is that, whichever view one takes, each agrees that Mary assumes responsibility for these children. Since most biblical scholars think Joseph died when Jesus was fairly young, Mary's responsibility becomes all the more significant.

Mary now has a vocation: she is to help nurture the faith of the girls (at least two) and boys (four plus Jesus). But, the names of the boys tells a story itself.

One of the deepest memories of Israel was that she was at one time enslaved in Egypt where the patriarch Israel (or Jacob) had twelve sons. According to Matthew, Joseph and Mary lived for a short while in that same Egypt. It is clear that while they were there they were immersed in Israel's former captivity and dreamed of the day they would return to the Land. It is no accident that the names of the boys under their care are the same names of the patriarch Israel's sons, those who were to lead Israel when she returned to the Land. In Hebrew the boys' names are: Yakov (James), Yosef (Joseph), Yehudah (Judah), and Shimeon (Simeon). With Jesus as Yeshua (or Joshua), they become five Jewish boys whose names tell the story of Israel's liberation from slavery.

Mary nurtures these children, and their names evoke her *Anawim* hope in the kingdom of God. These actions were part of the vocation God gives to her. Also part of that vocation is the secret that her son, Jesus (Yeshua), is to be Messiah.

4. I HAVE A VOCATION:
TO TEACH THE CHILDREN

And a part of that secret is how much Mary taught Jesus. Most Bible readers fail to connect Jesus with Mary when they think of the teachings of Jesus. This failure fulfills what I think should be the (tongue-in-cheek) correct translation of Luke 1:48: "From now on all generations (except Protestants!) will call me blessed." While some tend to adore Mary a little too much, Protestants tend to avoid her too often. Most Protestants have less respect for Mary than Frederica Mathewes-Green, who needed to adjust to Mary when she became Eastern Orthodox. She confessed,

> I like her [Mary] and everything. I respect her. She's his Mom. . . . I feel a formal distance, like we're still at the pleased-to-meetcha stage.

There is good reason, then, for many of us to reconsider Mary's impact on Jesus because the Gospels clearly show that she had a significant influence on his teachings.

On any reading of the *Magnificat* (Mary's Song), we find five of the major themes of Jesus' very own teachings and mission. It is not hard to figure which came first. *To begin with*, as Mary blesses the holy Name of God and asks God to fill the hungry, so Jesus hallows God's Name, prays for daily bread, and blesses the hungry. *Second*, as Mary is poor and from the *Anawim*, so Jesus blesses the poor and opens banquet doors to the poor. As Mary is a widow, so Jesus frequently shows mercy to widows. *Third*, as Mary prays for the powerful to be stripped of their unjust powers, so Jesus regularly tussles with unjust powers. *Fourth*, as Mary's prayer emphasizes

God's mercy and compassion, so Jesus is known for mercy and compassion. And, *fifth*, Mary's own prayerful concern for Israel's redemption is seen in Jesus' wrenching prayer for Jerusalem. These similarities are not accidents.

We must conclude that *Mary passes on her own vision and vocation to her son.* Our own vocations are not just to accomplish our special assignments, but to pass God's claim on our lives to our children and the next generation.

What is the secret to passing on God's claim on each of us to the next generation? The answer is as old as Moses, and it is certainly a custom adopted by Joseph and Mary. The fundamental confession of pious Jews is the *Shema.* Inasmuch as it is central to Jewish faith, and inasmuch as Jesus makes it his own *Creed*, we can infer that Jesus first heard the *Shema* in his home.

The secret of the *Shema* principle of training our children in the faith is simple. It is about *linking* generations. We are to pray for our children, be Christians before their eyes, include them in our lives, and include ourselves in their lives by linking our children to us in our faith. The holy family provides the first link, and the second link was forged as Jesus passed it on to his followers. We are to continue the links into the very world in which we live. It is through this linkage of generations that the story of vocation is told from one generation to another. As Mary's own past was taken up by God and transformed into a story of vocation, so many others have offered their pasts to God and have seen him create a vocation.

FICTION WRITER WITH A NEW VOCATION

Dorothy Sayers is known to many for her detective stories (centering on a certain Lord Peter Wimsey). She is also known for developing, later in her career, a pointed Christian pen, a pen that transformed the ink of detective stories into the ink of vocation.

What is less known is her past: Though from a Christian home (her father was a pastor), faith didn't come knocking until midlife. Before that time, she had a son out of wedlock with a married man. (His daughter later called him a charming rotter!) Dorothy decided her lifestyle and a young boy's needs could not coexist, so she persuaded her cousin, Ivy, to take in the child and nurture him. She never did live with her son, even though she "cared" for all his needs financially—which her success as a writer permitted.

Dorothy had a past that was not "conducive" to a spiritual calling. But, in his mysterious grace, God simply swept up this past into a new vocation for Dorothy. When she was asked to write a play for the annual Canterbury Festival (*The Zeal of Thy House*), her life powerfully shifted into a new vocation: in addition to her detective stories, Sayers' zeal shifted to the house built by Jesus Christ. If her past held her back, we'll never know, but her own comment provides a serious clue: "What has happened has happened, the past cannot be undone, only redeemed and made good." Hers was. There was not a day that she did not realize what had happened; there was also not a day when her pen was not "on vocation."

If the past of Dorothy Sayers surprises us, we simply have to stand back and let God do what he chooses. God takes this bitter experience, stirred up as it was by complicating bad decisions, and gives her a vocation. In the same way God gives a vocation to Mary, mother of Jesus.

If the neighborhood rumors about Mary shape what many at that time think of her, what God does through her speaks so loudly that little remains of the gossip. When Mary sits among the crowds and listens to Jesus, she surely thinks back to the days in Egypt, to the days in Nazareth, and to what God is now doing as the angel Gabriel had promised her some three decades earlier. What she had once sung about and yearned for is now being heard by is and coming to pass for a growing number of Israelites. This spindly band of believers is finding in her own Son not just another teacher but the one who will liberate Israel and turn rags into riches. Mary wears those riches, daily, over her wounds. With the generations, let us call her "blessed" for her vocation.

CHAPTER 10

Peter:
The Story of
Conversion

G O S P E L   R E A D I N G
Luke 5:1–11

Conversion, like wisdom, takes a lifetime.

For some, conversion is like a birth certificate while for others it is like a driver's license. For the first, the ultimate question is "What do I need to do to get to heaven?" For the second, the question is "How do I love God?" For the first, the concern is a moment; for the second, the concern is a life.

The *Jesus Creed* is more like a driver's license than a birth certificate. The difference between the two is dramatic. A birth certificate proves that we were born on a specific date at a given location. A driver's license is just that: a license to drive, permission to operate. If conversion is likened to a birth certificate, we produce babies who need to be pushed around in strollers. If it is like a driver's license, we produce adults who can operate on life's pathways.

The *Jesus Creed* is about the totality of life, and so conversion to Jesus and the *Jesus Creed* is total conversion—heart, soul, mind, and strength.

To see how total conversion is at the time of Jesus, we need to sit at the table with Jesus in first-century Galilee. At that table is one of Jesus' closest friends, who is also an apostle, one commissioned by Jesus to represent his mission. This friend's name is *Shimeon Kepha*, but we call him "Simon Peter." When we pull up to listen to Peter, we hear his story of conversion. A good place to begin is with Peter's own beginning: when, we might ask, is Peter converted?

WHEN IS PETER CONVERTED?

In which of the five scenes below do you think Peter is converted?

Is it when he is *introduced* to Jesus? Simon Peter's brother, Andrew, is at one time a disciple of John the Baptist. While in Jerusalem for a feast, John tells Andrew about Jesus, and Andrew spends most of the day with Jesus. Andrew tells his brother Simon that he thinks Jesus just might be the Messiah, the long-awaited king and liberator of Israel, and he introduces Simon to Jesus. When Jesus sees Simon, he reveals to him that someday he will be called "Peter." Is he converted here?

Or, is it when Peter *confesses he is a sinner*? After fishing all night, not catching anything and cleaning out his nets on the lake shore, Peter is asked by Jesus to oar his boat out into the water to listen to his teachings. Then Jesus asks Peter to let down his nets again. Peter, the fisherman, obliges Jesus, the carpenter. Peter's catch is wildly abundant. Peter falls to his knees and declares, "I am a sinful man!" How about now?

Or, is it when Peter, prodded by Jesus, *confesses Jesus is Messiah*? "But what about you?" Jesus asks Peter. "Who do you

say I am?" Peter gets it right: "You are the Christ [or, the Messiah]."
How about here?

Or, is he only converted *after the death and resurrection of
Jesus*? During the questioning of Jesus, Peter is asked three times
if he is one of the followers of Jesus and each time he flat-out
denies it. After the Resurrection, Jesus meets up with Peter, and
Jesus asks Peter to renew the *Jesus Creed*: Do you love, do you love
me, do you love? Peter says, Yes, yes, yes. How about here?

Or, is his conversion only complete when he and the others
receive the Holy Spirit at Pentecost? After the death and resurrection of Jesus, the next major Jewish holiday is Pentecost (the Feast
of Weeks). Some of Jesus' disciples are in a room together on
Pentecost when the group is bushwacked by the Holy Spirit, and
Peter is among them. The Spirit emboldens Peter to tell everyone
around about Jesus. Is this Peter's conversion?

Two other events can be mentioned—Peter's vision of a church
that is both Jewish and Gentile, and Peter's letters to churches. But
only celestial snobs who inspect others from back pews think Peter
isn't really converted until just before he writes 1 Peter, and it takes
someone with higher ideas than Socrates to think Peter can't be
called a convert until he embraces (what had been for him the
dreaded) Gentiles. But, serious Christians can make a case for each
of the first five events mentioned above.

The unserious can humor themselves with this: Number-
counting groups might like the first sign of life in Peter in scene
one, confession-oriented theologians hear "I am a sinner" and smile
ever so slightly, while creedal Christians stand up at Peter's confession
of Jesus as the Christ. Surely the charismatics finally find a brother
when Peter is flooded from above with the Holy Spirit's fire, and

the socially active churches are unenthusiastically satisfied when Peter finally embraces the multicultural acceptance of Gentiles! Only utopians wait until the end of someone's life to make a ruling. But this is humor . . . perhaps.

No one doubts *that* Peter is converted, but we may not be sure *when* the "moment" occurs, when he gets his birth certificate. And therein lies the mystery of conversion. Conversion is more than just an event; it is a process. Like wisdom, it takes a lifetime. Conversion is a lifelong series of gentle (or noisy) nods of the soul. The question of *when* someone is converted is much less important than *that* they are converting.

Some Christians are like the apostle Paul and know the date and time of their conversion. They tell a story of a "big moment." They get their birth certificate and their driver's license on the same day. As with Paul, the ground shakes, the sun flashes, voices boom, eyes twitter, and they've survived to tell us all about it. But few have such experiences. For most Christians, conversion is more like the evening soft-shoe dance of the summer shadows across the lawn. It's hard to see, but the shadow is moving, and at some point we see that it has, in fact, covered the lawn. Conversion, for these, is a series of gentle nods of the soul—from childhood through adulthood. There is no reason to think Paul's is the definitive model.

Peter's story is not Paul's, and Peter is as welcome to the table with Jesus, Joseph, and Mary as anyone. Here's his story:

I GROW IN MY UNDERSTANDING OF JESUS

A close reading of the biblical texts about Peter reveals an ongoing conversion, a developing understanding of who Jesus is. Here are seven chapters in that development:

1. Peter *suspects* Jesus might be Messiah.
2. Peter recognizes Jesus as someone *profoundly superior*.
3. Peter confesses Jesus as *the Messiah*. [But Peter disagrees with the Messiah on whether or not the Messiah ought to suffer.]
4. Peter perceives *the Messiah must suffer*.
5. Peter confesses Jesus *is Lord*.
6. Peter realizes that Jesus is not just the Lord of the Jews, but the Lord *of all*. Here Peter sees that the *Jesus Creed* is about loving *all* others.
7. Peter embraces Jesus' life as *the paradigm of Christian living*.

From *suspecting* Jesus might be the Messiah to making him the *example* of life is progress indeed. But, lest we get too systematic, Peter's growth is not consistent. Every time Peter learns something new about Jesus, he reorients his heart and life, but sometimes he lapses and falls backward.

Our perception of who Jesus is cannot be charted on a straight-line graph. Titles, definitions, and perceptions of Jesus are not the issue: response to Jesus is. If full understanding of Jesus Christ—including the later theological sophistications about his nature, person, and relationship to the Father and Spirit, backward in time and forward into eternity—is required for conversion, none of us will make it for one simple reason: No one really understands the fullness of the person of Jesus Christ! What is to be understood is that we are to respond, in love, to Jesus as we continue to grow in our perception of him.

Peter's conversion is a gradual growth of what he understood about Jesus. There is also a gradual growth in his willingness to go public with his faith in Jesus Christ.

I GO PUBLIC STEP BY STEP

Peter's conversion progressed (sometimes with baby steps) from the private to the public. In the first four "chapters" of Peter's life, his encounters with Jesus and others were more or less *in private*. But in chapters five through seven, Peter *went public* and, in fact, (to coin an expression) *he went Rome*!

In the public phase of his witness before others, Peter urged the Christians of Asia Minor to respect Roman authorities, to live lives of utter holiness, and to be ready to defend their faith publicly. Loving God, Peter said, means to follow Jesus—even to the Cross. So realistic was the Cross for Peter's "public confession" that tradition tells us that Peter was himself crucified in Rome. He asked that his crucifixion be upside down, knowing he was still inferior to the Messiah who told him to fish on the other side of the boat.

Peter was perhaps crucified upside down. What is certainly clear is that he left for us a wonderful example of how conversion progresses in understanding Jesus Christ and how it shifts from a private to a public courage. At the beginning of his life as an apostle, Peter thinks of converting fellow Galileans and Judeans; at the end of his life, he is thinking in terms of how to reach the Roman Empire.

A more recent example of progressive conversion can be seen in Frank C. Laubach.

A MISSIONARY GOES PUBLIC

In the annals of world history of the twentieth century, the most famous missionary in the mind of most was Albert Schweitzer. But many think the missionary with the most complete impact on the world was a man of much less fame: Frank C. Laubach (1884–1970).

Reared in the comforts of the farming communities of Pennsylvania at the hands of a Presbyterian father and a Baptist mother, Frank found faith with another group, the Methodists. But while serving as a Congregationalist missionary in the Philippines, Laubach had an experience while praying on Signal Hill behind his home in Lanao, where he was ministering to the Moros people. Experiencing total failure at the hands of a people who had no place for the gospel, he cried to the Father, "What can I do for hateful people like these: murderers, thieves, dirty filthy betel nut chewers— our enemies?" God answered him.

> My lips began to move and it seemed to me that God was speaking. "My child," my lips said, "you have failed because you do not really love these Moros. You feel superior to them because you are white. If you can forget you are an American and think only how I love them, they will respond."

Laubach's life was gradually but dramatically transformed in his understanding of the "others" he was called to love, and his work grew from a private to a public mission. The *Jesus Creed* formed the center of Laubach's life. Thus, he later confesses: "I choose to look at people through God, using God as my glasses, colored with His love for them."

His little book *Letters by a Modern Mystic* has sold nearly a million copies. Partly to his credit go the practice of "breath prayers" and the decision to live in the continual presence of God, which he had learned in seminary from Brother Lawrence. He went down from that Signal Hill experience with a mission "to respond to God as a violin responds to the bow of the master," and he believed that such "oneness with God is the most normal condition one can have." He found such oneness, for he confesses in April 1930 that "God was so close and so amazingly lovely that I felt like melting all over with a strange blissful contentment." One of his most potent statements about private, personal conversion is this: "Now I like God's presence so much that when for a half hour or so He slips out of mind—as He does many times a day—I feel as though I had deserted Him, and as though I had lost something very precious in my life."

"But the result of Laubach's prayer life was more than radiant being; it was also energetic doing." Laubach lived by balancing a love of God with a love of others: "It is as much our duty," he says, "to live in the beauty of the presence of God on some mount of transfiguration until we become white with Christ as it is for us to go down where they [needy people] grope, and grovel, and groan, and lift them to new life."

And just what did he do about moving, as Peter did, from the private to the *public*? Frank C. Laubach is not only a legend in prayer, but also a pioneer in literacy with his plan "Each One Teach One." His prayer: may everyone who learns to read teach one more to read. In his lifetime he tirelessly set up literacy programs in more than one hundred countries and, amazingly, was responsible for teaching over sixty million people to read!

Reading was more than a social act for Laubach. For him, teaching literacy was preparation for the gospel and for the transformation of society. For mission groups "he developed an approach for telling learners the story of Jesus" in the first person.

Like Peter, Laubach was transformed from the private to the public, and in the process he learned, like Peter, to love God and to love *all* others. Just the sort of thing that happens when we, at the suggestion of the Lord, toss our nets into unknown waters.

CHAPTER 11

John:
The Story of
Love

GOSPEL READINGS
Mark 10:35–45; Luke 9:49–56; John 13

Good biographies tell the truth.

Israel's once-famous King Saul is the Pete Rose of the Bible.
Propped up by magnificent gifts, he had some splendid successes
and some blatant failures. His end was tragic. Chosen by Samuel to
be Israel's first king, he's a shoo-in for hero in Israel's storybooks
for millennia to come; but, no, Saul breaks the rules. The Bible has
a knack for telling the truth about people. Think of Adam and Eve,
Abraham, and the kings of Israel.

At the other end of the spectrum is Christian biography, sometimes called "hagiography." Such Christian biographies often drift
into fiction as the authors wipe away every trace of sin in order to
make the person's life exemplary. But the Bible tells the truth about
people.

Telling ugly truths about leaders may encourage sin, so doting
biographers tend to hide the facts. But shading the truth may
exhaust other Christians who conclude that they could never live
such a perfect life. What is the solution? Tell the truth.

Telling the truth is exactly what the Christian leader and Old Testament scholar John Goldingay does in his book of reflections on faith, *Walk On*. John's wife, Ann, suffers from multiple sclerosis, and he explores the ups and downs of his own faith as he lives with her crippling disease. In his chapter on "Friendship," John says this:

> I have had several experiences of women telling me they have fallen in love with me when I had no such feelings for them. I have also had the experience of getting sexually entangled with someone and thus doing wrong by her, by Ann, by God—and by the people who think I am an upright man who does a good job of living with the loss involved in his wife's illness. [After quoting a letter from a student who found John and his wife's relationship an encouragement to marriage, John adds this line of truth:] I wish the student's letter were more unequivocally justified.

I don't retell John's story to pounce on him or to rationalize his behavior by appealing to the all-too-easy "we are, after all, sinners." Instead, this story is true; it is part of John's life. Because John is a clear-minded reader of the Bible, he told his own story the way Bible authors told the biographies of others.

Around the table of Jesus, his followers were telling the true stories of their lives. We've already heard the stories of Joseph, Mary, and Peter. Another one of those about whom the Bible tells a true story is the apostle John. John's own story has been shaded more than perhaps anyone's in the Bible.

DO YOU KNOW JOHN'S STORY?

Readers of the Bible rarely put together a complete picture of the apostle John. Instead, most readers focus on the glowing picture of what John was like later in life.

One word comes to mind when we think of the apostle John: love. But John's own "story of love" is not pretty. Love, for John, didn't come easy. In fact, if we sort out every reference to John in the Gospels we see this: John is with Jesus at some dramatic moments, but not once does John do anything that would lead us to think he would later become the celebrated apostle of love. We know this because the gospel writers told the truth about John's life.

If we were to ask John about his life, he would respond by telling us the story of learning to love. Here is where he would begin:

1. I LEARN ABOUT LOVE

The skinny on John begins with his family context. Many scholars think John was a cousin of Jesus. John's father, Zebedee, was a Galilean fisherman who employed John and his brother James. James was also an apostle of Jesus.

Jesus rocks the boat of all three when he calls James and John to "follow him." To follow Jesus means to travel with him, to learn from him, and to live as he lived. John will later write a gospel and a significant letter to Christians, explaining to them and to us what he had learned from Jesus. The one theme that consistently runs through John's writings is the theme of love. John sums it all up by telling us that Jesus gave to his followers a "new" commandment, and it was to "love one another." Why is it "new"? Because Jesus added the "love others" line to the *Shema* of Judaism when he taught the *Jesus Creed*. John even ties together the two parts of the *Jesus Creed* in another of his statements: "Whoever loves God must also love his brother." What John learned from Jesus was "love God, love others." When he sums up what he learned from Jesus, John says he learned about love.

But, learning *about* love doesn't mean *living* lovingly. Or *knowing* is not always the same as *doing*.

2. MY LOVE IS TESTED (AND I DON'T DO WELL)

In a moving, tender story of the love of a father and son, author Brian Doyle talks about the ups and downs of his own love for his parents:

> Like most children, I loved my parents without qualification until I was a teenager, when I began to hate them for the boundaries they placed about me; and then when I woke up from those years, at about age nineteen, I began again to love them without qualification but also with a deepening sense of the thousand ways in which they had given their lives for me, to me.

The rest of Doyle's book is a story of love, but a story incomplete if those five years are not mentioned. As Brian Doyle "learned" love from his parents, so the apostle John learned love from Jesus. But just as Doyle didn't always practice it, so John didn't either. As Aesop said about what really matters, "Deeds, not words."

John is about to be tested to see if his deeds match up to his words.

This young apostle of Jesus, the gospel writers truthfully tell us, had some love to learn. In fact, they tell us—if we listen to what they are saying—that John fails when he is *tested in love*. Three times. We blame Peter for his three denials. Let's not forget John's failures. What are they?

First, John and James approach Jesus and, banking on grace, state: "We want you to do for us whatever we ask." Jesus humors their obvious pettiness and asks them to proceed to their request. "Let one of us sit at your right and the other at your left in your glory," they say. We are not surprised to learn that the rest of the apostles bristle over the snobbish *chutzpah* of these two brothers. If love is service (which is what Jesus goes on to explain to the brothers), then John fails in love.

Second, John's love for others is tested when he doesn't recognize someone exorcising demons in Jesus' name. John tries to stop the person from doing miracles and "tells on him" to Jesus. To which Jesus gives the agelessly valuable response "whoever is not against us is for us." Anyone following the *Jesus Creed* would not denounce someone who is breaking down demonic walls. Except John.

Third, John hears that some Samaritans refuse hospitality to Jesus "because he was heading for Jerusalem." John's response: "Lord, do you want us to call fire down from heaven to destroy them?" Ouch! He prays for hell to fall on these people. John was in the Thunderbolt Gang before he was an apostle of love. Jesus explains that his followers are not to think of Sodom and Gomorrah, to call for "ash in a flash," every time they encounter someone who doesn't respond properly. When John's love for the Samaritans is tested, he fails.

For someone who spends his last days writing about love-love-love, John sure fails when his love is tested. John may learn about love, but as a young man, he is crusty and cranky. But he does have something going for him: he spends plenty of time with Jesus. Perhaps we need to join him with Jesus. "Example is better than precept," as Aesop also said. John has both precept and example in Jesus: Jesus keeps on loving John.

3. I AM LOVED ANYWAY

Nothing is more important for the development of love than being loved—we may be taught the importance of love, but *to experience it is to know it*. This is why Lewis Smedes, in his marvelous memoir of his own slow and painful growth in love of God and others, describes the love he looked for in his mother:

> Every comfort I was taught to see from my heavenly Father I looked for in her, my earthly mother, but, all the time I was growing up, she was working too hard and working too much to have either time or energy to get close to me long enough for me to find God's comfort in her. I was never conscious of my missing father whom I had never known, but I missed my mother all too often.

But Lew's growth in love all comes together when his mother was eighty-six and broke her hip for the second time. Lew is able (by providential accidents) to spend every afternoon with her. One afternoon Lew opens his heart of pain to his mother. After his mother expresses gratitude to the Lord for forgiving all her sins, Lew probes another serious issue.

Why had she never gotten married again? [He asked her,] "Didn't you ever want a man in your life? A man to take care of you? A man to talk to at the end of a day? A man to sleep with you?"

"Oh yes," she said, "I did; I felt so tired and so alone, and I sometimes wished that I had a husband, but I was afraid that if another man came into the house, *he might not care for my children as I did.*"

I knew then [Smedes continues] that I had found the love of my heavenly Father tucked into the love of my earthly mother.

For Lewis Smedes, a painful process leads to a personal knowledge that God loves him. That love had not been obvious in the love of his parents, but one day, many years later, he does see that God's love has been there all the time in his earthly mother. *To be loved is to know love.*

John learns that love is more than learning. He had learned the *Jesus Creed* from Jesus, and he had seen Jesus live a life of love, but he is struggling with loving others himself. What eventually circles him is Jesus' love.

John knows what it is to be loved. He is, after all, "teacher's pet." Jesus loves him so deeply he includes him in everything. Several incidents in the life of Jesus reveal how specially Jesus treats John. When Jesus goes to the synagogue ruler's home to heal his daughter, he takes John along. When Jesus is transfigured on the mountain, he permits John to see it take place. And when Jesus prays in the Garden of Gethsemane, he asks John to stay close by. In each of these, John experiences the special loving attention of Jesus.

So much is John the teacher's pet that John refers to himself in his Gospel as "the disciple whom Jesus loved." Perhaps the most fascinating dimension of John's calling himself the "disciple whom Jesus loved" is when he describes a famous meal with Jesus and says he was "reclining next to him [Jesus]." Literally, the text says that John was "reclining in his bosom." Now, it is a short step from this statement back to John's statement about Jesus: "No one has ever seen God, but God the One and Only, *who is at the Father's side*." Literally, this text says "who is in the bosom of the Father." Put together, John's own language suggests he thinks the love he experiences from Jesus is the same sort the Son experiences from the Father!

John knows what it means to be loved by Jesus, even though when tested, he goes belly-up. The love he experiences in the bosom of Jesus is what eventually transforms John's story from Thunderbolt to an apostle of Love.

4. FINALLY, I LEARN TO LOVE OTHERS

We know Mr. Thunderbolt became the apostle of love from John's later writings. Several considerations show the transformation of John's life:

First, John abandons his idea that he is the most important apostle. In fact, so profound is John's own self-humiliation and service to others that he *doesn't even identify himself* in the narrative of the Gospel he wrote. John gives himself only one name: the "one Jesus loved." The would-be MVP becomes the anonymous loved one.

Second, John writes for us a theology of love. The young apostle who wanted to turn Samaritans into ash and who thought gifts of exorcism were limited to one small group of disciples comes full circle. It doesn't take much imagination to know how John would have responded to each test later in his life.

Third, we need to count some words. The epistles of John are about 2 percent of the New Testament, yet they contain more than 20 percent of the instances of the term "love." It is not just usage. It is about *centrality*. John learned from Day One that Jesus wanted his followers to love God and love others. If Jesus adapts the *Shema* in his *Jesus Creed*, John adapts the *Jesus Creed* ever so slightly: "This is his command," John says, "to believe in the name of his Son, Jesus Christ, and to love one another as he commanded us." That is, love God, *believe in Jesus*, and love others.

This is the story of John: the rascally thunderbolt becomes a tender apostle of love. This is the true story of John's life, and by telling the truth, we see the fullness of God's gracious work in his life. We need to tell the truth about our lives too.

By telling the whole story of our lives, we awaken sleeping paragraphs in our own lives and in the lives of others, and when they awaken, they give to our lives a fullness, a continuity in time, and a richness.

In the community of Jesus there are many stories, none more exemplary than this story about the apostle John. As an old man, it is said, all John wanted to talk about was love. His own students were amazed at how loving he was. He would have been the first to remind them that "it was not always so."

CHAPTER 12

Women:
The Story of
Compassion

Compassion is a story everyone loves to hear.

In the community of Jesus we sit at table with one another and learn
to embrace the stories of others as our own, even when those stories raise eyebrows. Jesus, in his radical actions of compassion,
does not permit his followers to embrace the stories of only those
who are similar—we are to love all those who sit at Jesus' table.

At the table with Jesus is an unusual collection of people.
Some have done wicked things—like prostitution and theft—and
need forgiveness and redemption. Some have fallen victim to tragic
fate—like disability and poverty—and need healing and help.
Jesus, oddly enough, seems "anxious to get them [gathered round
his table] and have the difficulties begin"—to hitch a ride on an
expression from Flannery O'Connor.

Sometimes we treat the needy as if they are pariahs, as if they
have done something to deserve their fate. Sometimes our social
allergies to others are the result of a moral judgment. More often
they come from a profound inner disturbance of not knowing what

to do with people who have profound needs. Even when we believe that God loves everyone, we still don't know what to do with some people. The distance between "us" and "them" creates hostility between the haves and the have-nots. And any effort to move "from hostility to hospitality," as Henri Nouwen dubs it, is not easy.

But Jesus, with eyes abrightin' and heart awarmin' and hands astretchin' and feet amovin', does offer hospitality to persons at the edges of society. He enters the safety zone, walks to the edges, takes the needy in his hand, escorts them back across the zone, offers them a spot at his table, and utters the deepest words they are to hear: "Welcome to my table!" He offers them a "free space where the stranger can enter and become a friend instead of an enemy."

The gospel writers use the term *compassion* for this kind of behavior by Jesus. The *Jesus Creed* is to love God and to love others. Jesus exhibits both, and love sometimes manifests itself in mercy shown to those with deep needs.

Some women, stories of whom are tucked into the narrative of Luke 7–8, are part of the community of Jesus, and from them we hear and embrace the story of Jesus' compassionate love for others. The Gospels show a genre: a story of compassion. It has three chapters.

1. MY GRIEF IS OBSERVED BY JESUS

When Jesus and his disciples enter Nain, a place for nobodies going nowhere, they encounter a funeral procession. A dead son is being carted away in a casket. A woman customarily walks first in a Jewish funeral procession to remind Israel that Eve, a woman, sinned first and kick-started this "mortality thing." Leading the procession that Jesus and his followers come upon is a widow.

Jesus knows widowhood firsthand because his mother is widowed. Even though Judaism developed a small bundle of laws protecting widows, the label "widow" (Hebrew: *almanah**) quickly became synonymous with poverty. Jesus' Parable of the Widow Demanding Justice, who badgers the judge until he listens to her case, illustrates the all-too-common powerlessness and poverty of a widow. The widow from Nain had already seen the death of her husband, and she is now losing her "only son." And thus she is probably losing her income. She is weeping in grief when Jesus observes her.

Sometimes the grief observed by Jesus is caused by the suffering of leprosy, by spiritual and physical malnutrition, by the helplessness of epilepsy, or by the misery of blindness. Whether it is caused by physical or spiritual issues, Jesus observes the grief because his "compassion radar" is set on high. He is a walking emergency room, so it seems. Others are like this.

A story is told of the famous Rebbe Wolfe of Zbaraj who was known for finding the needy and showing them compassion. One day he

> was attending a circumcision. Stepping outside for a moment, he noticed the coachman shivering with cold:
>
> "Inside it is warm," he told him. "Go in, warm yourself, have a drink and something to eat."
>
> "Who will watch the horses?" [the coachman says]
>
> "I will," [the Rebbe answers.]
>
> The coachman did as the Master wished. Several hours later people saw Rebbe Wolfe, half frozen in the snow, jumping from one foot to the other, at a loss to understand why the guests were making such a fuss.

Rebbe Wolfe, like Jesus, was a famous person, held in honor by many. And also like Jesus, he sees a person in need because he observes the need.

The story of women who find compassionate mercy begins with Jesus observing their grief. Their story quickly turns to Jesus' emotion and empathy.

2. I SEE JESUS' EMOTION AND KNOW HIS EMPATHY

When Jesus sees the widow, Luke tells us that "his heart went out to her," or "he had compassion on her." The next words he utters he had probably spoken many times to his own mother: "Don't cry." We have a picture of Jesus here that is profoundly emotional. How do we know when a person is filled with compassion? Clearly, "his heart went out to her" is virtually synonymous with "tears filled his eyes." Jesus shows the woman emotional empathy, an empathy he derives from his mother and from his God.

Love and compassion, as they say, start in the home. Jesus knows the realities of widowhood at home because Mary was a widow. Mary, steeped in Israel's Scriptures, found help in the *Torah*. Because Jesus has also heard the Psalms over and over, he knows that his *Abba* will defend the needy because he is the "*Abba* of the *abba*-less." Both Jesus' experience at home and his theology prompt his emotional response and empathy to widows.

Jesus' empathy extends to many others in need. In the home of Simon the Pharisee, Jesus encounters a prostitute (*zonah*) who lavishes her gratitude and adoration on Jesus. She weeps at his feet, wipes them dry with her hair, and then pours ointment on them as a gesture of gratitude. Preoccupied with "Bulls and Cycles" from the authorities on how to treat the impure, Simon is not happy with Jesus' behavior. But, Jesus sees the prostitute for what *Abba* made her to be. In the words of Thomas Kelly, Jesus could see that all humans are "tinged with deeper shadows" but also "touched with Galilean glories." That includes everyone, to swipe a line from William Griffin, "from the wormy to the pachydermy." And, to grab a line from Nancy Mairs, "for even the grudgingest of creatures," like us. That's how Jesus sees this *zonah*.

But not Simon. He has already failed to be courteous to Jesus, which Jesus brings to the surface because Simon is in need of some moral instruction. Simon also fails to show this woman compassion. He wonders about her character, but Jesus marvels at her love. Simon forgets that Rahab the *zonah* entered the community of *YHWH*, so Jesus encourages this *zonah* to enter his community. For Simon, the woman is "guilty until proven innocent," but for Jesus, she is guilty *but now* forgiven.

She is forgiven because Jesus sees her grief and reaches out to her in empathy. As we enter the third chapter of the story of compassion we need to pause to remind ourselves of the awkwardness that empathy sometimes creates. We may see someone in need, and we may feel empathy, but compassion asks for one more thing.

3. I AM RESTORED BY JESUS' ACTION

All of us are caught on the horns of a dilemma at times: we observe grief and we empathize. But do we have time? Do we want to be bothered? What will it cost us? Once again, a story of a compassionate rabbi, *Abba* Tachnah the Pious, shows the way.

> When he was entering his city on Sabbath eve at dusk [with scarcely enough time to get home], a bundle slung over his shoulder [which if Sabbath begins he violates by working], came upon a man afflicted with boils lying (helplessly) at a crossroads. The man said to him, "Master, do an act of compassion—carry me into the city." . . . . Abba Tachnah set his bundle on the road [risking theft] and carried the man into the city. . . . Everyone was astonished to see someone so pious carrying a bundle, with Shabbat about to begin. . . . The Holy One, feeling his suffering, caused the sun to continue to shine a while longer, delaying the onset of the Shabbat until Abba Tachnah arrived home with his bundle.

When grief is observed and empathy expressed, the next stage is set: a person who loves others *acts to alleviate the need*. Observing grief for what it really is and emotionally empathizing with it is not enough. In the words of Frederica Mathewes-Green, compassion without action is "one of those truths that run out of gas halfway home." The love of the *Jesus Creed* prompts the action of compassion.

Notice how Jesus' compassion for these women turns into *action to resolve the problem*: he *raises* the widow's son, he *forgives* the prostitute and gives her a new vocation, he *exorcises* demons from Mary Magdalene, and he *heals* Joanna, Susanna, and others. On other occasions, Jesus' compassion prompts other *actions*: he cleanses a leper, he feeds a crowd, he heals an epileptic, he sends out the disciples to evangelize and heal, and he gives sight to the blind. Jesus' kind of compassion is not abstract commitment. It is real and personal and concrete. Compassion moves from the heart to the hands and feet.

Jesus doesn't act in compassion in order to dazzle people into adoring him. He acts out of love and to transform the life of the grieving person. The widow gets her son back and has an income again. The prostitute's life is transformed from impurity to purity. Each woman of Luke 8—Mary Magdalene, Joanna, Susanna, and others—has a special story to tell about what Jesus has done: one tells a story of spiritual cleansing, another of physical healing, and others (if I may guess) of learning that Roman money is to be distributed to the needy, including Jesus. Wealthy people at the time of Jesus—and these women were evidently wealthy—did not pay taxes. Instead, if they had good hearts, they distributed their funds to charities. The chosen charity of these women was Jesus, whom they support and follow his entire life. It is these same women who become witnesses of Jesus' death and resurrection. We know some of their stories, and we know what became of them.

We don't know what became of the widow or of the prostitute, but we can guess that their lives were also changed to form a coherent story of compassion at the table of Jesus.

THE CYCLE OF COMPASSION

Not only do these women have stories to tell, they have a challenge for us: If we are to live according to the *Jesus Creed*, we, too, will have to love others by observing grief, empathizing, and acting compassionately. Compassion is not only a story to tell but also a cycle to repeat.

By the age of twelve, Agnes Gonxha Bojaxhiu of Skopje, Albania, was persuaded she was called by God to be a missionary. (It is a good thing she changed her name, because it would have been quite a handle.) Twenty-four years later, in 1946, Agnes felt a further call: to leave the comforts of her cloistered life to serve the "poorest of the poor" in Calcutta. So was born Mother Teresa.

The theology of Mother Teresa comes from Matthew 25:31–46. Here Jesus tells the Parable of the Sheep and Goats and reveals a profound understanding of his own presence. He says, "Whatever you did for one of the least of these brothers of mine, you did for me." That is, Jesus identified himself with those in need. Mother Teresa learned in that passage that she was to serve Jesus who is present among the poor. One of her biographers explains her single-minded focus on compassion:

> The call to change political structures or seek justice, though recognized as valid, was not hers. Hers was to deal, one by one, with those whose horizons had shrunk to the bowl of rice they craved. . . . Those seeking to understand were put to work because "love was best proved in deeds" but also because in order to understand poverty you had to "touch" it, you had to touch the body of Christ.

Mother Teresa's story of love for the poorest of the poor in Calcutta is well known. Like Clare of Sciffi (associate of St. Francis) and her Poor Clares, Mother Teresa explored her vocation with such rigorous commitment that she attracted others to the vocation. "Attraction" may be the wrong word: her discipline was so rigorous that her more than four thousand Sisters (the Missionaries of Charity) themselves live on almost nothing. (To be exact, they are permitted to own two sets of clothes, a pair of sandals, a bucket, a metal plate, the basic utensils, and sparse bedding.) Her perception that Jesus was among the poor, however controversial, sustained her vision: "Christ crying out for love in the broken bodies of the poor and simultaneously offering himself as sustenance."

Mother Teresa observed grief, empathized, and acted to show the love of God. Living in the slums of Calcutta, she observed grief everywhere and all the time. As an illustration of her empathy, an English volunteer once said of her: "Whoever she's talking to, that person becomes the most important person." For Mother Teresa, love is only of use if it is seen in action. Her famous words are: "Do ordinary things with extraordinary love: little things like caring for the sick and the homeless, the lonely and the unwanted, washing and cleaning for them." And, "You must give what will cost you something."

Her creed—call it her *Shema*—is simple:

> The fruit of silence is prayer.
> The fruit of prayer is faith.
> The fruit of faith is love.
> The fruit of love is service.
> The fruit of service is peace.

In Mother Teresa countless persons have encountered the compassion of Jesus Christ, demonstrated long ago to the widow, to the prostitute, and to some wealthy women. Each of them had a story to tell—some of them quite lengthy, and not a few of them enough to raise plenty of eyebrows.

PART THREE

The Society of the *Jesus Creed*

THE *JESUS CREED*
"Hear, O Israel, the Lord our God, the Lord is one.
Love the Lord your God with all your heart,
with all your soul,
with all your mind, and with all your strength."
The second is this: "Love your neighbor as yourself."
There is no commandment greater than these.

A spiritually formed person loves God by following Jesus and loving others.
In addition, the spiritually formed person embraces the stories
of others who love Jesus.

Because Jesus' mission was to establish the kingdom of God—
the society in which the *Jesus Creed* transforms life—
a spiritually formed person lives out kingdom values
in the Society of the *Jesus Creed*.

As navigators need the North Star for direction, as hikers need a compass,
and as vacationers need a map and a goal, so the followers of Jesus
need a clear vision of what the *Jesus Creed* looks like when lived out.

Jesus has given it. His category for spiritual direction is the term kingdom.
Jesus uses kingdom for the society in which the *Jesus Creed* transforms life.
Those committed to the kingdom form a society,
which we now call the church.
The kingdom's values are transformation,
a mustard seed,
justice,
restoration,
joy,
and an eternal perspective.

If we want to reshape our image of Jesus by turning to the real Jesus to see what he was all about, then we will have to make this term *kingdom* a close friend.

Jesus said, "I must preach the good news of the kingdom of God."

CHAPTER 13

A Society of Transformation

GOSPEL READINGS
Matthew 6:10; 11:28–30; Luke 17:20–21; Mark 3:31–35

Our ultimate goal shapes our each and every step. When humans live without goals, they get lost.

As a high school senior, I was a cross-country runner on the second-to-worst team in the conference, and I've shaded this in our favor. What I won't shade is that I wasn't very good. My high school was the Freeport Pretzels—and I'm not joking. But another team in our conference was called the E-Rabs (for **E**ast, **R**ed **a**nd **B**lack). "Pretzels" isn't at the top of anyone's list of favorite nicknames, but, hey, it's better than being an E-Rab. Back to cross country.

Before a meet with the Rockford Guilford Vikings, the best team in the conference, my father and coach called us two seniors into his office and told us that the Pretzels had never been skunked in a meet—that is, never had the other team's six top runners beat each of our runners. Our direction was simple: we had to beat one of their top six runners. We both took it as a challenge.

Rather foolishly, when we got to the course, I assumed I would not need to know the turns of the course. Knowing I'd never be in the lead, I knew there'd always be someone to follow.

The race began normally. I was running along (trotting might be a good term) in fourth place, with two Vikings nipping at my heels. I was some distance from third place—in fact, too great of a distance. I came upon a fork in the path, didn't know the course, and a Viking runner was there pointing to his right, my left. It was nice of him to be helping us all out. I veered left, and twenty yards down that path I realized I was running alone and had been duped by a Viking. (They were known for this sort of stunt.) I sprinted back to the jerk, gave him an earful on my way past, recovered my place, and (against all odds) . . . well, you can probably guess the end of the story.

If you have a goal, and know where you are going, you can prevent getting lost.

KINGDOM MISSION

Jesus, too, knew where he was going, and he had a term for it—"*kingdom* of heaven" (*malekutha shamayim*). This expression of Jesus provides a goal for his followers and, by living out that vision in heart, soul, mind, and strength, life is transformed.

But what does he mean by "kingdom"? Ask a Christian "What did Jesus mean by 'kingdom'?" and you will get something like this: "heaven, eternity, life after death." Or, you might hear: "heaven on earth, the millennium, a perfect world, a paradise." (On my unscientific questionnaire, the responses are about fifty-fifty.)

"Kingdom of God" is Jesus' favorite expression for his mission. The Gospel of Matthew sums up the entire ministry of Jesus like this:

> Jesus went throughout Galilee, teaching in their synagogues,
> preaching the good news of the *kingdom*, and healing every disease
> and sickness among the people.

Underneath Jesus' kingdom vision is the *Jesus Creed*, and next to it, the Lord's Prayer, which puts the *Jesus Creed* into prayer form. In the Lord's Prayer we repeat over and over, to remind us of Jesus' vision, "May your kingdom come, may your will be done, on earth as it is in heaven."

So, if "kingdom of God" is so important to Jesus, what does it mean? I offer this thumbnail definition: *the kingdom is the society in which the* Jesus Creed *transforms life*. Three parts here: first, it is a *society*; second, the content shaping that society is the *Jesus Creed*; and third, the impact of the kingdom is that it *transforms life*.

It is important to understand that for Jesus the kingdom is about a *society*. Jesus did not come merely to enable specific individuals to develop a solo relationship with God, to run about on earth knowing that they, surrounded by a bunch of bunglers, were the only ones getting it right. No, he came to collect individuals into a big heap, set them in the middle of the world, and ask them to live out the *Jesus Creed*. If they live out that *Jesus Creed*, they will be personally transformed, and they also will transform the society around them.

The kingdom would be a society that is transforming life *in the now*, and that's the extraordinary thing about Jesus. At the time of Jesus, it was not hard to find Jews pining for, pondering over, or planning for the kingdom. It was impossible to find one who believed that the long-anticipated kingdom was already *present*. Of all the radical claims Jesus made, this one stands the tallest: "The kingdom of God does not come visibly . . . *because the kingdom of God is* [right now and here] *among you*"(author's translation). Jesus' saying-satchel is full of radical comments, but this tops 'em all. Jesus believes the kingdom of God is present. This can mean only one thing: he expects his followers to *live in the kingdom in their daily lives*—right now. Thus, a spiritually formed follower of Jesus lives the values of the kingdom now.

And so we come to the most important observation we can make: Jesus' claim is that *the kingdom transformation of life has begun.*

KINGDOM HERE: LET THE TRANSFORMATION BEGIN!

It was a good time to begin. Had God waited much longer, there wouldn't have been a temple to stand in. Israel, according to Jesus, was in need of transformation. Its temple officials were corrupt; its teachers, especially the Pharisees, were overly concerned with the wrong things. Rome had its big mitt on Jerusalem and the Land. For the long-awaited kingdom to come, a transformation had to occur.

Jesus offered to these very people, to those who saw the plight of Israel as he did, an opportunity to enter the kingdom of God now: enter it, and the transformation will begin. Enter it, and a new society will be created. Enter it, and life will be transformed.

This society of transformation begins by turning to Jesus, continues by following Jesus, and is sustained by fellowshipping with others committed to the *Jesus Creed* that shapes the heart of Jesus' new society.

Kingdom transformation begins by turning to Jesus

Jesus said:

> Whoever acknowledges me before men, I will also acknowledge
> him before my Father in heaven. But whoever disowns me before
> men, I will disown him before my Father in heaven.

If Jesus thinks that confessing him is how one enters the kingdom, then it is no wonder that Jesus stands up in the synagogue in Nazareth, reads from Isaiah, and then announces that Isaiah's kingdom predictions were about him. It is also no wonder that some in that synagogue wanted to end his life right then. So it is: Jesus says the kingdom begins by turning to him.

When pastors and theologians speak of the "personal" or "relational" nature of the Christian faith, they've got it right. Jesus' kingdom can neither be ratcheted tightly into a cold-edged system of logical propositions, nor can it be downshifted into a set of social virtues. Kingdom transformation begins by recognizing that the kingdom is about a personal connection to Jesus, it begins by *turning to Jesus.*

Most remember the day Payne Stewart, a professional golfer, and four friends eerily coasted in a plane fourteen-hundred miles from Florida to South Dakota. Shortly after take-off, a problem occurred, all the occupants of the plane were deprived of sufficient oxygen, and all died. So with the plane on autopilot, they coasted over the country. Aware that those in the plane were in some kind of serious trouble, the military inspected the jet and concluded that all were dead. The plane nose-dived into a field in South Dakota. Payne, the charismatic, fun-loving, knicker-wearing PGA Tour golfer and two-time U.S. Open champion, had recently turned to

Jesus and his life was being transformed. The testimonies at his funeral had a powerful impact on his fellow touring professionals, but what few know is how it was that Payne Stewart became a Christian.

It began in 1965 when six professional golfers came to the settled conviction that they needed regular Christian fellowship on the tour, and they wanted to support one another in sharing their faith with family, friends, and fellow golfers. Those golfers—hardly household names—were Kermit Zarley, Babe Hiskey and his nontouring brother Jim, Joel Goldstrand, Paul Bondeson, and Dave Ragan.

For nearly forty years now, Christian golfers on the tour have shared their faith with other players, and the numbers of those who have turned to Jesus have steadily grown into a lengthy list. Payne Stewart is but one example of a professional golfer whose life was transformed by turning to Jesus because of the decision of some golfers to offer the kingdom to friends.

Because the *Jesus Creed* calls for the whole person—heart, soul, mind, and strength—entering the kingdom is just the first step. A whole person won't be transformed overnight—the transformation continues by making a lifestyle out of following Jesus.

Kingdom transformation continues by following Jesus

At the time of Jesus, a respectable Jewish lifestyle was all about *Torah*—we could call it "*Torah*-style." Jesus teaches that "*Torah*-style" needs a kingdom upgrade to "Jesus-style," what Jesus once called his "yoke":

> Come to me, all you who are weary and burdened, and I will give you rest. Take my yoke upon you and learn from me, for I am gentle and humble in heart, and you will find rest for your souls. For my yoke is easy and my burden is light.

In Jesus' day, the observant spoke of *Torah*-style as the "yoke of the *Torah*." Some considered the *Torah*-yoke to be a source of joy. But the average Israelite frequently found the *Torah*-yoke to be anything but a joy; instead, he or she found it burdensome. The apostle Peter complained about this at a public convention about twenty years later.

In a world where spiritual formation is measured by conformity to the *Torah*, Jesus offers an alternative. The "Jesus-style" is "easy" and "light" and brings "rest" because Jesus himself is "gentle and humble in heart." Jesus' words strike his followers as good news, the best news they've heard in some time. G. K. Chesterton gets to the heart of how many felt: this is "something that would be much too good to be true, except that it is true." If the "Jesus-style" is easy and light and brings rest, and the "*Torah*-style" is not, is Jesus dismissing the *Torah*? Surely not. The Law is not dismissed; it is fulfilled. An analogy clarifies what I mean.

My father bought our family a typewriter, made by Royal, when I was about ten years old. It clunked in at about fifty pounds, but bless its heart, it was durable. It has been since thrown away. Deep in my heart I sense that it rests at the bottom of some garbage heap, waiting for some old codger to find it, take it home, dust it off, give it a new ribbon, and set it on a table so it can get back to its chores.

We now type on a computer. What a manual typewriter is to a modern dressed-up computer, so *Torah*-style is to Jesus-style. Put differently, everything the *Torah* wanted to be when it was a little guy is exactly what Jesus' teachings are.

As the *Torah* was the lifestyle for Israel under the covenant with Moses, so following Jesus personally—loving God by following him—is the lifestyle for the kingdom. The transformation Jesus announces in the kingdom is deepened as a person follows Jesus. The central element of "Jesus-style" is the *Jesus Creed*.

Kingdom transformation is not a solo act. The kingdom is the *society* in which the *Jesus Creed* transforms life. All societies are sustained by fellowship; so also is Jesus'.

Kingdom transformation is sustained by fellowship

The *Jesus Creed* creates a society of people who love God and who love others. *Jesus Creed* people don't merely shuffle off to the shade of a fig tree to be alone. They gather together around a table. Together they learn from one another what the fellowship of Jesus is all about. Two words describe this fellowship: *family* and *upside-down*.

Once, when Jesus is teaching, Mary and her other sons come to the door of the home in which Jesus is teaching. They are looking for him. They send someone inside and interrupt his teaching. Some of those in the home inform Jesus that his family wants him. Jesus asks a stunning question: "Who are my mother and my brothers?" Then he looked at those seated in a circle around him and said, "Here are my mother and my brothers!" The new society Jesus creates around the *Jesus Creed* is like a *family*—they share their lives with one another, they care for one another, and they do all of this around Jesus.

As a family they learn from Jesus about this new transforming: about boundary-breaking table fellowship, about forgiving one another, about financial responsibility for one another, and about equality within the family of God. What they learn most is the *upside-down* nature of the kingdom itself: instead of acting with power, his family serves one another. And, instead of living in self-absorption, his followers *love one another*. In other words, they live out the *Jesus Creed* as a society—and when they do, life is transformed.

Jesus may have heard an earful—if he went home after that little lesson in his kingdom family, but his point is clear: He is forming a family fellowship clasped together by the *Jesus Creed*. The kingdom is the society in which the *Jesus Creed* transforms life.

CHAPTER 14

A Society of Mustard Seeds

G O S P E L   R E A D I N G
Matthew 13:31–32

Jesus has a thing for paradox.

Paradoxes surprise. Jesus thinks paradoxes best explain the kingdom.

Here's one of them. Some tend, as I said at the beginning of the last chapter, to think of the kingdom of God as paradise. "When God's kingdom comes," they say, "surely things will be put right. Sin will be squashed in the pit; injustices will be readjusted; cruelty will collapse; and the loving and peaceful will direct society—and we'll be in the middle of it all!"

But, instead of defining "kingdom" as paradise, Jesus defines it with a paradox. If you want to see what the kingdom is like, look at a mustard seed. This surprises everyone because it asks everyone to think of "kingdom" in a new way. We should look at what they were already thinking—and be honest enough to admit that what they were thinking is what we are thinking—before we look at what Jesus means by a mustard seed.

HARD GROUND FOR
A MUSTARD SEED

Jesus' audience knows the great kingdom dream of the Bible: The kingdom will be the day when *YHWH alone is King*. Everyone will obey the *Torah* from the heart. Instead of Gentiles' surrounding Jerusalem to conquer it, Gentiles will make pilgrimages to worship in it. Creation itself will join in on the fun: wild animals will frolic in the house with household pets. Only one word sums up what his audience thinks: paradise.

In place of paradise, Jesus offers a paradox: the kingdom, Jesus says, is not quite like that. Instead,

> The kingdom of heaven is like a mustard seed, which a man took and planted in his field. Though it is the smallest of all your seeds, yet when it grows, it is the largest of garden plants and becomes a tree, so that the birds of the air come and perch in its branches.

A mustard seed is considered by Jesus' contemporaries the smallest of seeds. The kingdom, Jesus is saying, is not like a palatial paradise but a small seed. It is like a mustard plant, not like a tall sequoia or a powerful oak. Jesus (according to our standards) apparently knows nothing of marketing strategies or attractive packaging, for he markets his kingdom in the little spiritual paradox called a mustard seed.

Why does a mustard seed attract comparison to the kingdom of God? Because for Jesus the kingdom is about the ordinariness of loving God and loving others. The kingdom is as common as sparrows, as earthy as backyard bushes, as routine as breakfast coffee, and as normal as aging. He hallows the ordinary act of love, making it extraordinary. Instead of finding it in the majestic, Jesus sees God's kingdom in the mundane. The kingdom of God is the transforming presence of God in ordinary humans who live out the *Jesus Creed.*

Our proclivity for paradise makes it difficult for us to see through Jesus' paradox. As Thomas à Kempis says, "humongous doesn't count" with Jesus. We should see in Jesus' kingdom what June Sprigg, in her chronicle of her summer with the Shakers in New Hampshire, says about her elderly Shaker friend: "Lillian . . . was the real item, the water of life in a plain tin cup." A plain tin cup filled with living water, or a mustard seed about to sprout into a bush, or a kingdom—take your pick, because each opens to us a window onto Jesus' vision of a new society.

The *Jesus Creed* shapes the society of Jesus, and when it does, the society of Jesus takes on the look of a basket full of mustard seeds. A big basket, full of ordinary acts of sacred love that demonstrate the extraordinary transformation of life.

The mustard-seed paradox of Jesus surprises in many ways. The first surprise is that Jesus finds the presence of his kingdom at work in the most unlikely of persons.

The mustard seed sprouts among the unlikely

Time and time again Jesus chooses odd people to follow him, and then he holds them up as examples of what the kingdom is all about. Instead of gathering together the Pharisaic leaders or a few well-heeled Sadducees, or even a convert or two from the Herodian powers, Jesus chooses four unschooled fishermen, a tax collector, a woman with a bad reputation . . . I could go on but you get the point. The kingdom is not made up of Roman giants and gladiators or the Jewish elite and their entourage, but of ordinary, gritty folk and ragamuffins. As Herb Brooks, coach of the United States's hockey team in the 1980 Winter Olympics, now the focus of the movie *Miracle*, says, "I don't choose the *best* players; I choose the *right* players." So also Jesus: he found the right ones, each a mustard seed.

Our natural tendency is to search for the perfect, for the powerful, for the pure, and so prepare for paradise. But Jesus' kingdom is about tiny mustard seeds, not big coconuts; it is about the ordinary act of loving God and loving others with a sacred love that transforms.

The kingdom is as ordinary as a mustard seed, and it spreads quietly, as a mustard seed grows quietly.

The mustard seed spreads from person to person

Jesus' Parable of the Mustard Seed tells us that the mustard seed, though small when it is planted, becomes a large bush. It grows. So also the kingdom of Jesus: *it spreads like seeds, one at a time, from person to person.* Don't get me wrong, sometimes Jesus speaks to large crowds and gets large responses, and other times he engages in intense discussions with the powerful in the temple courts. But mostly Jesus just meets people—breezy mornings with his disciples, sultry afternoon walks with his followers, cool evenings around the table with all sorts. Nothing about Jesus breathes the need for the gymnasium in Tiberias, or the Sanhedrin's audience in Jerusalem, or a daily platform in the courts of the temple. Nor does he need Rome's theater in Sepphoris. The paradox of a mustard-seed kingdom means that all Jesus needs is a person and an opportunity.

His is not a ministry of the big and beautiful, but of the little mustard seed passing from person to person, pocket to pocket, heart to heart. Jesus does not develop a human system dictating a personal ministry, because his ministry develops the person at the heart of a divine relationship. This is because for him the big event is the little person.

Again, though, it is the "little person" focus of Jesus that surprises his contemporaries. What also surprises them is that his method for bringing in the kingdom is peaceful.

The mustard seed grows peacefully

In the world of Jesus, there are only two ways the kingdom can be established: either wait *patiently and peacefully* for God's time or *force* the rule of God with violence. Jesus is offered by his contemporaries, as it were, two symbols of the kingdom: a sword or a mustard seed. He pulls the little seed from his pocket and leaves the sword to others. He opts for peace and against violence.

At the time of Jesus, the sword is wielded by the sort of people who are later known as the Zealots*. They believe it is necessary at times to use violence to establish God's kingdom. Jesus knows his society, characterized as it is by the *Jesus Creed*, is not compatible with violence.

His Parable of the Wheat and Weeds explains his choice of peace. The kingdom, Jesus says, to surprise us with another paradox, is like a farmer planting wheat seeds in a field. Overnight his enemies plant weeds in the same field. When the farmer's servants discover weeds are growing with the wheat, they offer to yank the weeds out by the roots (a violent image, and an allusion to the *Zealots*). But Jesus informs them that this is not the way of the kingdom: let the weeds and the wheat grow together, peacefully coexisting until the Day of Reckoning. Then God will pull out the weeds.

Mustard seeds, wheat seeds, and weeds, paradoxically, reveal the stuff of the kingdom of Jesus. It is a society in which the *Jesus Creed* transforms life. That life, Jesus says, is not characterized by violence but by patient, peaceful waiting on the work of God. When weeds and wheat coexist, sometimes the weeds become wheat—as the following story shows.

A MODERN MUSTARD SEED

On May 13, 1993, the Chicagoland section of the *Chicago Tribune* ran a story about the violent death of a Cabrini-Green resident, thirteen-year-old Brian Dixon, impressing upon its readers that this poor, tough, defiant kid was little more than a typical victim of gangs. But Bob Muzikowski, his Little League coach, knew better. As Bob said it:

> I barely recognized the boy in that newspaper article—the description just didn't fit. I never once thought of Brian as "tough." And he certainly didn't defy the authority of his Little League coaches.
>
> On the contrary, his craving for our time and attention was so transparent we had to laugh about it—the way he always schemed to be the last one delivered home so he could have one-on-one time in the car with me or with Bill. And the times he'd call the house just to say hello and ask what we were doing, obviously hoping for an invitation to come over.

Bob knew more than the reporter because Bob was personally involved in Brian's life. He had taken Brian's team, in Little League uniform, to a White Sox baseball game; he had driven Brian's team to Lake Michigan to swim; he had barnstormed with Brian's team in Iowa, camping out and having a fire, around which the boys told stories. Bob awoke one morning to find Brian asleep as close to him as he could get. It was also Bob whom the family asked to speak at Brian's funeral—a funeral funded by Bob and his small group of mustard-seed volunteers.

Bob was, and is, a mustard seed. After anything but a moral life in New Jersey and New York City, a newly converted Bob and his Christian wife, Tina, moved to the Harrison neighborhood of Chicago—known for its crime rate—where Bob found a dilapidated ball field awaiting mustard-seed growth. With Al Carter and others in tow, they turned the old place into a well-lit baseball field for kids in the toughest of neighborhoods—Cabrini-Green.

As a member of the local Alcoholics Anonymous chapter called Mustard Seed, Bob gave his heart to others—because, as Bob expresses the mustard seed–like *Jesus Creed*, "I loved God, kids, and baseball. I wanted to be a good neighbor. And I was just trying to do the next right thing." He devoted himself to "help one kid at a time" because he had learned "that connections change lives." An unlikely family working with unlikely people in a person-to-person mustard-seed ministry.

Neither Brian Dixon nor Bob Muzikowski is a household name, though many Americans have watched a Hollywood movie about Bob's inner-city mustard seed. *Hardball* was based on the story of Bob's inner-city work as told by Daniel Coyle. The movie distorted facts and dropped faith so it could be rated R and make money. Out of respect to the kids and the volunteers, Bob told the "true story" in his moving book *Safe at Home: The True and Inspiring Story of Chicago's Field of Dreams*. It is a story of a mustard seed—of a society transformed when love of God and love of others shape a person's life.

From Jesus' Parable of the Mustard Seed, we are challenged to join Bob Muzikowski and fill our pockets with mustard seeds and plant them when we get a chance. Jesus does not just talk about mustard seeds; he is one.

THE MUSTARD SEED IN PERSON

Jesus was from backwoods Nazareth in the humble region of Galilee, not the upscale Judea and its big-city Jerusalem. As we've already seen, Jesus' father was a disgraced *tsadiq* (righteous man), and his mother, a lowly member of the *Anawim* (humble poor) who was considered by many to be a *na'ap* (adulteress). Jesus' cousin, John the Baptist, was wired hot and a bit off his rocker, living in the wilderness, eating bugs, and calling the nation to repentance. John was imprisoned and beheaded.

Jesus himself was unschooled. Even more, he was considered by many of his contemporaries to be a *mamzer* (an illegitimate child). The Jewish elites didn't care for him, and they began the besmirching process by labeling him with all sorts of innuendo and slander. It became something of a risk just to be around Jesus.

Even more, Jesus often wetted his finger to find the direction of the acceptable winds, and instead of going with them, headed straight against them. So instead of finding secluded spots in Galilee to dig a foot in for his kingdom, he set out for Jerusalem. He knew his fate would be that of John's. He went anyway.

It is this "anyway" that provides yet another dimension of Jesus' model of the mustard seed. As a seed dies and then (mysteriously) grows into a large plant, so Jesus knew that he, too, must die—but it was his body (like that of the mustard seed) that would die, germinate in resurrection, and soon explode into a worldwide growth.

Nothing is more like a mustard seed than the kingdom, and that kingdom is Jesus himself. He is the Mustard Seed in Person. We might think of the kingdom as paradise, but Jesus doesn't. Paradise, Jesus says, is a Mustard Seed.

Jesus has a thing for paradox. The thing is that it works.

CHAPTER 15

A Society for Justice

GOSPEL READING
Luke 4:16–30; 6:20–26

Jesus Creed-ers love justice.

By virtue of entering the kingdom of God, we Christians make the astounding claim that we live under a different order—God's order. Living in that order should make a difference in our day-to-day living and in our society. After all, the kingdom Jesus describes is a *society* and not just a personal nest.

Spiritual formation is not all contemplation and meditation, or Bible study groups and church gatherings. Spiritual formation, *because it begins with the Jesus Creed*, involves loving God *and* others. We need not choose one or the other; we need both, because loving others includes brushing up against the thorns of injustice in society. Love wants them removed.

That kingdom living has an impact on society itself has not always been a welcome idea among some Christians. Some worry about working for social justice because they have seen many get lost in the "love others" stuff to the degree that they forget about "loving God." Others worry about the "love God" types who don't often enough lend a helping hand to their neighbors. There have been lots of arguments back and forth, but instead of describing these debates, let me tell a story about how Christians can become involved in "loving others" to build a society with a greater justice.

In the 1960s, a man in our church decided to run for mayor because he thought he could make a difference. Some in our church thought a Christian serving in politics was a sacred calling. Others thought he would be wasting his time in a secular calling. In the 1980s evangelical Christians awoke to the prospects of political agitation, but this was still the sixties, and a concern for social justice in our church was just beginning.

Our church member was elected. On the first payday of his mayoral duty, the garbage men were all standing outside his office waiting for him when he came out at the end of the day. They informed him that for years on Friday afternoons they handed over their checks to the former mayor who promptly gave them a portion in cash. That mayor had kept the rest for himself. When the new mayor told the garbage men those days were now over, like the lepers who had been healed, they hoofed it home in joy. Justice, a characteristic of the society of Jesus, had arrived for these workers.

We live in a society racked by social injustices like this, even if we (as I do) believe that the American system, with its emphasis on personal freedom and civil rights, is as noble a social dream as any in the world. Still, our society has not achieved a peaceful justice. Because it hasn't, it is our Christian duty, as those who are striving to live out the *Jesus Creed*, to pursue justice. We are learning, as Jim Wallis illustrates time and time again, that "faith works."

To convert the kingdom dream of Jesus into justice realities, we need to answer this simple question: what is kingdom justice?

JUSTICE: WHAT IS IT?

Justice is a faded entry on a dog-eared page of our society's lexicon. When someone is the victim of a heinous crime, we sometimes hear someone say, usually in emotive, unflinching terms: "I want justice." What they often mean is the death penalty. When civil liberty spokespersons talk about "justice," they tend to think in terms of Robin Hood: dismantling systemic exploitation and redistributing money and power. They often intend to be the beneficiaries of this "justice."

Because the term *justice* is used like this so often, it has acquired the sense of being negative and nasty. It seems to be little more than recrimination, retribution, and punishment. But in Jesus' kingdom, justice is deeper than retribution. Any look at the Bible will reveal to you that kingdom justice concerns *restoring* humans to both God and others.

In the Bible, *justice* (Hebrew, *tsedeqa* or *mishpat*) describes "making something right," and for something to be "right," there has to be a standard. For the Jewish world the standard is God's will, the *Torah*, and so justice for Israel was to "make things right" according to Scripture. In our American society what makes something "right" is if it conforms to the United States Constitution or to a decision made in a court of law. Jesus operates in the Jewish world. What makes things "right" for him? What is his standard? Here is where a Christian restorative sense of justice parts company with standard social understandings.

The standard of justice for Jesus is the Jesus Creed. What is "right" is determined by the twin exhortation to love God (by following Jesus) and to love others. For Jesus, justice is about restoring people and society to the love of God and love of others. This vision of restorative justice clobbers, with a padded stick of love, any retributive sense of justice. The follower of Jesus is to "hunger and thirst for righteousness [or justice]," but that "justice" is defined by the *Jesus Creed*, not the Constitution. To get things right in our world, according to Jesus, is to love others and work for a system that expresses such love.

JUSTICE FROM INAUGURATION DAY TO JUDGMENT DAY

That justice is central to Jesus can be discovered by looking at Jesus' "inaugural" statements. We can begin with Jesus' first public sermon, when he returns to the synagogue in Nazareth.

At his home synagogue, Jesus stands up to read. It is on this day that Jesus goes public with his unpopular opinions in order to annoy the powerful. What gets them going is this:

> The Spirit of the Lord is on me,
>> because he has anointed me to preach good news to the *poor*.
>
> He has sent me to proclaim freedom for the *prisoners*
>> and recovery of sight for the *blind*,
>
> to release the *oppressed*,
>> to proclaim the year of the Lord's favor.

In Jesus' "second inaugural address," Jesus keeps up the same focus on justice with a medieval tenacity:

> Blessed are you *who are poor*, for yours is the kingdom of God.
>
> Blessed are you *who hunger now*, for you will be satisfied.
>
> Blessed are you *who weep now*, for you will laugh.

Blessed are you *when men hate you*, when they *exclude you* and *insult you* and *reject your name as evil*, because of the Son of Man. Rejoice in that day and leap for joy, because great is your reward in heaven.

What Jesus promises with this odd box of chocolates is justice, a justice prompted by love for God and others. Look at the texts: to the poor he promises "good news," and to the imprisoned, "freedom." To the blind he promises "sight," and to the oppressed, "release." To the poor he promises "the kingdom of God," and to the hungry, "satisfaction." To the mourners he offers "laughter," and to the hated, "rejoicing," "leaping in joy," and a "great reward." In these inaugural statements, Jesus is concerned with *restoring humans so that things are just plain right*.

But he said such things not only in his inaugural statements. At the end of his life, Jesus gives us a clear view of the Judgment Day in the Parable of the Sheep and Goats. As a shepherd separates his sheep from his goats at the end of a day—shooing them into their respective locations so the goats (who are less hardy) can be protected with more warmth—so the Son of Man will separate humans on the basis of who acted justly and who did not. If sheep and goats can be distinguished by a cocked tail (goats), so humans can be distinguished by their treatment of others.

"For I was hungry and you gave me something to eat, I was thirsty and you gave me something to drink, I was a stranger and you invited me in, I needed clothes and you clothed me, I was sick and you looked after me, I was in prison and you came to visit me." Then the righteous will answer him, "Lord, when did we see you hungry and feed you, or thirsty and give you something to drink?

> When did we see you a stranger and invite you in, or needing
> clothes and clothe you? When did we see you sick or in prison and
> go to visit you?" The King will reply, "I tell you the truth, what-
> ever you did for one of the least of these brothers of mine, you did
> for me."

What distinguishes a follower of Jesus is a *Jesus Creed*–inspired love that lives out the value of justice for the hungry, thirsty, estranged, unclothed, sick, and imprisoned. From Inauguration Day to Judgment Day, *Jesus Creed*–justice is what Jesus teaches.

Think through your own country in one sitting. And think how Jesus' understanding of justice is or is not at work in our world. Where do we see our world falling short of the *Jesus Creed*? Inasmuch as I am a citizen of the United States, my perspective is shaped by my country, but similar questions apply in various parts of the world. Thus we could ask: Are all groups being treated with equity—the elderly, the immigrants, the young, the poor? Where do we see subtle (or not so subtle) forms of racism? Are we aware of the potential dangers of the growing, insidious cycle of hate between the races in the United States? Is the gospel preached by established churches a subtle form of racism, as has been suggested in the widely read book *Divided by Faith*? Is there adequate medical care, housing, and food for all? Are workers being paid adequately and treated fairly? Does office help receive the same benefits as others? And where do we even begin when it comes to international tensions?

The *Jesus Creed* calls us to love God *and* to love others, and loving others means that we seek to *restore* humans to God and to one another. We all fall short, so we need to ask: What can we do? What can we do to restore humans to one another? To make things right? We can look, we can see, and we can act. I limit myself to one brilliant example of someone who is doing what he can (as a mustard seed) to bring about a greater sense of justice, and he is doing so within the legal system in the state of Texas.

NEXT DOOR TO THE DEATH HOUSE

The city of Huntsville, Texas, surrounds the state of Texas's death house; Texas happens to be the state where the most executions occur in the United States. Virginia Stem Owens, with her husband, David, lives in Huntsville, and the two have written an account of the state's system of justice. They tell the story of a man who is working to restore humans. He is working at one small crack in the road.

Dan Doerfler is someone who, like Jesus, lives close enough to the people to find them in the cracks. Is it time, he is asking, for us to think of how crime impacts those family members who survive the crime? Can we help them? Doerfler gets it right in his interview, saying:

> "I think we grab the whole business of justice by the wrong end of the stick," he says. "Currently we ask who did it and how we can punish them. But it makes more sense to ask who was hurt and how we can restore them. . . . But the victim's emotional needs, which are most important, have been totally ignored."

Some progress is being made for surviving victims. For instance, in current courtrooms, laws have ruled that judges can permit Victim Impact Statements in the sentencing phase of the court. For many, a sense of justice is restored when the victim is permitted a voice in the court. Progress is also being made at other levels.

Doerfler, a Lutheran pastor, developed a Victim-Offender Mediation program through which humans can seek restoration. Criminals who participate in this program do not benefit in the commutation or alteration of their sentences for participation, in order to rule out ulterior motivations on the part of those participating. Doerfler's entire concern is with personal health and spiritual restoration, so far as it is possible between the surviving victim and the criminal. After a lengthy, careful process of introspection, preparation, and communication—and only if successful with both parties—Doerfler leads both criminal and victim into a room where they meet. Doerfler observes that 60 to 75 percent of offenders earnestly seek the process—as an opportunity to confess. But the program is designed for victims, and many surviving victims yearn for the opportunity to look the criminal face-to-face and engage in some form of communication.

In eight years, Doerfler has had over six hundred victims ask for mediation. He has learned plenty. Both the criminal and victim come to realize, through the process, that "you have to face life on life's terms" because the dead person cannot be brought back to life. They know that the criminal on death row is unlikely to gain a reprieve.

Doerfler's vision of helping victims is a genuine contribution to society, to finding a way to bring about a sense of justice, to letting humans be genuinely human and honest with one another. Many victims report a profound measure of restoration by participating in the program.

He illustrates the value of restoration with an example of a mother of a young woman who had been raped and murdered. The mother is a Christian and thought she had forgiven the man who had abused her daughter—until she met the man through Doerfler's mediation services. There she realized that she has some much deeper levels of forgiveness to explore. The process aided deeply in her healing and led to profound changes on the part of the offender. Here is the final comment by Virginia Stem Owens about this case:

> The man who had raped and murdered her daughter did indeed die in the death chamber. Asked for his last words, he recited the thirteenth chapter of 1 Corinthians. For his last meal he requested the sacrament.

Not all of us are called to work in the justice system, but we are empowered to restore justice in our society. One person at a time; one change at a time; wherever we can.

A Society of Restoration

G O S P E L   R E A D I N G S
Matthew 23:8–12; Mark 5:24–34; Luke 5:12–16

Miracles have a life of their own.

Especially Jesus' miracles. Plenty of Christians think they are proofs—proofs that Jesus is God, proofs that Jesus is the Son of God, proofs that Jesus is right. And I suppose they are "at least" proofs of these beliefs.

They are proofs for lots of thinking Christians. Frank Morison, a British journalist, went to his desk to demonstrate that the resurrection of Jesus was a myth. But combing through the Gospels, he says,

> effected a revolution in my thought. . . . Slowly but very defi-
> nitely the conviction grew that the drama of those unforgettable
> weeks of human history was stranger and deeper than it seemed.

He was convinced by the gospel accounts of Holy Week that Jesus really did die and was raised.

> The whole thing reads like an actual, unvarnished, and even
> naïve transcript from real life. Yet directly we turn over the page
> to the events of the succeeding days we run into a situation

which . . . would be utterly unbelievable by any student accustomed alike with history and the conclusions of modern thought.

What about those events? Morison thinks the evidence is clear: the tomb was empty. Who, he asks memorably, moved the stone? Morison concludes that it was moved by God. It was a miracle—and because he believed the miracle was true, he turned his life over to Jesus Christ.

There may be, and I think there certainly is, a deep and profoundly historical basis for that much-disputed sentence in the Apostles' Creed: "the *third day* he rose again from the dead."

The *fact* of the miracle of Jesus' being raised from the dead convinced Morison to believe. A miracle led him to faith.

Right here's where some clear-thinking Christians let miracles take on a life of their own and cut them off from their original context. Just because the *impact* of a miracle creates faith does not mean the miracle occurred to make that impact. Whether we are thinking of the big ones (like the Resurrection) or the little ones (like healing a leper), God isn't in the show-off business or in the convincing business. Miracles, again speaking generally, are not done to *prove* the truth about God or about Jesus Christ. They may reveal plenty about Jesus (as our next chapter will show), but their intent is often otherwise.

I must emphasize this: Miracles do reveal things about God and His Son. That is beyond dispute; that they are always *designed* to prove something is disputable. I'm on the side of those who think Jesus did miracles, and on the side of those who think miracles tell us something about Jesus and about truth. But I am also on the side of those who think the miracles had intents other than proving something.

It is quite easy to see the normal intent of Jesus' healing miracles. Any glance at the many records of Jesus' miracles in the Gospels reveals what the miracles normally do: *They restore people.* Miracles are performed by Jesus *out of love* and are done *to restore humans to God and to others.* Miracles are what happens when the *Jesus Creed* becomes restorative.

Not observing the social impact of miracles is the main reason why many Christians are confused about miracles. Jews at the time of Jesus, however, were not confused.

MOSES, JOB, AND JESUS

Jews at the time of Jesus knew that there was a connection between one's standing with God and one's health. They knew all about what Moses had said. They had heard and read Deuteronomy 28, the chapter that details what happens to Israel when she obeys (good things happen) and when she disobeys (bad things happen). When Israel lived outside the bounds of the *Shema* and *Torah*, Israel experienced sicknesses and distresses and exiles. Rather importantly, however, Moses didn't have the last word about social location. Sometimes, the book of Job tells us, sickness is a test from God and not a punishment from God.

We can say summarily that in Jesus' Jewish world, when people became seriously sick, they could understand the sickness in one of two ways: either they could say they had sinned, or they could say God was giving them a test. They could classify themselves as sinners or as saints.

A good example of this sort of classifying can be found in John 9. The disciples of Jesus encounter a man blind from birth, and they ask, "Rabbi, who *sinned*, this man or his parents, that he was born blind?" Jesus counters: "Neither this man nor his parents sinned, . . . but this happened so that the work of God might be displayed in his life." The disciples play the all-too-typical "who's-to-blame?" game of classifying sinners and saints. Jesus knows better and has the power to do something about it. Jesus performs a miracle for this man, to restore his sight and to restore him to society, and through that miracle the glory of God is seen. Jesus does this so that the man can be reclassified and placed on the healthy side of society.

CLASSIFICATIONITIS

Jewish society at the time of Jesus was one of classifications, as modern anthropologists often observe. Priests are classified: the high priest, chief priests, regular priests, and Levites. Other Jews are classified: observant and nonobservant, *tsadiq*, Essene, Pharisee, Sadducee, Zealot, *Am ha-aretz*, proselyte, and *God-fearer*.* Females are distinguished from males, adults from children, old from young, and sick from healthy. The temple and the Land are distinguished, and within the temple there are various courts: for Gentiles, for Jewish women, for Jewish men, for priests, and for the high priest only. Humans are classified into the clean and unclean—that is, who is fit for the temple and who is not. Animals are classified into the clean and unclean as well.

All these classifications seem to us today like a disease itself, what we might jovially call *classificationitis*, the inflammation of orderly distinctions. Mind you, Jesus' contemporaries perceive this as *Torah* obligation, as forms of expressing love for God. Jesus thinks it has gone too far and applies the brakes. He wants some classification walls to come down, and he heals people to get the tumblin' started.

THE WALLS COME DOWN

Jesus heals *to restore others into a society without the age-old classifications*. He heals to knock down walls between people. We will look at two walls the *Jesus Creed* knocks down.

Wall #1: Women Join the Table (Mark 5:24–34)

A woman has been bleeding for twelve years and, though she has emptied her moneybag to doctors, she is getting worse. She hears about Jesus, the healer, and sneaks up to him, touches him, draws healing from him, and is set free from her burden. In this story we see what miracles are all about, and it begins with the woman's social location.

What for us is largely a private matter (menstruation) is for Jesus' world a public reality and leads to classifications. A menstruating woman is classified as a *niddah** (nee-dah). A woman who bleeds beyond the normal cycle is classified as a *zavah.** The woman in our story is a *zavah*. Most in her society would see her extreme condition as divine discipline. She is probably restricted from marriage, and if married, her husband can divorce her. Her social location defines her. Jesus knows all about the impact of being defined by social location: his mother is poor and is considered by some to be an adulteress, and Jesus himself is considered a *mamzer* (an illegitimate child). This woman, too, is defined as a *zavah*.

Until Jesus passes by. Desperate, she comes to Jesus in the hope of healing, and should she be healed, she could be restored to the community, to marriage, and to a normal life. Restoration is her primary concern. Because Jesus is intent on creating a society that transforms life as we know it, he wants her to be restored.

This *zavah* touches "the edge" of Jesus' cloak, and his power to heal flows to her. Her bleeding stops and her impurity finally comes to an end. She's back.

One wall down.

MODERN WALLS BETWEEN MEN AND WOMEN

The walls of classification that separate people have not vanished with the march of centuries. No, there remain those in our world who maintain rigid walls between women and men. Merrill Joan Gerber, a (not all that observant) Jewish woman, spent a few months in Florence, Italy, home of the illustrious Dante Alighieri. She is invited to Rosh Hashonah (as she spells it) and so wends her way through Florence to the synagogue. When she finally finds the majestic green dome over the *sinagoga israelitica*, she needs to pass by a female security guard who wants an ID and her camera. She gives her ID but not her camera. "I push past her—camera and all—into the house of worship, where I feel fully entitled to be."

But Merrill's sense of entitlement to be in the synagogue soon stares into the face of exclusion. Instead of the sanctuary having a *mechitza** (a separating wall in the sanctuary), it has an upstairs (for women) and a downstairs (for men). The "dance of piety" takes place downstairs, often completely out of view of the women. She peers through the "bars that—on this important night—keep the women isolated from the men, who below us are invited to pray to God while their women chatter and admire each other's jewelry."

I admit to enjoying her defiant action of taking a forbidden picture, but most of us empathize when she says, "For some reason, tears rise to my eyes, surprising me. In the place where I thought I would be welcome, I feel most alienated." Her experience in the *sinagoga israelitica*—if you suspect that I criticize the exclusion of people in either synagogue or church, you've got me pegged—continues the ages-long practice of exclusion by classification. Harmless? Hardly.

We are wired in such a way that being excluded or classified by religious institutions influences our perceptions of God. When humans see women excluded this way, they can hardly come to any other conclusion than that women are inferior. When it all gets wrapped in the official "dance of piety," humans become convinced that God perhaps loves all, but he has a special place in his heavenly heart for males.

But that wall comes down with Jesus' healing of the *zavah*. Now to a second one.

Wall #2: Lepers Come to the Table (Luke 5:12–16)

A *metsora'** (leper) approaches Jesus, kneels before him, and asks to be made "clean"—that is, restored to society. A wall, metaphorical or not, exists between the leper who is classified as unclean and anyone who is clean. What we need to observe is that the classification *metsora'* is less a medical diagnosis than a purity status. The leper is in many instances a pariah and excluded from society.

Jesus, by the power of the Spirit, heals the leper and so reclassifies him. Jesus directs the *metsora'* to go to the temple and offer the levitical gift of restoration "as a testimony to them." That is, Jesus says, show to them what I have done for you, and be a witness of me at the very center of the purity system in Judaism: "Tell the temple priests that I made you clean."

In these two cases of walls tumbling down, we see Jesus doing a miracle, and we see why he performed miracles: He is restoring the marginalized to the center of society and reclassifying them as pure. The kingdom of God is the *society* in which the *Jesus Creed* transforms life—and one way to transform life is to restore humans to God and to others by performing miracles.

That society comes through Jesus.

JESUS, A CONTAGION OF PURITY

Everyone in Judaism knows that impurity is contagious. It spreads to whatever touches it. That is why humans are classified and segregated into the pure and impure. In contrast, purity is not contagious. Until Jesus comes.

Jesus is the first *contagion of purity*. Jesus lives for us, and he becomes impure for us so that he can touch us and "infect" us with his purity. We've seen above that Jesus absorbs two blows of impurity: from a *zavah* and from a *metsora'*. But the really odd thing about Jesus is that he absorbs the impure blow, transforms it, and then marvelously "infects" the impure person with his own purity. By sending back a flow of purity, Jesus restores the person to the community and ushers the person to a seat at his table.

The table of Jesus must look like a big bowl of jambalaya to some contemporaries of Jesus. At his table are ordinary Jews, along with a menagerie of others, all tossed into the kingdom cooking pot of Jesus and allowed to simmer until a spicy brew develops: lepers, women, Gentiles, prostitutes, tax collectors, and nondescript sinners sitting with the observant.

Jesus is in the middle of it all, grateful for this society of ordinary people who come to terms with his *Creed*. This kind of society, Jesus is saying, is what *Abba* wants: He loves all and welcomes all to the table where they can find healing, restoration, and a new community of God's declassified people. And anyone today who is committed to the *Jesus Creed* will be committed to a ministry of restoring humans to God and to others.

CHAPTER 17

A Society of Joy

GOSPEL READING
John 2:1–11

Yearning for more can be a good thing.

There aren't many of us who wouldn't admit that we'd like to have more of something (money, cars, clothes, success, time, children, joy, love). Most of us think life could be better with that "more." *Someday*, we yearn. Yearning, in and of itself, is worth exploring. Why do we yearn?

Craig Barnes, in *Yearning*, observes: "The deep yearnings of the spirit are part of what makes us human." Barnes has me in his grip with this: "The confession that we are unable to get the life of our dreams is the first step toward authentic spirituality." And with this: "What distinguishes humanity in creation is not moral superiority but the *mark* of a need—a craving to have meaning that is eternal and thus able to sustain us through the shifting tides of our years. . . . This godlike *mark*, then, serves two functions. The first is that it is the source of our hunger for life's meaning, and the second is that it refuses to be satisfied with any meaning other than the eternal."

Our yearning indicates our hunger for something eternal.

We are all looking for the "Great Someday." If we dig deep enough in our hearts to discover what our yearning thirsts for the most, we will discover that we are yearning for the *eternal joy* that comes from knowing God. This yearning "simply leads us back to the world with the strange message that our limited humanity is the mark of our need for God." We are, in other words, soul-thirsty for a drink of joy that will satisfy us eternally and infinitely. The kingdom is the society in which the *Jesus Creed* transforms life. One feature of that transformation is that what humans yearn for they find in Jesus. This joy is not giddiness; it is inner contentment that comes from knowing that what we yearn for is loving God and others.

Here's the good news: Jesus claims that the yearned-for joy is already here, that he's provided us with an abundant drink of it, and that his offer will satisfy our thirst forever and ever. To reveal that joy, Jesus *performs miracles* that draw down a little bit of heaven's joy to earth, that suddenly make life in this world light up in glory, and that convert the humdrum routine of reality into the joy of life.

The Gospel of John calls some miracles "signs."

A sign is a miracle that is at the same time a flash of revelation. But this flash is seen only by the person who looks at the sign with the eyes of faith. For this person, the miracle of Jesus is a window into what God is doing.

These flashes of revelation, like aha! moments in life, occur unpredictably. Jesus provides such a flash at a wedding, when no one is expecting it.

WEDDING WINE AS SIGN

I'm a curmudgeon when it comes to weddings. I'd prefer not to go, but compared with Kris, I rarely offer the better argument, so I tag along. There are three exceptions: I loved the wedding when our daughter Laura was married, and I'm looking forward to our son Lukas's wedding.

I can only wish I had attended the wedding in Cana of Galilee. The whole village and other villages such as Nazareth turn out in their Sabbath best to wish the young man and woman, as Jews say today, *Mazel Tov* (good luck). Not too long into the wedding, the hosts run out of wine. Running out of wine is not so much tacky as it is a mood killer. Wine is to weddings what a tree surrounded by presents is to a family Christmas, what fans are to a sports contest, and what discovery is to a search. Without wine the wedding falls flat; the joy vaporizes. Without joy a wedding is just not a wedding.

Mary thinks, with good reason, that Jesus can do something about the lack of wine and suggests he do something. But he slows her step a bit with this: "Dear woman, why do you involve me? My time has not yet come." She thinks Jesus ought to step forward and show his powers. Jesus thinks not. The Messiah, he is suggesting, is not a tame lion; he roars and roams when and where he chooses. And he is about to choose to do so, but not until Mary clears herself from the picture.

The miracle of transforming water into wine itself is triggered by Mary's wonderful surrender to her son's timing: "Do whatever he tells you," she tells the servants. Nearby, the Gospel of John continues, there are six large earthenware vessels—"each holding from twenty to thirty gallons." Jesus has the servants fill them with water, and he changes the water into wine. For the one who sees with an eye of faith, as the joy of the wedding returns to the wedding guests, so the yearned-for joy of the kingdom is present. This is what John means when he calls the wedding miracle a "sign." The eye of faith sees through the miracle to what the miracle reveals: the joyous glory of the Son.

MIRACLE AS SIGN

The apostle John also tells us that the vessels at the wedding are "for ceremonial washing." John's decision to state this is not the persistent jottings of a journalist who records everything he or she sees. No, John wants to make a point: The water in these stone jars is not for hygiene. This water is sacred. This water is used to purify people and things. People and things are made pure to get them in the proper order before God, to render them fit to enter into God's presence. Observant Jews wash their hands in this water so they can eat their food in a state of purity.

Of Joy

Jesus *transforms the water of purity into the wine of joy, eternal joy.* The eye of faith sees through the wine to its inner mystery, the way families see beyond a Christmas present's material benefit to its inner expression of love. In Jesus' sign, ceremonial purification rites are being swallowed up by the joy of the new society's wedding feast. Purity comes, not from water, but from drinking in the wedding wine of Jesus.

Jesus not only transforms water into wine, he does so *in abundance.* If the guests have already consumed the prepared drink for the wedding, then the miraculous transformation of water into about 120 gallons of wine is more than enough. Abundant joy is a feature of the kingdom, just as abundant love is often a feature of a family Christmas. Whoever said Christmas is about only what we need is missing what the celebration is all about. So also, the kingdom of God, which is the society in which the *Jesus Creed* is practiced, is a kingdom where there is more than enough of all the joy we truly need.

Of Jesus

What this sign reveals, John tells us, is "his glory." Jesus, who is himself the manifestation of God's glory, reveals his own glory—who he is and what he is here to do—in this miracle. When the water turns to wine and the eye of faith peers into the purification vessels, it sees not sacred water but sacred wine. The eye of faith sees not an image of itself but the image of Jesus floating on the surface of the wine. Jesus is seen in this wine for who he really is: the one who not only provides but is himself the joy of the kingdom.

All human yearning is ultimately a yearning for an abundance of the sort of wedding wine that is Jesus himself. This is to say that our yearning is really to know the joy that comes from knowing the love of God (in Jesus). The *Jesus Creed* reveals that what humans ultimately yearn for is love for God and others. To know that love is to know the joy of the wedding wine Jesus alone provides.

POTLUCKS AS SIGNS OF THE SIGN

When I was a little boy and tagging along to church with my parents, the only Wednesday-night prayer meetings I enjoyed were the ones that started with a potluck. (I found prayer meetings to be a source of joy later in my life.) Our Wednesday-night feasts were a "pot" of "luck" because, instead of listening to some boring sermon while bobbing around on an uncomfortable wooden pew, I could sit at table with my friends and eat and tell stories. Good food, too. Stews, chicken, hams, casseroles, potatoes, fresh vegetables from the local farmers. There were always homemade pies and cakes. Occasionally someone cranked ice cream in a rock salt–lined ice-cream maker.

What I vividly remember is this: no matter how many people came, there were always pots of food left over. There is something about church people: when they get together for a potluck, the vegetarians sample the other side, the calorie counters transgress, and the food flows. Why? Because when Christians get together, somehow they are showing off what they think the final kingdom is all about; they act out the joy and the love of God's new society. Jesus can't hold back at the wedding, and humans can't hold back at potlucks. Potlucks, for the eye of faith, are imitations of that sign Jesus performed long ago to show that he can provide more than enough.

More than enough is exactly what Jesus provides at the wedding at Cana. And through that abundance he offers a glimpse into who he is. He reveals himself as the abundant provider of the joy that comes from knowing the love of God.

SURPRISED BY JOY

C. S. Lewis also found the joy of the wedding wine. Lewis tells us that from his earliest days he yearned for those occasional tastes of joy he experienced in his reading and writing of stories and myths. But, he confesses, the stories and myths offered only snatches of joy. There was more, so he thought, and he was chasing it down.

What he was chasing, however, he learned was actually chasing him, and he first became aware of it at Oxford.

In a late night discussion on September 19, 1931, some fellow intellectuals asked Lewis some pointed questions. They were both Christians, and one of them was the (now quite famous) J. R. R. Tolkien, who wrote *The Lord of the Rings*. The other was Hugo Dyson, a lecturer and tutor at Reading. Both were to become fellow members with Lewis of a literary group called The Inklings. Their questions that night settled into one: Why are you, they asked C. S. Lewis, mysteriously moved by the notion of sacrifice when you read it in pagan stories, but not also moved when you read of it in the story of Jesus? For Lewis, as the English (or Irish) might say, "the penny dropped." The weight of the question and its answer dawned on him, and he began to ask if maybe the story of Jesus was the joy he was chasing.

Lewis writes, after he embraced the answer to Tolkien and Dyson's question, in a letter to his good friend Arthur Greeves, "Now the story of Christ is simply a true myth: a myth working on us in the same way as the others, but with this tremendous difference that *it really happened* . . . remembering that it is God's myth where the others are men's myths." This is a well-known passage of Lewis, asking us only to accept a fiction writer's understanding of the term "myth"—the truth, this time, in story form *and* historical reality.

Importantly, Lewis calls what he found that night "Joy." He occasionally had caught a glimpse of this joy in pictures of nature, in reading about Nordic myths, and in wandering about on hillsides or seeing moonlit landscapes. These momentary, sense-flooding visitations of joy drove Lewis to find their source, because they left him dissatisfied with the present world.

That joy did not come to him until he came to faith in Jesus Christ. Its presence and discovery surprised him, for it was not, in fact, joy that he was yearning for, after all. It was the Person to whom this joy was pointing all along. As Lewis himself explains his quest, "But what, in conclusion, of Joy? . . . To tell you the truth, the subject has lost nearly all interest for me since I became a Christian." Why? Because the joy Lewis found is only the effect of drinking the wine of Jesus—it is not the wine itself. Joy is a person, and his name is Jesus.

When Jesus transforms the waters of purification into the wine of celebration he is saying that the daily grind of yearning for joy through purity has come to an end. "You need search no longer," Jesus is saying, "the wedding wine is at the table, drink it, all of you. Drink of me, for I am the wedding wine of joy, for the forgiveness of sin. I am what you yearn for. I make all things pure."

CHAPTER 18

A Society with Perspective

GOSPEL READINGS
Mark 14:25; Matthew 25:31–46

The Bible gives us only an occasional glimpse of heaven.

So Christians have guessed about it for nearly two millennia. Guesses have a habit of becoming paintings. Because humans are visual, paintings impress our minds powerfully, and before long our guesses become convictions about heaven.

Even so, from century to century our convictions about heaven have changed. Shifts in perceptions of heaven have occasionally been so drastic that one image of "heaven" is placed in the attic of embarrassment and replaced by a more tasteful "heaven." One of the classical presentations of Renaissance "high society heaven" was painted by Peter Paul Rubens (1577–1640). It hung in a church in Neuberg on the Danube River and influenced the convictions of many worshipers, until the Jesuits of Bavaria came to a different conviction in the middle of the eighteenth century about what heaven was like. When they did, they removed the painting. Rubens's famous piece depicted plump (unclad) females and (barely clad) muscular males either entering the light of heaven or descending into the abyss of darkness.

The Jesuits, in a rare agreement with the Reformers, judged Rubens's famous painting distracting. Indeed, irreverent. While Mr. Baroque and Ms. Renaissance thought of heaven as an extravagant cultural display of their own society, the Msgr. Jesuit and Mr. and Mrs. Reformer saw heaven as more than an improvement of high society. They thought heaven was a place of worship.

Because these reformers thought heaven was for worship, their lives were conducted to ready themselves for that worship—so they focused on worship and the sacred love of God. Their view of heaven, in other words, *gave them a perspective on life.*

A perspective on life gives us a spiritual center around which to organize our lives and a moral filter through which we can judge the good from the bad. By speaking about heaven, about eternity, Jesus gives his followers such a perspective.

WORSHIP OR SOCIETY?

Some argue that heaven will be all God—all praise, worship, blessed union, and repose. The final kingdom will be total absorption in the Triune God. The chief end of humans, the Reformers teach in the *Westminster Confession*, is to glorify God forever. Many in all the major Christian traditions agree with them. Such a heaven appeals to the theologian, the mystic, those who love solitude, and those who prefer (especially classical) music during travel time. Their heaven is "heavenly."

Other Christians depict heaven as a glorified world, as society perfected—as worship, family, and society. Parents will be reunited with children, and friendships will be renewed. Each person will have a gloriously eternal vocation of service in the perfect society. Such a heaven appeals to interpersonal sorts, to those who love committee work, to those who crave the bustle of big city life, and to those who prefer (especially cultural) talk shows during travel time. Their heaven is "earthy."

Our vacation of choice, so I've heard, corresponds to our view of heaven. Those who hike into the mountains with their tents to secluded spots seem to think of heaven as a place of solitude and worship. Those who take vacations to big cities or to Disney World or to crowded beaches or to tourist locations with groups on tour buses seem to think of heaven as a place of society and worship.

Well, which is it? Do we have to choose? Could it perhaps be both? A two-story paradise where there is both an upper-story worship center in the presence of God as well as a lower story for the delight of human society and the pleasure of perfect culture? How does the *Jesus Creed* shape our view of eternity?

How can we know what eternity is like? I suggest, once again, we ask Jesus. He doesn't have to guess. To find out what he says about heaven, we need to turn once again to the Bible.

JESUS AND HEAVEN: A BIBLICAL SKETCH

Jesus teaches that heaven, or the eternal kingdom, begins with a judgment; that heaven is entered by the followers of Jesus; that heaven involves table fellowship between *Abba* and his people; and that heaven is magnificent in its glory, intensity, and splendor. In short, heaven begins with the judgment and then, once that is over, the whole place is decked out for eternal fellowship with God and others.

First the Judgment . . .

Judgment, in the Christian scheme of the future, follows resurrection. Christians have argued about the Resurrection as much as they have guessed about heaven. Resurrection only makes sense if it means that, after death, our present bodies are transformed into bodies fit for eternal fellowship. I join hands with Alan Jacobs, who admits: "I'm not interested in any reconfiguration of the notion of eternal life that doesn't at some point—I don't mind a long sleep—*get me out of the grave*, and I doubt that many other people are either."

The judgment is described by Jesus as the Son of Man judging humans as a farmer separates the "sheep" and "goats"—sending sheep to eternal life and goats to eternal fire. Eternal standing matters a great deal to Jesus, and he talks about it quite often.

Sincere Christians differ wildly about other issues. Some, on the basis of 1 Thessalonians 4–5 and Revelation, argue (rather confidently) for a complex arrangement of rapture, tribulation, Second Coming, millennium, final judgment, and heaven. Others, less confidently, keep the scene far simpler and know less and think that less is better.

While Christians differ on specific events, they don't differ on what is next.

Then the fellowship

Following judgment, there follows *an enormous banquet of fellowship*. Jesus promises a resumption of fellowship with his disciples, and he speaks of that fellowship as an eternal banquet. Whether we are to think of physical tables, crystal glasses, expensive china, sturdy goldware, and padded gold thrones is unimportant: What matters is that the eternal state is one of fellowship in the love of God and love of others. If the present kingdom is imperfectly shaped by the *Jesus Creed*, then surely the final kingdom will be perfectly shaped by it.

Anything established around Jesus, whether earthly or eternal, will be a *society*. A glimpse of the eternal society can be seen when Jesus describes the twelve apostles as somehow presiding. They will, he says, "sit on twelve thrones, judging the twelve tribes of Israel."

We may not know all the details of the eternal painting, but we do know the broad strokes, and what we also know is that these broad strokes are clear enough. What needs to be made more clear is that *these broad strokes give us a perspective on life now*. They give us a place to stand.

PERSPECTIVE: THE END IS THE BEGINNING

The place to stand, the perspective it gives us, is this: *The end is the beginning*. That is, one's view of the eternal (the end) *gives one perspective in this life* (our beginning each day). The most potent incentive to spiritual formation is to see the end of history, to ponder God's eternity, and to realize that this *end* shapes our *beginning* each day. So, in the words of Thomas à Kempis, "Practice now what you'll have to put into practice then."

We can turn the argument of this book on its head now: the *Jesus Creed* is the creed of life now because the *Jesus Creed* is the creed of the eternal kingdom. We are to live the *Jesus Creed* now because it is the eternal plan of God. Knowing this gives us a perspective and shapes an entire society around Jesus with that perspective. That society has a perspective on life that begins with knowing and loving God.

KNOWING AND LOVING GOD

J. I. Packer, in his potent study of what the Bible teaches about God, develops the subtle distinction between knowledge *about* God (mind) and knowledge *of* God *personally* (mind *and* heart—as well as soul and strength). If eternity is eternal fellowship with the Father (and not a theology test), then we need to get started right now in knowing this One with whom we will share the table. As Packer says it, "The rule . . . is that we turn each truth that we learn *about* God into a matter for meditation *before* God, leading to prayer and praise *to* God."

Some in the Christian tradition have taken the "love God" part of the *Jesus Creed* so seriously that they devote their entire lives to adoration of God. Kristin Ohlson, a journalist struggling for faith, wanted to understand why it was that the Poor Clares of St. Paul Shrine in Cleveland spent so much of their lives in silent prayer. She asked one of the Poor Clares, Mother James. "It was the perpetual adoration," Mother James said. "We're going to be doing that for all eternity, adoring God. When you do this, it's like your heaven begins on earth." We can agree that Mother James gets at least this right: if eternity is about eternal communion with God, then we can prepare ourselves by learning to fellowship with him now.

A concrete suggestion to aid us in preparing for eternal fellowship with *Abba*: we need to *read the Bible Abba-centrically*, or "Father-centered." Christians sometimes read the Bible too often to "figure things out," to come to terms with a theological debate, or to settle an old score. They read it for *information*.

But as M. Robert Mulholland explains in his very important book, *Shaped by the Word*, in reading the Bible for knowledge, we can (and often do) miss the mission: for *Abba* to love us and for us to love *Abba*. When we let *Abba* speak to us through the Bible, we come to know him (and not just about him), and our reading moves from communication from God to communion with God, from "*information* to *formation*," from learning about love to learning to love.

My suggestion is simple: put away study aids, commentaries, group Bible-study materials; get out a piece of paper and a pen and write down what we learn about God in a passage of Scripture. Just what we learn about the *Abba*. We read, we meditate, and we pray. In time these parts of spiritual reading can become indistinguishable. When they do become one, we are reading *Abba*-centrically. There is no substitute for reading the Bible in order to hear from God. It has changed the lives of many, including St. Augustine.

Augustine was converted when, groaning in prayer to God in a garden, he heard a voice—as from a little boy or girl—say, "Pick it up and read it." So he picked up the Bible, opened it, and read two verses. "No sooner had I finished," he says, "than it was as if the light of steadfast trust poured into my heart." Reading the Bible with one's heart open to *Abba*, as did Augustine, can unleash the flooding power of God's Spirit.

In addition to reading the Bible, many have strengthened their fellowship with God by reading the spiritual writings of giants in the Christian tradition. I must mention here a few of those giants (and their books) from four different Christian traditions, whom many have found helpful: *The Philokalia* of the Orthodox tradition, Thomas Merton's *Inner Experience* from the Roman Catholic tradition,

J. I. Packer's *Knowing God* from the Reformed-Evangelical tradition, and A. W. Tozer's *The Knowledge of the Holy* from the Holiness-Evangelical tradition.

Finding a regular source of fellowship by reading the Bible and reading giants in the Christian tradition prepares us for what the eternal kingdom is all about: *loving fellowship with God*. This is a perspective on life that the *Jesus Creed* gives us. That perspective also encourages us to know that the "end is the beginning" when it comes to fellowship with others who live the *Jesus Creed*.

FELLOWSHIP IN THE KINGDOM SOCIETY OF JESUS

If the end is the beginning, and the end is about loving God and loving others in eternal fellowship, then we are challenged to make fellowship with Jesus' society a regular feature of our lives—in the now. In fellowship with others we can begin our eternity. I am reminded of this in my commute to my office. Perhaps my experience is not yours, but it can serve to remind us of what daily fellowship can be.

This commute begins with a walk of about ten minutes to the train station, where I grab a cup of coffee at the local café. At that café on Tuesdays and Thursdays, I see a group of three to four men poring over some passage in the Bible; sometimes I see them in prayer, sometimes in discussion, and sometimes in quiet reflection. On the train I sit across from a man who sometimes is with a young man; they pray together (sometimes in tongues), but mostly the younger man listens to the older man explain how to live the Christian faith. At times I see a man, whether Roman Catholic or Eastern Orthodox I am unable to determine, who reads a line or two from what appears to be a devotional guide and then crosses himself, sometimes once and sometimes thrice, but always in big motions: head to belly button, shoulder to shoulder. I generally pray and read.

This year I have worked my way through *The Journals of Father Alexander Schmemann*, Richard Foster's *Streams of Living Water*, Henry Carrigan's *Eternal Wisdom from the Desert*, Thomas Merton's *The Inner Experience*, and David Larsen's *Biblical Spirituality*.

After the train, I climb aboard Chicago Metra Bus #92, and more often than not I sit near an elderly lady reading a daily devotional in some Eastern European language. Sometimes she is with another woman, and they speak to one another between reading paragraphs. I assume their whisperings are not about my being a nosy Parker!

For three years an elderly Indian man met me at the bus stop, mostly to ask me questions about the Bible, but our times were more often than not little more than the gentle, daily comfort of a Christian brushing up against another Christian and experiencing the kinship that is itself a brush with the Age to Come, the end that can begin each day.

PART FOUR

Living the *Jesus Creed*

THE *JESUS CREED*
"Hear, O Israel, the Lord our God is one.
Love the Lord your God with all your heart,
with all your soul,
with all your mind, and with all your strength."
The second is this: "Love your neighbor as yourself."
There is no commandment greater than these.

A spiritually formed person loves God by following Jesus and loving others.
A spiritually formed person embraces the stories of others who love Jesus.
A spiritually formed person lives out kingdom values,
and
a spiritually formed person loves Jesus.

What does it mean to love Jesus?

It means to believe in him,
to abide in him,
to surrender to him,
to be restored in him,
to forgive others in him,
and
to reach out with the good news about him.

This is how a disciple of Jesus loves Jesus.

CHAPTER 19

Believing in Jesus

GOSPEL   READINGS
Mark 7:24–30; Matthew 15:21–28

The goal of a disciple of Jesus is relationship, not perfection.

There is no better example of a person who confused relationship with perfection—and got ahead of himself—than Ben Franklin, America's icon of the homespun man with a mindspun religion. "It was about this time," he confesses, "I conceived the bold and arduous project of arriving at *moral perfection*. I wished to live without committing any fault at any time."

Franklin listed thirteen virtues and began to tame one moral lion per week, hoping he would master one a week. In a journal he assessed himself every evening, marking a • for each failure in a given virtue. Franklin's list of moral virtues was this: temperance, silence, order, resolution, frugality, industry, sincerity, justice, moderation, cleanliness, tranquility, chastity, and humility.

After sweating his way through his system for a while, he admits: "I was surprised to find myself so much fuller of faults than I had imagined." Indeed! When the moral life becomes a system of dots on a chart of moral progress toward perfection, the moral life unravels into externalism and futile attempts to tame wild lions. If a person is telling the truth, what he or she discovers in the human heart is an unconquerable sinful disposition that is in need, not of taming, but of *renovation*, as Dallas Willard has explained so well. Or, in the words of John Ortberg, we are to "morph indeed"—we discover that we are to be changed from the inside out.

It is this "morph indeed" business that leads Christians to make the claim that discipleship is about relationship and not perfection. Lest I be given a D for moral standards, let me quickly add that the relationship will inevitably create good, moral persons. The issue is one of order—and discipleship begins, Jesus says, with relationship.

BELIEVING IS A RELATIONSHIP

Everyone knows that anyone claiming "I am a disciple of Jesus" had better be a good person. In fact, we'd all agree that such a person would have to be extraordinarily good. We might shy away from saying they have to be perfect, but we might as well admit that inside we are holding any person making such a claim to a pretty lofty standard. But Jesus, so it seems to me, would not have joined us in these thoughts. He thinks the primary point is about "believing."

According to the Gospel of Mark, the very first expectation of Jesus for a disciple is this: "Repent and *believe* the good news!" To "believe" is to have "faith" and to "trust." (Each is a translation of the same Hebrew or Greek term.) Faith and trust are what Jesus wants, and these express a relationship to Jesus rather than moral perfection.

Faith can be analyzed theoretically, but it is best understood when it is seen in action in the real world. A good place to begin, therefore, is Jesus' encounter with the Syro-Phoenician woman.

Jesus is "on a vacation" from his ministry demands in Galilee and needs rest. This woman is "on a mission" from her daughter, who is spiritually ill with demons tormenting her and needs help. The mother hears that Jesus is in town, finds him, and disturbs his vacation—and herein lies the gateway to the biblical idea of faith. Jesus at first puts her off, but her faith won't let go, and Jesus responds to her persistent faith by healing her daughter.

If we describe a disciple as one who believes in Jesus, which this woman does, we also need to remind ourselves that believing is a dimension of love. This is clear if we substitute "trust" for "believing" or "faith." Love and trust are constant friends. The *Jesus Creed* calls people to love God (by following Jesus) and to love others. To follow Jesus as an act of love means to trust him.

The *Jesus Creed* is not a system for moral improvement like the one used (temporarily) by Ben Franklin. This is not to say that any of Franklin's virtues is unacceptable to a disciple of Jesus. But, a disciple is someone who engages Jesus as a person by trusting him, and because of that relationship, begins to live out the virtues Jesus talks about. It all begins here, in this order, and if it doesn't begin here, it doesn't begin at all.

FAITH AND ITS FRIENDS

Faith is an ongoing relationship and therefore like a marathon. The *Jesus Creed* is not for someone who believ*ed*, in the past, but someone who believ*es*. Christians are called believ*ers* not believ*eders*.

Relationships have dimensions. When two people begin a relationship, they come to know one another mentally, emotionally, psychologically, spiritually, physically, financially—and the list goes on. The relationship of a disciple to Jesus also has its dimensions,

and I call them the "friends" of faith. There are at least three elements, or three constant friends, of faith. Each is always present in
the relationship.

The *Jesus Creed* exhorts us to love God with our "all." The
Syro-Phoenician woman who interrupts Jesus' vacation responds to
Jesus in mind, body, and heart.

Faith's friend of the mind: affirming kingdom truths

The Syro-Phoenician woman, the mother of a spiritually
tormented daughter, hears about Jesus and thinks he is the person
who can heal her daughter. We can assume that the mother doesn't
know what the disciples know about Jesus. She probably doesn't
know all that much about *YHWH* or the *Torah*. But she knows Jesus
can heal and that God is doing great things through him. If she did
not believe these things *about him,* she would stay home and attend
to her daughter. Her knowledge about Jesus is "mental faith," the
affirmation of certain truths about Jesus: He can heal; he is sent
from God, he will help.

This is why Christians have, at times, reduced a dimension of
their faith to certain creedal statements. Faith may transcend the
creedal statements, but it surely involves those creedal statements.
To believe in Jesus Christ is to believe at least this one irreducible
Truth: *Abba* redeems in Jesus' death and resurrection through the
power of the Holy Spirit.

Not all of this would have been known by the Syro-Phoenician
mother in detail, but like a big backyard satellite dish, she was
pointing in the right direction so she could receive the power Jesus
could send. In effect, she believes that God's kingdom was now at
work in and through this Jesus, this Son of David. She goes to

Jesus; she gets near Jesus; she spends time with Jesus; she wants to be in his presence.

A great rabbi, a contemporary with Jesus, was named Shammai. Once a potential proselyte asked Shammai to summarize the entire *Torah* while he stood on one foot—a sort of fast-food *Torah*. Shammai repulsed the Gentile. Hillel, a more merciful rabbi, converted the man by teaching him a summary creed: "What is hateful to you, do not do to your neighbor." We can summarize our faith while we stand on one foot with this: "I believe in Jesus Christ." This creed defines the object we love when we recite the *Jesus Creed*. But we need to remind ourselves of this: the *credo* ("I believe") of the creed is a relationship with the subject of the creed, Jesus.

Reminding ourselves that a genuine creed is a relationship does not minimize the importance of the mind, which is a "friend of faith." In fact, ongoing orthodox Christian thinking is what keeps our gospel true to the New Testament shape of faith. Even more, sound thinking makes the relationship with Jesus a relationship with the person he really is. So yes, the mind is always present in faith—and one can even say that the relationship can't exist without our orthodox friend being present.

The mind has a friend in the body, our second dimension of faith.

Faith's friend of the body: acting on kingdom truths

Notice the evidence of the Syro-Phoenician mother's faith. Jesus is seeking privacy, but she physically seeks him out. She falls at his feet in an act of total desperation and begs him on behalf of her daughter. This woman's faith does not simply reside in the mind as a set of cognitive affirmations ("I believe that . . . "). Faith, in other words, is seen in action, in the concrete deed of trust.

Genuine faith prompts action. When I was in graduate school, I worked at a local warehouse packing orders for a company that supplied local stores. Mark, a fellow worker, spent his off days parachuting. He came in on Mondays with stories—and we all sat on the edges of our seats listening to them. I became interested in parachuting. He began to explain how it worked—where the airport was, what days they jumped, what the price was, what the air felt like, and (as my imagination got into it) what I would see, what I would need to wear, and so forth. He gave me ample sta-stistics (as he called them) on safety. I grew more interested as I became more convinced of the safety. I decided I'd try it. Then one day, after explaining it all again, he said, "We're going tomorrow. You wanna go?" I was confronted with a decision—I was mentally persuaded it was safe, and I knew it would be cool, but my body wasn't cooperating with my mind. My answer: "No. I'm not getting in the plane." What he called me is not repeatable here, but you get the point.

I believed in my mind, but not with my body. My *actions* betrayed my mental faith. Genuine faith not only believes in the mind, it also beckons the body to act.

Perhaps we do not notice our actions for what they are, but we often express our faith "bodily": we *give* money, believing God will use our gifts; we risk financial security by *changing careers*, believing God has called us to something new; we *make that difficult, emotional phone call* to someone, hoping on reconciliation among God's people; and we *turn our backs on temptation*, trusting God will honor our obedience in the kingdom.

Faith acts out its mental affirmations in the body. And it also has heart.

Faith's friend of the heart: persisting in kingdom truths

The Syro-Phoenician mother's faith is not only in her mind and in her body. It has settled deeply into her heart—and heart-rooted faith shows itself as *persistence*. She knows enough about Jesus to know that he can heal, and so she steps out on behalf of her daughter. But Jesus permits two challenges to test her heart.

First challenge: When the disciples of Jesus come to the conclusion that this woman is pestering Jesus, they ask Jesus to send her away. After all, she's a Gentile and a woman, and her daughter has demons. She doesn't budge. She meets the first challenge.

Second: Jesus challenges her faith with a riddle. Jesus says: "Let the children of Israel eat from the kingdom table first. Wait your turn." Not to be denied even by Jesus, the woman pulls a remarkable twist out of her own bag of riddles: "Even the dogs [Jewish code word for "Gentiles"] eat the crumbs that fall from their masters' table" Challenge met again.

Jesus unleashes power: "Woman, you have great faith! Your request is granted."

Jesus responds to her because her faith has heart; it is persistent and will not back down when challenges block her way to the Great Healer.

Speaking of persistence, the lake around which Kris and I walk has now spawned a separate pond—the beavers have created it. In the spring we observed the daily growth of a beaver dam at the neck of the lake on its western end. After a rain we noted that the water level was a bit high on the western side of the beaver dam. Before long the neighbors were flipping open their little cell phones to register concerns with the Parks & Recreation Department. Rob, our hard-working and good-natured supervisor, was soon on the scene dismantling the beaver dam. I could imagine the beavers huddling together to plot their next move. Beavers are like that.

Not to be deprived of their need for security, the beavers rebuilt the dam that very night—only a little higher, a little better, and a little stronger. Rob dismantled it again, this time leaving the debris on the bank to "show 'em." That night the beavers were back at it—fooling with Rob by leaving the debris where it was and using other sticks, twigs, and even a small pole they found. About a week later we noticed the dam was untouched, filled with mud and growing weeds; apparently the dam was settling into a quiet life on the lake. We asked Rob about it. His comment: "I gave up. The beavers can't be denied." The neighbors and the beavers have become friends.

FAITH IS. . .

Like the persistent family of beavers, the Syro-Phoenician woman, begging Jesus to heal her daughter and banish the powers of darkness, overcomes obstacles to reach Jesus' power to heal. Her faith—a relationship with Jesus—is accompanied by a sound mind, an active body, and a persistent heart.

Faith is a relationship with Jesus Christ. A friend of mine and author of many academic books, Mark Allan Powell, is writing a book about loving Jesus in a complicated world. In that book, he speaks about the relational nature of faith:

> We cannot have a relationship with our *christology*—we can have a relationship with Jesus Christ.
>
> Our *soteriology* cannot save us from our sins—our Savior can.

Our *ecclesiology* does not make us one—the Lord of the Church does.

Our *eschatology* will not transform this flawed universe—Jesus the King of kings and Prince of Peace will do that.

And, no matter how much we love *theology*—it will never love us back.

Only God in Christ loves us, and that is why believing is a relationship.

Abiding in Jesus

G O S P E L   R E A D I N G S
Luke 10:38–42; John 15:1–17

Sometimes it takes a jolt to get the point.

And sometimes Jesus is the one who has to provide the jolt, even to
his closest friends. Martha, a close friend of Jesus and his disciples,
needs a jolt, and Jesus gives it to her. In her own home, with Jesus
sitting in the "living room" teaching her sister, Mary, Martha finds
herself in the "kitchen" toiling away. Martha is "distracted" with a
Wall Street share of groaning and grunting, and she lets Jesus know
that Mary could poke her spoon into the pot to help. Jesus responds
with wisdom drawn from deep wells:

> Martha, Martha, . . . you are worried and upset about many
> things, but *only one thing is needed*. Mary has chosen what is
> better, and it will not be taken away from her.

What is that "one thing needed"? What distinguishes Martha's
distraction from Mary's devotion? I suggest it is not so much their
location as their posture.

THE PROPER POSTURE

Martha flits about the kitchen with her mind on many things, mostly herself, while her sister, Mary, sits in front of Jesus at his feet, with her mind on anything but herself. There you have it. Mary's posture tells the story. Her posture is that of a student, of someone who wants to listen to what Jesus has to say, of someone who can wait for dinner. It is the posture, in fact, of someone who is so enthralled with Jesus that dinner might not even happen. What Peter and others experience on the mountain when Jesus is transfigured is what Mary experiences at the feet of Jesus.

Disciples at the time of Jesus didn't sit in chairs and listen to teachers who lectured behind *Torah*-lecterns with each *Torah*-point on the screen. Instead, teachers often taught in homes. When they did, their students sat at their feet, the way kindergarten students gather round their teachers in a circle and open up their minds for learning, like little birds in a nest with open beaks waiting for food. Because this posture is the custom for disciples, "sitting at the feet" of someone becomes an idiom for "being a disciple." The apostle Paul, when he was a budding rabbi, sat at the feet of Gamaliel. Mary sat at the feet of her rabbi, Jesus.

At the feet of Jesus, Mary is seemingly serene. Mary's serenity derives from *attending to Jesus*, an expression that sums up Mary's posture. Humans, Jesus says, are defined not by their labor for him, as Martha thinks, but by their relationship to him, as Mary learns. Catherine Clark Kroeger, who has devoted her academic life to studying women in the early church, concludes in a sentence just shy of pure poetry that a woman in Jesus' kingdom society "is not ultimately defined by the excellence of the table she spreads but on spreading her heart open to God's Word."

CONSTANT ACCESS

An analogy may help us understand what "attending to" Jesus means. The *first* Internet service in our home required that we dial into the server whenever we wanted to access the Internet. At peak times the phone line was sometimes busy, and so at those times we weren't able to gain access. Once on, if we weren't active on the service for fifteen minutes, the company disconnected us. Our children informed us one evening, in order to ruffle our feathers, that our form of access was more obsolete than Morse code. We made a change.

Our *second* service (which we still have) comes through a cable, and our computer is now on "constant access." We simply have to click the appropriate buttons and we have access. *However*, we do not have access if we are in another room, or if we get in the car, or if we go on a trip.

Our son, still not satisfied with our system, has a *third* kind of service that gives him greater access. He calls it cellular access, and it is rigged up to our cable modem through a device that sends off a remote signal. Lukas can sit in his bedroom, in our living room, and even on our back porch, and be "online."

And this still is inadequate as far as the "techies" are concerned. Lukas has greater access to the Internet than do we, but he still must be within 150 feet of the "router" to have access. The days are coming, he informs me, when Internet access will be constant—like a cell phone. "Way cool," as he might say. "When," we ask, "can we get used to something before it becomes obsolete?" Never mind change: We've got access and that is what matters.

God's love for us in Christ is like a cellular connection: It is constantly available. He calls us to sit at his feet, attend to him, and absorb his life and love for us. How might we attend to Jesus so we have constant access to his love and life?

ATTENDING TO JESUS

We can best attend to Jesus in at least three ways: listening to the Word, participating physically in worship and the sacraments, and engaging in Christian fellowship.

Attending to the Lord in the Word

One of the most common disciplines that shapes our lives according to the *Jesus Creed* is to spend regular time in the presence of Jesus by reading the Bible and listening to his teachings. As mentioned in a previous chapter, M. Robert Mulholland Jr. has devoted his ministry (and life) to the spiritual reading of the Bible. He calls attention to the distinction between "informational" and "formational" reading of the Bible. The difference has to do with *how* we read the Bible and *why* we read the Bible. Either we read the Bible informationally (to learn more) or we read the Bible formationally (to be changed). Mulholland provides a set of comparisons of the two kinds of Bible reading that can provide for us a checklist of what we do when we open the Bible.

In Informational reading, we:	In Formational reading, we:
Cover as much as possible	Cover what we need to
Read line after line	Read for depth, perhaps only a word
Have a goal of mastering the text	Have a goal of being mastered by the text

Treat the text as an "object"	Treat ourselves as the object of the text
Read analytically	Read receptively
Solve problems	Are open to mystery

As a trained and certified "informational" reader, I am keenly aware of the accuracy and importance of Mulholland's comparison of these two kinds of Bible reading. I am also convinced of the absolute importance of formational reading.

His suggestions to read formationally push us away from the yen to know and shift us to the yearning to become. Formational reading implies readiness for kingdom transformation. We perhaps need to remind ourselves, when reading the Bible, that kingdom is the society in which the *Jesus Creed* transforms our very lives.

Those who are devoted to the formational, as Mary clearly is, *attend to Jesus* because when they read the Bible *they both learn and listen*. Attending to Jesus creates a society where he is adored, and that is a second form of attending to Jesus.

Attending to the Lord in worship

Any form of liturgy, whether structured or spontaneous, is designed to be both a spiritual *and* physical encounter with Jesus himself. Thus, praying together, observing an act of worship, or even walking around the church building in prayer (as some traditions do) is a way of attending to the Lord.

At an Easter service we attended, the worship team had constructed a large bridge on the stage. The pastor's sermon addressed our need for reconciliation with God and others, and he explained how the power of the Resurrection makes that reconciliation possible.

When the joyous celebration of Easter was coming to an end, the pastor encouraged anyone who desired to do so to "walk the bridge" with someone as a reenactment of a recent experience of reconciliation.

To our amazement, many walked forward and walked over the bridge—some hugging each other, some in tears, and some in the joy of a renewed relationship. For those who participated, and for those who observed it, that act was a form of *attending to Jesus in a concrete act of worship.*

In fact, just being together, fellowship itself, is being in the presence of Jesus himself. He says so.

Attending to the Lord in fellowship

Of all Jesus' amazing statements, this one might rank at the top:

> For where two or three come together in my name, there am I with them.

Every time we fellowship with other disciples, we are in the presence of Jesus, and he is in our presence. What I mean here by "fellowship" is any connection of Christians where, because they are together, they are in the presence of the Lord. Because the church is the body of Christ, each gathering of believers offers a whisper of his presence or the lingering aroma of his fragrance. This means that when we are in fellowship with others, we are actually *attending to Jesus.*

These three considerations on how we can "attend to" Jesus—reading the Bible, worshiping together, and fellowshipping together—are as simple as they are wise. Both parents and the great spiritual classics teach them. We are called by Jesus to the

Jesus Creed, and that means loving him. The one needful thing for such love is *to attend to Jesus*, and another expression for this is *abiding in him*.

WE ATTEND TO JESUS BY ABIDING IN HIM

Abiding is the central theme of Jesus on the last night he spent with his disciples. Abiding is Jesus' own commentary on what he means by the "one needful thing." On that last night, Jesus taught:

> I am the true vine, and my Father is the gardener. . . . Remain [or, Abide] in me, and I will remain [or, abide] in you. No branch can bear fruit by itself; it must remain [or, abide] in the vine.

As a branch draws its sap of life from the vine from which it grows, so also the disciple of Jesus draws spiritual life from Jesus. The *manner* of drawing life from Jesus is profoundly simple: Abide in him, or open up to the flow.

Abiding in Jesus is a *discipline* of prayer and receiving life from Jesus; it is a way of life. We don't stumble onto it accidentally; we have to make it a conscious pattern of life. Abiding in Jesus as constant prayer *takes practice* if it is to become a constant mode of life, as one notable saint in the church taught us.

PRACTICING THE PRESENCE OF GOD

Brother Lawrence lived in a monastery, but he found that he struggled to recite formal prayers meaningfully. To overcome his problem, he decided he wanted to practice "continual conversation with God." The location where this legendary man of prayer established his discipline was the kitchen. For fifteen years he found constant access to God in kitchen service through simple conversation with God. Brother Lawrence let everything in his life become a path of expressing his love for God.

His wisdom for prayer can be summarized in three points. First, he wants us to learn that God "is closer to us than we think." Second: "No one sees anything of it [our prayers]; there is nothing easier than to repeat these little interior acts of worship throughout the day." And, third: "We can make our heart a prayer room into which we can retire from time to time to converse with Him gently, humbly, and lovingly." "I do this simply by keeping my attention on God and by being generally and lovingly aware of Him." Perhaps his greatest success is seen in this: "My fixed hours of prayer are no longer anything other than a continuation of this same exercise."

Jesus calls us to the *Jesus Creed*—to be people who love God and who love others. We can be spiritually formed people if we learn to abide in him, for then the great love focus of the *Jesus Creed* begins to appear in our lives. Jesus promised this is what would happen to those who would abide in him.

THE FRUIT OF ABIDING

Jesus makes a claim for abiding: The branch that remains in the vine produces "fruit." That fruit is God's love energizing us.

God is love. And because his life is coursing down through the vine (Jesus) constantly toward the branches (the disciples), when that life gets to the branches, it produces the fruit of *love*: "Now remain in my love. If you obey my commands, you will remain in my love."

If abiding in Jesus produces love, that love expresses itself as self-sacrifice for others. A disciple of Jesus is called to the *Jesus Creed*, to love God (by following Jesus) and to love others. What Jesus says about "abiding" clarifies how the love of the *Jesus Creed* works: God loves us, his love flows to his Son, and by abiding in him (following him), God's love flows to us. We, in turn, can let that love flow to others. It couldn't be simpler.

CHAPTER 21

Surrendering in Jesus

GOSPEL READING
Mark 8:34–9:1; 12:28–31

A disciple of Jesus holds aloft the white flag of surrender.

The white flag is actually a prayer. Here's the simple white-flag prayer a disciple carries each day: "May your will be done."

The *Jesus Creed* teaches us that a disciple's responsibility is to love God by *following* Jesus. You only follow someone else when your own lights or sense of direction are not good enough. When a disciple of Jesus utters that white-flag prayer and begins to let Jesus show the way, the disciple admits that he or she has lost the way and needs direction. This disciple is living a life of surrender. Sometimes it hurts, but disciples will tell you right away that surrendering to Jesus is a good kind of hurt.

My colleague at North Park University, Rajkumar Boaz Johnson and his wife, Sarita, know the good hurt of surrender. Boaz himself was converted to Jesus Christ while studying in a Hindu seminary, and he suffered ostracism for his commitment, but we will focus on Sarita here. Sarita's well-to-do family was Hindu, and social status mattered to them. When Sarita began to consider the

Christian faith, she knew the implications. Still, she surrendered herself to Jesus Christ. When she was publicly baptized, she received from her family an official notice that she was to vacate the home within one week or renounce, in the newspaper, her new-found faith.

With a little flick of her sari, she left home with bags packed. It is amazing that a woman named Sheila had just opened a hostel for converted women from Hindu and Sikh backgrounds who were struggling with their families. Because Sheila knew the danger of seeking out such young women, she prayed that if it was God's will for women to learn from her, they would find her home. Sarita showed up at her doorstep on a miserably hot day and learned faith at the feet of this dear woman.

Sarita and Boaz met when both were studying in a seminary and then married some years later. To prepare for an academic career, they moved to the United States, finished their degrees, and developed an international ministry. Now I am privileged to work alongside the Johnsons. They minister throughout the world because they weighed the cost and surrendered themselves to Jesus. It hurt, but it has turned out for the good.

Surrendering to Jesus is a dimension of what it means to love God. All genuine love involves surrender.

JESUS AND SURRENDER

It was Jesus' own love for *Abba* and for his disciples that led him to die for them. His love for them set the tone for how they were to love God, him, and others. Jesus says, "If anyone would come after me, he must deny himself and take up his cross and follow me." In historical context, this statement of Jesus suggests martyrdom. But a careful reading of similar statements by Jesus leads to the conclusion that he is speaking of an *orientation in life*: a life of surrender, whether it involves martyrdom or not. Letting Jesus show the way, as Dallas Willard says, "is the controlling principle of the renovated heart and the restored soul." But as John Stott observes, this life of surrender paradoxically is a life of blessing, a good hurt:

> Only if we serve, will we experience freedom. Only if we lose ourselves in loving, will we find ourselves. Only if we die to our own self-centredness, will we begin to live.

The *Jesus Creed* is about loving God with the heart, soul, mind, and strength—with the entire person. In short, Jesus is calling us to total surrender: personally (heart and soul), mentally (mind), and physically (strength). Or as Dale Allison puts it, "with every globule of one's being."

SURRENDERING PERSONALLY

Surrender begins in the heart and soul. Jesus calls the disciple to surrender his or her heart because it is in the heart that the inner self is located. As Thomas Merton describes it,

> The inner self is not a part of our being, like a motor in a car. It is our entire substantial reality itself, on its highest and most personal and most existential level. It is like life, and it is life: it is our spiritual life when it is most alive. It is the life by which everything else in us lives and moves. It is in and through and beyond everything that we are.

Contrary to reports, surrendering our hearts and inner selves to God does not mean God will make us wear itchy wool garments in one-hundred-degree humid conditions, while holed up in some godforsaken hut without air conditioning where the major sport is swatting man-sized diseased mosquitoes. This bizarre image fueling our fears is the opposite of what surrender is. Surrendering is the secret to every genuine love, and surrendering our hearts and souls to God (by following Jesus) unleashes our personalities to become what they are really meant to be. Surrendering the heart is really about our identities being transformed. It is what Jesus saw in his family, in Joseph and Mary.

The Christian story of surrender as transformation of self-identity is told often. For Alicia Chester, who was a ballet dancer, surrender has to do with her heart's commitment to dance:

> [My parents] were actually more surprised when I told them I wanted to stop dancing. Ballet had become a sort of religion for me, an all-encompassing way of life that required a single-minded devotion I was no longer willing to give. . . . But what worried me most was that dance had become my whole identity. It defined not just my schedule, but my sense of self; I hardly knew who I was without it and the recognition it brought. My ballet teacher worried that I was throwing away a God-given gift. I knew it was a gift, one which, once given up, could never be retrieved. Yet God was calling me—not as a dancer, or a student, but simply as me—and I knew this was a break I had to make. In the first few weeks of not going to ballet class, I had a sense of peace I had not felt in many years. Body and soul, it was a tremendous liberation.

And Alicia also knows that surrendering to God is a lifetime disposition of love, not a one-off act. As Jesus says it, a disciple "must deny himself and take up his cross *daily*."

The Lord's Prayer contains a gentle reminder of ongoing surrender: "May *your* [not *my*] will be done." Love of God is a sacred love, a total love, and it involves not only the heart and soul, but also the mind.

SURRENDERING MENTALLY

The apostle Peter has trouble surrendering his mind. After Jesus predicts that he will die in Jerusalem, Peter pulls Jesus off to the side and gives him an earful of rebuke—this according to the Gospels. Jesus' response gets to the heart of what loving God with the mind means: "Get behind me, Satan!" he says to Peter. "You do not have *in mind* the things of God, but the things of men."

What kind of *mind* did Jesus think we should have? The sort of mind that *followed Jesus* with the mind, the sort of mind that *surrendered* to Jesus mentally, the sort of mind that knew that it was lost—mentally. And it was that sort of mind that Peter didn't have when he rebuked Jesus for thinking God's plan for him involved the Cross. A mentally surrendered disciple of Jesus *follows* Jesus even with the mind.

How can we surrender mentally? It begins with what we hope to accomplish with our mind. Wise Christians *devote themselves to wisdom*—a mind shaped to please God, as Dallas Willard has emphasized. Wisdom begins when we reverence God. We gain wisdom in several ways, but one well-worn path is *reading the Bible* in a disciplined manner with a disposition to learn about and hear God. When Christians think Joan of Arc is Noah's wife, that

Sodom and Gomorrah are husband and wife, that Mary sings the *Magna Carta*, and that Jesus eats with the *R*epublicans—when these things are going on, I need to say one more time that surrendering mentally to God begins with reading the Bible.

Wise Christians also *learn the history of the Church*, from the days of the apostles to our own day. They learn about the theological conclusions of the first five hundred years, the major moments of church history (like the missionary movement of the nineteenth century), significant locations (like Carthage), and "heroes" of the faith (like Perpetua or the Anabaptists).

Wise Christians also *comprehend their own culture*. They read newspapers, they read magazines, they seek to comprehend all sides of the political frays of our day, they grapple with influential philosophers and thinkers, and they come to terms with modern cultural expressions. They want to understand what the current "postmodern" view of reality is—which is exactly what it isn't—there is no right "view" of reality. Many thinkers today are attempting to comprehend the culture, such as J. Richard Middleton, Brian J. Walsh, and Brian McLaren. Mental surrender involves this sort of response to culture, and it should be a priority.

To surrender mentally is to give up thinking we know everything. After her conversion from her own brand of bohemian feminism, Frederica Mathewes-Green describes the beginning of her own mental surrender in these terms:

> I felt a pressing need to read a Bible. If this guy Jesus is going to be my boss, who the heck is he? I bought a small King James Version in London and plunged into the Gospel of Matthew. I wasn't pleased. I found a lot to argue with. *But a conviction was*

*slowly seeping into me: I didn't make the world, I didn't know
everything, and it was time to sit down and listen.*

Because Frederica wisely did sit down and listen and accepted
what she learned, a career in journalism became a vocation of
addressing Christian issues, telling her own story of conversion and
grace and of an ongoing mental surrender to gospel truths—even
when unfashionable.

SURRENDERING PHYSICALLY

The *Jesus Creed* also says we are to surrender in love to God
"with all our strength," a Jewish idiom for physical strength and
physical resources.

A disciple of Jesus recognizes the significance of what is physical. As Dallas Willard makes clear in several of his books, "the body
lies right at the center of the spiritual life." The challenge for spiritual
formation is for our *bodies to love God and others* so that they "honor
God." While some people need to discipline the body more than others, the extravagances of some forms of monasticism, however well
intended, express a fundamental misconception of the proper place of
the body in spiritual formation. Having said that, however, the
disciplines of the Christian life are "body acts of love" and cannot be
set aside if we are being spiritually formed. In fact, the body cries for
the opportunity to surrender itself to the *Jesus Creed*. How so?

We surrender our bodies by recognizing that *body and spirit
are related.* Jesus says, "Nothing outside a man can make him
'unclean' by going into him. Rather, it is what comes out of a man
that makes him 'unclean.' . . . For from within, out of men's hearts,
come evil thoughts," etc.

That is, humans work from the spirit to the body but the two are connected. Cultivation of the interior life is the only path to transformation of the exterior—with the goal of a body that is fully surrendered to loving God.

We surrender our bodies by relinquishing our quest *for agelessness*. We do this by embracing our mortality, by learning how to live the *Jesus Creed* in each "phase" of life, by denouncing the rampant "youthism" of modern culture, by honoring senior citizens as not only fellow human beings but as storehouses of wisdom, and by preparing not only to live and retire well but also to die well. Aging isn't so bad, as Mark Twain observes with a twinkle in his eye.

> When I was younger I could remember anything, whether it happened or not; but my faculties are decaying now and soon I shall be so I cannot remember any but the things that never happened. It is sad to go to pieces like this but we all have to do it.

We surrender our bodies to the legitimate use of *power*. We surrender our bodies to God by tending to our *physical health*. We surrender our bodies when we jettison our yearnings *for vanity*. We surrender our bodies to the goodness of *sexual pleasure*. To do so, we accept our sexuality as a gift from God and protect ourselves from temptation.

Jesus' call for each of us to surrender to him—personally, mentally, and physically—when sifted through the *Jesus Creed*, reveals what surrender really is: a total expression of love. The white-flag prayer that Christians utter each day, "May your will be done," is a white flag that speaks of a total love for God (by following Jesus) and for others.

Surrendering ourselves to love God is not giving up things *for* God so much as giving ourselves *to* God.

CHAPTER 22

Restoring in Jesus

G O S P E L   R E A D I N G S
Mark 4:35–41; 9:14–19; John 21:1–25

When we fall, Jesus picks us up. He's busy.

A disciple is called to love God and to love others, *and this means:* trust *completely*, abide *constantly*, and surrender *totally*. This is difficult. No one sitting at the feet of Jesus listening to the Beatitudes, or to his incisive comments on hypocrisy, or to his profound concentration on righteousness, gets up and says, "Give me a challenge!"

In fact, those who hear Jesus say "Be *perfect* as your heavenly Father is perfect" walk away with an acid pit in their stomachs. Some dilute the acid by contending that "perfection" means "maturity" or "mercifulness." The problem here is not the term "perfect," but the expression *"as God is . . . "*—whether the call is to be "mature" or "merciful" or "perfect," the *standard is God*. We fall and we get lost morally.

Whether we look at Jesus' demands for us through the lens of the *Jesus Creed*, or whether we dig into the categories of trusting completely, abiding constantly, and surrendering totally, or whether we take our hands away from our eyes to see that testy little word "perfection," it all comes down to one fundamental problem: we fail.

The best news yet is that we can be *restored in Jesus*. Yes, even leaders fail and leaders sometimes need restoration in Jesus.

FAILURE BY ANY OTHER NAME IS SIN

A professor at a Christian college finds time in his schedule of teaching and writing about the faith to have an affair with a friend's wife. Roman Catholic priests are presently being scorched in the media for their sin and for their response to their sin. Sometimes Christians, leaders or not, simply fall apart in their love for God and others.

Michael Green, currently Advisor in Evangelism to the Archbishops of Canterbury and York and noted author of more than forty books, confesses that he and Rosemary, his wife, at one time had serious marriage difficulties and jeopardized their family of four children. Such upheaval occurred in the middle of two thriving ministries, and it almost shipwrecked their lives and ministries. As a friend put it: "Rosemary and Michael are walking in broadly the same direction, but on different sides of a river."

Both had busy schedules. Psychological issues were running deep for Rosemary while ecclesiastical demands were running high for Michael. He who on the outside was a pastor of pastors describes the inside of his home:

> After all, it was my over-busyness and neglect which had been a
> substantial part of the trouble. We reached a very low point

during that year, and Rosemary's thoughts sometimes turned towards divorce, sometimes even to suicide. She graphically described her affection towards me as being like one solitary little white flower crushed in on every side by brambles. The love was flickering and almost gone. We began working on it, however, and the leadership team in the church helped us. By the end of the year we were very much together again, and have been ever since. Nobody meeting us now would ever imagine that we had ever had any difficulties in our marriage. . . .

We have a very good relationship, but it would all have been thrown away, and both our ministries would have been ruined, had we yielded to the impulse to break away from each other. . . . We worked at it, prayed about it, deliberately set about serving one another and allowed others to help us—and, because of these things, the marriage was restored and is the joy of our lives today.

Not only does Michael put a "fallen face" in a biography with many glorious chapters, and not only does he show that restoration of marriage does occur, he also reveals that failure in discipleship can accompany a life of ministry and that failure can be addressed and overcome. Admission of failure and addressing failure can lead to restoration for the one who loves Jesus.

FAILURE FROM THE GET-GO

Failure is an element of being a disciple, and that is why the disciples are shown for what they really are. The disciples exhibit enough examples of failure to suggest a pattern. They fail to understand Jesus' teachings, they scream in the middle of a storm, they don't understand how Jesus can provide for others, . . . and that's just a start! As for the final failure, when they fall asleep on Jesus in Gethsemane, Thomas à Kempis has it right: at first "they become bellicose, then lachrymose, then comatose."

This *pattern of imperfection* found in the gospel stories reveals that a disciple of Jesus is not sinless. Without minimizing the demand of Jesus, we can say that we will fail, even if failure gradually weakens. In the *Jesus Creed* is a basic recognition of human sinfulness: love is not about perfection but about relationship. This pattern of *im*perfection should manifest itself in every understanding of spiritual formation shaped by his *Creed*.

A careful reading of any of the Gospels reveals what I call the "pattern of *im*perfection": *failure* is followed by *rebuke*, and rebuke by *repentance*, and repentance by *restoration*. These are the Three Rs of Failure. If Peter is a good example of the process of conversion, he is also a good example of the pattern of imperfection.

Failure

Peter's reputation is established by a life of good things: his confession of Jesus as Messiah, his leadership of the apostles, and his role in the early church. But this fisherman does not always experience smooth sailing. Thinking he's the bee's knees, Peter tries to walk on water but plunges into the water of failure. When Jesus is transfigured on the mountain, Peter desecrates a revelatory moment with words sounding like a child pleading to go potty during a sacred moment in church. When Jesus needs him the most, Peter publicly denies any association with Jesus at all—the worst sin against Jesus a disciple can commit. The honesty of the gospel writers make Peter's failures public.

Some judge public declaration of failure a taboo. If so, Phillip Yancey breaks the taboo as he describes his own racism. "I grew up in Atlanta," he begins. "I grew up a racist," Yancey continues. "Stores in downtown Atlanta had three restrooms: White Men, White Women, and Colored." When the Civil Rights Act made restaurant segregation illegal, Yancey tells us, Lester Maddox (later Governor of Georgia) "sold clubs and ax handles in three different sizes—Daddy, Mama, and Junior—replicas of the clubs used to beat black civil rights demonstrators." In a painful moment of truth, Yancey confesses his failure: "I bought one of those ax handles with money earned from my paper route."

Because of escalating racial tensions, Yancey's church quickly founded a private white school and shooed away a little black daughter of a Bible professor,

> . . . but most of us approved of the decision. A year later the church board rejected a Carver Bible Institute student for membership (his name was Tony Evans and he went to become a prominent pastor and speaker).
>
> We used to call Martin Luther King, Jr. "Martin Lucifer Coon."
>
> . . . Today as I look back on my childhood I feel shame, remorse, and also repentance. It took years for God to break through my armor of blatant racism—I wonder if any of us sheds its more subtle forms—and I now see that sin as one of the most malevolent, with perhaps the greatest societal impact.

Phillip Yancey knows that racism is a Christian moral failure that is standing, like the proverbial elephant, in front of us. Yancey tells the truth. Failure is not confronted until we tell the truth, but sometimes that truth doesn't come to the surface until someone points it out—someone like Jesus.

Rebuke

After Jesus predicts his death, Peter butts into Jesus' disclosure of the plan of God with an alternative strategy: "kingdom without death" is his "strateegery." To this suggestion, Jesus gives Peter what he needs: a clear *rebuke* that his mind is grubbing around in diabolical and fiendish places.

Sometimes we, too, need to see the argumentative index finger of Jesus. Sometimes we *sin*, some things are *wrong*, and however much it hurts and potentially "damages" our self-esteem, the truth has to be told. Whether we call it admonishment or instruction, the point is the same: sinful behavior must be pointed out.

Here are two examples from the Bible. Jesus promises that the Holy Spirit will invade our hearts, and that one of the Spirit's missions is to rebuke us of our sins. And Paul will later tell Peter, with the finesse of a Scud missile, that Peter is doing something grossly inconsistent with God's gospel love for all. Sometimes, the Bible tells us, the truth needs to be told—and it tells us to relate that truth in love. When we do, good things can happen.

Repentance

The best result is that the person who needs to hear the truth swallows the pill of truth and repents. Peter was offered a pill, but like a child examining that first adult-sized aspirin, it took him a while to down it. After denying Jesus, Peter hears the rooster that Jesus predicted, remembers the words of Jesus, and weeps bitterly. Then Peter and Jesus meet up in Galilee. Jesus probes Peter's heart in terms of whether or not he is willing to live out the *Jesus Creed*. Peter is led to think through his disastrous night three more times, absorb each failure as his own, and verbally recommit his love for Jesus. Genuine repentance, seen here, involves three more Rs: taking *r*esponsibility, making *r*estitution when necessary and possible, and *r*ecommitment.

Phillip Yancey, now years later when repentance from racism was beginning to crawl into public places, continues his journey in and out of racism and illustrates repentance:

> Even my childhood church learned to repent. As the neighborhood changed, attendance at the church began to decline. When I attended a service several years ago, I was shocked to find only a few hundred worshipers scattered in the large sanctuary that, in my childhood, used to be packed with fifteen hundred. The church seemed cursed, blighted. . . .
>
> Finally the pastor, a classmate of mine from childhood, took the unusual step of scheduling a service of repentance. In advance of the service he wrote to Tony Evans and to the Bible professor, asking their forgiveness. Then publicly, painfully, with African-American leaders present, he recounted the sin of racism as it had been practiced by the church in the past.

Yancey and his fellow Christians, because they recognize their sin and repent from it, stand in a long line of those who need restoration, beginning with the apostle Peter.

Restoration

After the Resurrection, at the Sea of Galilee, Jesus meets up with Peter to deal with his repentance after denying him. Jesus requires Peter to answer his soul-searching question of the *Jesus Creed* again: "Peter, do you love me?" Three times Jesus says to Peter some variation of "Feed my lambs." To cap it off, standing on the same seashore, Jesus returns to the original call: "Follow me." Peter is restored to his call to serve Jesus.

These two commands were the best words Peter ever heard in his life. With Jesus *there is always room at the table of restoration for the one who will remember the words of Jesus and repent.*

Yancey, in another brush with the restoring grace of God, continues his story:

> [The pastor of the Atlanta church] confessed—and received their forgiveness.
>
> Although a burden seemed to lift from the congregation after that service, it was not sufficient to save the church. A few years later the white congregation moved out to the suburbs, and today a rousing African-American congregation, The Wings of Faith, fills the building and rattles its windows once more.

Restoration, one learns, doesn't necessarily mean we can set the clock back. But, there is forgiveness.

Lauren Winner, whose spiritual path led her from liberal Judaism to Orthodox Judaism to an evangelical Episcopal faith, tells of the time she nervously wrote out her sins on a legal pad so she could remember them when she confessed to Father Peter. She had a six-page list of sins by the time she got to her confession and then processed through them, embarrassed by what he might think. Father Peter said after her confession, "The Lord has put away all your sins." "Thanks be to God," Lauren responded. "Go in peace and pray for me, a sinner," said Father Peter. Then he asked her for the sheets of paper.

I clutched my yellow sheets . . . and, reluctantly, handed over my sins, and then I watched as Father Peter ripped my six sheets into shreds. . . . "It's funny," said Father Peter, as we walked out of the church, "it happens whenever I hear a confession. After I leave the altar, I can never, for the life of me, remember a single thing the penitent said."

Phillip Yancey, standing next to Lauren Winner, reminds us of the possibilities of social and interpersonal restoration and forgiveness with this:

The Benedictines, for example, have a moving service of forgiveness and reconciliation. After giving instruction from the Bible, the leaders ask each one attending to identify issues that require forgiveness. Worshipers then submerge their hands in a large crystal bowl of water, "holding" the grievance in their cupped hands. As they pray for the grace to forgive, gradually their hands open to symbolically "release" the grievance. . . . What impact might it have if blacks and whites in . . . the United States of America plunge their hands repeatedly into a common bowl of forgiveness?

Jesus and Peter plunged their hands into the bowl, Jesus' hands came out empty, and Peter was restored.

That night, along the shore of the Sea of Galilee, between the water and the fire, more than one shadow was seen dancing to the song of restoration. All the disciples had tasted the fish, and it breathed new life into their flagging hearts.

CHAPTER 23

Forgiving in Jesus

G O S P E L   R E A D I N G
Matthew 6:12, 14-15; 18:21–35

The *Jesus Creed* expands forgiveness.

In the Old Testament, God's gracious forgiveness is center stage, but we don't find a challenge for humans to forgive. With Jesus, since he believes that what God does is what humans are to do, humans join God in the action. They, too, are to forgive.

Because many are so accustomed to hearing about the importance of forgiveness, it surprises to hear that forgiveness gets a new shape with Jesus. Forgiveness doesn't appear in any of Moses' lists of commandments. In all the prayers of David, we don't find the prayers concerned with forgiving one another. And, the prophets don't call Israelites to forgive one another. This is not the way these biblical figures talk.

One of the rare instances of human forgiveness concerns the patriarch Joseph. After they buried their father Jacob, Joseph's brothers worry that Joseph may turn on them, so they concoct a falsehood and claim their father said:

"This is what you are to say to Joseph: I ask you to forgive your brothers the sins and the wrongs they committed in treating you so badly."

When they throw themselves at Joseph's feet, Joseph simply asks, "Am I in the place of God?" The Scripture continues, "And he reassured them and spoke kindly to them." This story is really the only instance in the Old Testament of humans forgiving one another.

If human forgiveness figures so prominently in Christian teaching, why is it so rare that humans are urged to forgive one another in the Old Testament? What does it teach about forgiveness?

A "GOD THING" AND A "REPENTANCE THING"

The simplest answer to that question is that *forgiveness is something God does*, not something humans do. If forgiveness is the objective reality of wiping the slate clean of one's sinful behaviors and thoughts, then most of us would agree that *only God* can wipe the slate clean. This is why the vast majority of references to forgiveness in the Bible describe this process: Israel sins, *YHWH* forgives.

There's another consideration. Forgiveness is generally granted in the Old Testament *on the condition of repentance*. One doesn't walk around Israel handing out pardons or amnesty certificates to sinners *unless and until* they repent. This requirement of repentance prior to forgiveness expresses an important system of justice in Israel. It is (at some level) simply unjust to forgive because it would be giving someone something they don't deserve. (Herein is found the secret to forgiveness.)

Forgiveness, in the Old Testament, is a "God thing" and a "repentance thing."

In this understanding Christianity and Judaism differ significantly. The Jewish scholar Solomon Schimmel has written the most complete study of forgiveness. While he respects the differences among Jewish thinkers on forgiveness, he represents a representative viewpoint of how Jews understood their tradition about forgiveness. And Schimmel observes a fundamental difference between Judaism and Christianity when it comes to forgiveness:Judaism overall is more concerned with guaranteeing justice than with forgiving incorrigible sinners, whereas Christianity, at least in its foundational prayer and creeds, if not in its actions, talks more of forgiveness as an act of grace, given even to the undeserving and not-yet-repentant, than of justice.

In what probably strikes Christians as a bit slender on mercy, Schimmel adds:

> We have to imitate God, and God, for the most part, punishes
> unrepentant sinners and forgives repentant ones.

Schimmel's understanding of Judaism's essential view is grounded in the emphases we find in the Old Testament.

There is something different about Jesus when it comes to forgiveness.

THE PREEMPTIVE STRIKE OF FORGIVENESS

Because forgiveness is such a familiar idea, we run the risk of missing just what Jesus was saying. To begin with, forgiveness begins with God's loving act of forgiving. It suspends any system of justice: Instead of sinful humans getting what they deserve (a system of justice), they are granted forgiveness (a system of forgiveness).

This loving act of forgiveness reveals God's inner nature: he is a forgiving God. He preemptively strikes the human condition with an offer of grace. That strike of God's forgiving love to us produces in us a cascading flow of forgiveness to others, which is where the *Jesus Creed* begins to expand what forgiveness is all about.

Notice these statements by Jesus:

Forgive us our sins, for we also forgive everyone who sins against us.

For if you forgive men when they sin against you, your heavenly Father will also forgive you. But if you do not forgive men their sins, your Father will not forgive your sins.

If your brother sins, rebuke him, and if he repents, forgive him. If he sins against you seven times in a day, and seven times comes back to you and says, "I repent," forgive him.

If you forgive anyone his sins, they are forgiven; if you do not forgive them, they are not forgiven.

[From the cross,] Jesus said, "Father, forgive them, for they do not know what they are doing."

A brief summary of each: *First*, Jesus innovates in his world when he urges his followers to have a *disposition* of forgiveness rather than of strict justice. *Second*, so important is forgiveness to Jesus that *forgiving others* is a litmus test of whether or not one is a follower of Jesus. *Third*, forgiving others *knows no limit* for Jesus' followers. *Fourth*, forgiving others is *effective* in his society of followers. The ultimate observation we make is that *Jesus is the example*: On the cross Jesus looks to those who are crucifying him and forgives them.

What Jesus says about forgiveness is rooted in the *Jesus Creed*: God loves us, so we are to love others and to love God. Loving others means *forgiving them*. Put succinctly, the *Jesus Creed* manifests itself in gracious, preemptive strikes of forgiveness.

FROM *YOM KIPPUR* TO FORGIVENESS SUNDAY

Jesus innovates within the lines of Judaism and declares that the sacred *Shema* needs to be more than a "love God thing." The *Shema* of Jesus (the *Jesus Creed*) is a "love God" and "love others" thing. Jesus also says the *Kaddish* needs to be expanded to include others, and thus he gave us the Lord's Prayer. And now *forgiveness* is expanded: *both* God *and* humans are to forgive.

I am not a historian of liturgy, but I do know that in the Orthodox tradition there is a day in the church calendar called Forgiveness Sunday, and at the Vespers service initiating the days of Lent, at least one Orthodox church has a custom of forgiving one another publicly. (The Orthodox do a lot of things publicly.)

After a lengthy series of liturgical prayers and gestures, these Orthodox form two lines facing one another. Bowing before one another, they ask one another for forgiveness. Then they shift so that each person in the congregation asks forgiveness from everyone.

The parade of forgiveness begins when Frederica Mathewes-Green's husband, Gary, and her son, David, embrace one another, speaking to one another words of grace and forgiveness. Frederica's emotions begin to well up inside her as she sees her own flesh and blood participate in the grace of God and watch the people of God extend to each other what God has offered to each. Then her two sons, David and Stephen, forgive one another in a public act. Walls between humans, between family members, begin to tumble as grace blows through the congregation.

"One at a time I bow to people I worship with every week, looking each one in the eye, men and women, children and aged. Each interchange is an intimate moment, and I feel on the wobbly border between embarrassment, laughter and tears."

Forgiveness, sometimes, is easier between strangers than between family members. And it is easier to watch than to do.

The challenge to forgive is now a family member standing in front of Frederica: her daughter, Megan, about whom Frederica has told many stories, now faces her mother. Here's an encounter that can't be faked; there are things between them. Frederica asks her daughter for forgiveness; Megan asks for the same grace from her mother. And Frederica caps it off with this, "Can a mother do such a thing? You bet. A moment later we are in a marshmallowy embrace." Forgiveness on a Sunday is a good custom, but not a new one.

This is a custom that has a deep root not only in Church history but in the very teachings of Jesus: not only do we ask God to forgive us, but we are to forgive one another, and to do so preemptively.

DISTINGUISHING SORTS OF FORGIVENESS

C. S. Lewis once said, "Every one says forgiveness is a lovely idea, until they have something to forgive." Some take the words of Jesus to mean that Christians are to forgive whomever for whatever at all times. But there are some issues to think about first.

Simon Wiesenthal, for instance, is a Jew who was brought face-to-face with a young, dying Nazi officer who described an atrocity—herding hundreds of Jews into a home, blowing the home up with grenades, hearing the screams, and watching small children die. When the Nazi officer, to make peace with himself, pleaded for forgiveness from Wiesenthal because he was a Jew, Wiesenthal walked away without offering the man one ounce of hope for forgiveness. It has been asked of many: is the Christian to offer such a person forgiveness?

A woman is abused by her husband—she is a Christian and he is not (does it matter?). Is she to forgive him? A neighbor is asked to care for a home when a family is on vacation, rifles through the drawers, steals some money, and the family learns of it. Is that Christian family to forgive the neighbor and ask him to care for the home the next time they leave?

These questions lead to this fundamental issue: *What is forgiveness?* Even though the Bible never sorts out the various kinds of forgiveness, I believe there are two fundamental dimensions of forgiveness that need to be distinguished: *objective* forgiveness and *subjective* forgiveness.[1] "Objective forgiveness" refers to the elimination of the offense in the relationship, that is, it refers to "reconciliation." The "subjective" includes both a *disposition* to forgive and an *experience* of forgiving: release of anger, hatred, and resentment—ending the internal recycling of the offense.

I will attempt to make a complex discussion as simple as possible: Because a disciple of Jesus loves God and loves others, the disciple develops a disposition to forgive that is ready to release the negative emotions caused by offenses (subjective) but reconciliation is not always possible (objective). So much for definitions.

How do we go about forgiving others?

FORGIVING OTHERS

The *disposition* of a follower of Jesus is to forgive others so that all relationships are reconciled to reflect the *Jesus Creed*. To move through the process, from the subjective disposition and experience to the objective, involves the following:

First, the victim of an offense *really confronts the offense and the offender's responsibility*. There can be no genuine reconciliation or forgiveness until a person confronts "who did what." Shoving an abusive situation into a hidden pocket of the heart only lets it fester until it abscesses. The victim meets the offender and the offense by naming it what it really is: stealing, sexual abuse, fraud, etc. The offense is a moral wrong, and it is not minimized by an effort to reduce the pain or hurry a reconciliation. This takes time, sometimes lots of time.

---

1   Because forgiveness is so important and emotional a topic, let me state the difference I see in what I say above from some other discussions. Some make a substantial difference between "forgiveness" (subjective) and "reconciliation" (objective), and believe Christians are always to "forgive" even when they cannot "reconcile." Where I would differ, and I do so because I think the Bible does, is that I think human reconciliation is an aspect of human forgiveness. I am not sure that "reconciliation" and "forgiveness" are always distinguishable experiences.

Second, the victim *recognizes the impact*. A victim does not subjectively forgive until he or she recognizes what the offense has done to the relationship: whether it "merely" harmed the relationship or actually destroyed it (as infidelity can do). Forgiveness admits into view the real emotions that have emerged because of the offense.

Third, the victim *chooses to pursue (objective) forgiveness*. Even with the disposition to forgive, a victim still needs to decide to "get over it" or "get it behind me" or "release the anger" or "let it go." To do so the victim will need to absorb injustice by accepting the offender as a human who has sinned. Then the victim suspends justice and offers (subjective) forgiveness. The offer of grace sometimes melts the heart of the offender.

Fourth, the victim *strives for justifiable reconciliation* (or, objective forgiveness). The lovely idea, as C. S. Lewis states, suddenly becomes even harder now. The disciple of Jesus knows God's immense love for sinful humans and Jesus' shining example of asking God to forgive those who were crucifying him. Because of these truths, the disciple is challenged to reconcile with the offender. Again, this can take time. Furthermore, the degree of reconciliation is shaped by other factors: our hurts, whether or not the offender has repented, how long the offender may have served time in prison, if the offender is a dangerous person, if the offender is even alive, etc.

Finally, *forgiveness creates an alternative reality: those who forgive unleash a flow of love for others*. The simple fact is this: When we are forgiven by those whom we have offended, we suddenly become alive internally in a way we did not expect, and it creates a "cycle of grace" and a "moral cease-fire."

No one said the *Jesus Creed* was the easy way.

CHAPTER 24

Reaching Out
in Jesus

G O S P E L   R E A D I N G S
Matthew 9:36–11:1; 28:16–20; John 20:21

Love has arms that reach out—always.

As I was shoveling the snow out of my driveway before dawn today, it occurred to me, because of what I had been reading the night before, that I was facing a typical day: approximately 90,000 people would turn their lives over to Jesus Christ. The Church continues to extend its arms to others. In the Christian world today, 1.06 billion are Roman Catholic, 386 million are Independent-Pentecostal, 342 million are Protestant, 215 million are Orthodox, and 79 million are Anglican. There are more nonwhite Christians than white, more in the Southern Hemisphere than in the Northern, and the center of gravity is shifting to the South and to the East. By the year 2050 only about one-fifth of the world's Christians will be non-Hispanic whites; the vast majority will be conservative and charismatic. These changes will have occurred all because missionaries have reached out.

While shoveling, I gave thanks to the Lord as I pondered these mind-boggling statistics. I also thought back to where it all began.

THE ORIGINS OF
MISSIONARY WORK

Here's the "official" moment: "Come, follow me," Jesus said, "and I will make you fishers of men." A fisherman of that era pulled a net of fish into his boat, then hauled the fish ashore to separate the bad from the good. Fishing, then, is about netting and separating. Fishing "for others," then, involves *declaring* (netting) and *offering forgiveness* or *warning of judgment* (separating).

Jesus regularly called his disciples to "fish for others." After his resurrection, he commissioned the eleven remaining disciples to "make disciples of all nations." In another context, he said, "As the Father has sent me, I am sending you." And, then just before the Ascension, he said, "you will be my witnesses in Jerusalem, and in all Judea and Samaria, and to the ends of the earth." We call this the "missionary task" of the Church: The Church is to reach out with good news.

This missionary task is the inevitable manifestation of the *Jesus Creed*: those who love others reach out with the Good News of God's love, just as a medical person always reaches out to those in need.

FROM JESUS TO OTHERS

To get a firm grip on what the missionary task of the Church is, we need to examine several texts in the Gospel of Matthew; once we connect these texts, we will see that the missionary task is very specific: it is to *reach out with the mission of Jesus to new people*. First, Matthew describes Jesus' ministry: "Jesus went throughout Galilee, *teaching* in their synagogues, *preaching* the Good News of the kingdom, *and healing every disease and sickness among the people*." Then he describes the disciples' mission in identical terms: "[Jesus] called his twelve disciples to him and gave them authority to drive out evil spirits and to *heal every disease and sickness*." In other words, *what Jesus, does the Twelve are to do.*

This understanding of mission becomes even more direct in a fourth text, the instructions of which I have numbered:

These twelve Jesus sent out with the following instructions:

[1.] Do not go among the Gentiles or enter any town of the Samaritans. Go rather to the lost sheep of Israel.

[2.] As you go, preach this message: "The kingdom of heaven is near."

[3.] Heal the sick, raise the dead, cleanse those who have leprosy, drive out demons.

[4.] Freely you have received, freely give. Do not take along any gold or silver or copper in your belts; take no bag for the journey, or extra tunic, or sandals or a staff; for the worker is worth his keep.

Each of these instructions asks the disciples to do exactly as Jesus did in other chapters of the Gospel of Matthew.

Add up all these instructions and we arrive at this important understanding of the missionary task of the disciple of Jesus: the mission of a disciple is *to reach out to others with the mission of Jesus.*

This is our task too.

TEACHING JESUS IS
REACHING OUT

Each of us can reach out with Jesus in our own ways, through our vocations. My vocation gives me a direct way of reaching out, and from it I share this story. After eleven happy years of teaching seminary students, I sensed a leading to teach college students. So, nine years ago I began teaching at North Park University. The *students* I encountered changed dramatically: thirty-five-year-old (mostly) men with (in the case of the men) moustaches, drinking cups of coffee became men and women eighteen to twenty years old. College students, bless their hearts, attend early classes in their pajama flannels, wear baseball hats to mask their not-yet-combed hair, slouch their trousers low enough that all can see their undies (or where some undies ought to be), dye their hair in previously unseen colors, and pierce and tattoo their bodies in public places. These things are fine, I suppose, as long as the person in question is not your own child.

When I began teaching at North Park, the students changed, but the subject didn't. And this time I knew the subject would have a different impact.

Because North Park does not require that students follow the Christian faith, and because it is successful in attracting students from Chicagoland, about half of my introductory students are not Christians. We go through the Bible in two chunks: the Old Testament and the New Testament. In the New Testament portion, we focus on Jesus and Paul. I cannot tell you how many students become Christians, but end-of-course assessments show that many students either gain or renew their faith. The class is not evangelistic; Jesus, the *subject*, is.

Like a centripetal force, Jesus attracts. One student, Asha Gandhi, came to my office a few years ago to inform me that she was Hindu and didn't want to take the required Bible class. I explained to her that the course was mandated by the Board. She said "OK" and left my office. She walked down the hall to her advisor and promptly lied: "Professor McKnight told me I didn't have to take 1850 because I am Hindu." To which her wise advisor said, "Professor McKnight does not have that option. You'll have to take the course." The next morning Asha sat in the back row with that sweet look of mandated misery. By the second week she was listening; by the fourth week she was interested. Later in the semester she approached me: "Are there any empty seats in your Jesus class next semester? I need to take a second religion course, and I really like Jesus." Asha took the second class, did well, and showed dramatic signs of turning her life over to Jesus. The *subject* matter, Jesus and his *Creed*, drew her in.

I am privileged, by vocation, to be able to extend Jesus through teaching about him. Each of us is privileged to be persons who can reach out to others.

FROM VILLAGE-TO-VILLAGE TO SEEKER GROUPS

When Jesus reaches out through his disciples to others, he expects them to go from village to village declaring the "kingdom of God"—this expression is Jesus' code word for what God is doing.

Kingdom, it will be remembered, is the society in which the *Jesus Creed* transforms life. That kingdom is seen in loving God and loving others, in table fellowship, in restoring persons to the table of God through forgiveness and healing, in the paradoxical smallness of mustard seed–like power, in working for justice, and in an abundant joy. As Dorothy Sayers asks, "If this is dull, then what, in Heaven's name, is worthy to be called exciting?"

Those who respond favorably to Jesus' first disciples' declaration of the kingdom of God invite the disciples home. There the new disciple sees the kingdom story and observes kingdom people. The kingdom's most visible trait in the first century was not renovation of the synagogue but revolution in the home, not a program hoping for change but a person making changes, not the distant seat of Moses but a close seat at the table. This is how the first followers of Jesus extended the mission of Jesus to others. This is how they "evangelized," or "declared the good news."

Evangelism is not always a positive term among Christians today. Indeed, because the Western Church has become hesitant to declare the Good News about Jesus, it needs to be called back to the task of reaching out to others. The Anglican leader and evangelist Michael Green cuts through church cant: "God's church exists not for itself but for the benefit of those who are not yet members. . . . [and] the church which lives for itself will be sure to die by itself." The church is not a religious club and it does not have a secular mission. Instead, it is a worshipping *and* sending community.

Most writers about spiritual formation tend to dwell on what happens in the inner life, on what happens to an individual in the heart, but M. Robert Mulholland gets it right:

> Christian spiritual formation is the process of being conformed
> to the image of Christ *for the sake of others.*

A part of "for the sake of others" is reaching out with Jesus' mission to others. This is why "spiritual formation" needs to be understood as Jesus understood it: A spiritually formed person loves God and loves others.

In one of my first classes teaching seminary students was a blonde-haired, good-looking young man from Indiana University who had the gift of evangelism more than any student I have ever taught. His name is Garry Poole.

After graduating from seminary, Garry and I kept in touch. When I was teaching an extension course in Indianapolis, Garry, then church planting, would pick me up at the airport to chat, take me to a restaurant for an early dinner, and then take me to my classroom. When I stopped teaching those courses, I lost contact with Garry until I bumped into him in one of Willow Creek's mazelike lobbies. Garry, to my delight, was on staff and directing Willow's seeker Bible studies.

He has since informed me that there are over one hundred seeker small groups with at least ten people in each group. These successful Bible studies build a bridge of friendship to seekers, hoping to present the Good News about Jesus through a holistic ministry (as Jesus had). The *Alpha* course, directed in England by Nicky Gumbel, has been anointed in a similar manner, and over two million have become Christians through its ministries.

Recently, Garry Poole published *Seeker Small Groups*, and he gave me a copy, signed it, and capped it off by writing Acts 20:24.

> However, I consider my life worth nothing to me, if only I may finish the race and complete the task the Lord Jesus has given me—the task of testifying to the gospel of God's grace.

This verse captures Garry's life.

In the introduction to his book Garry says this:

> I have spent my whole life on the lookout to develop and implement the best ways to convey the compelling message of the gospel of Jesus Christ. Along the way, however, I've come to discover one of the greatest challenges within the evangelism process: to find and strike that important balance between presenting the truths of the Bible with boldness and clarity while, at the same time, keeping my treasured friendships with seekers safely intact.

This vision began when Garry was offered an opportunity to lead a group on the campus of Indiana University, but the offer came with this hitch: He'd have to find the people. His leader had one question: "Who knows what God might do through you? Just give it your best shot." Little did he know. Garry advertised his group and nine people showed up. The problem was that Garry was ready for an in-depth Bible study for Christians, but no Christians came.

In a stroke of wisdom that altered his life, Garry let the "seekers" talk. Soon they were sharing hurts and questions; bridges were built. The group met for the rest of the year. Six of the original nine came to faith. What Garry learned there now shapes the heart of his entire ministry: the way to reach out is to build bridges to others so they can cross that bridge to Jesus.

Whether we are talking about Willow Creek's Garry Poole and its seeker studies, Anglicanism's Michael Green, or Nicky Gumbel's *Alpha* course, or any one of us, each of us has a task: through our vocations to reach out with the Good News of the kingdom. Reaching out to others is what happens when a person lives the *Jesus Creed*; that person loves others, and love means seeking God's best for someone.

PART FIVE

Jesus and the *Jesus Creed*

THE *JESUS CREED*
"Hear, O Israel, the Lord our God is one.
Love the Lord your God with all your heart,
with all your soul,
with all your mind, and with all your strength."
The second is this: "Love your neighbor as yourself."
There is no commandment greater than these.

A spiritually formed person loves God by
following Jesus and loving others.
A spiritually formed person embraces the stories
of others who love Jesus.
A spiritually formed person lives out kingdom values.
A spiritually formed person loves Jesus personally,
and participates in the life of Jesus.

The events in the life of Jesus are often a mystery:
Why, we sometimes ask, was Jesus baptized?
Why was he tempted? Why was he transfigured?
Why did he give the Last Supper? Why did he die?
And why was he raised?

One thing is for sure: Jesus was radically committed to his own *Creed:*
He, too, loved God and loved others.
Every event in the life of Jesus is an expression of that *Creed.*
Because he lived his own *Creed* perfectly,
he lived the life God calls each of us to live.
By participating in his life, we live out the *Jesus Creed* today.

Theologians speak of Jesus' "active" and "passive" obedience. "Passive obedience" refers to Jesus' suffering for us; his "active" obedience is his perfect life before God. It is Jesus' "active" obedience that is the focus of part 5.

Notice these words of Jesus:
"A new commandment I give you: Love one another. As I have loved you, so you must love one another."

The life of Jesus is an act of love for others. We do not see what his life is all about until we see it as the perfect life of love.

In the Jordan with Jesus

G O S P E L   R E A D I N G
Matthew 3:13–17

> Sometimes we need someone to pave the way for us.

Such was our situation when the Blizzard of 1979 socked Chicago. It snowed persistently from Friday night through Sunday morning. The snow accumulated up to four feet, and it drifted in some spots even higher.

Our daughter, Laura, was almost three. On Sunday afternoon, peering out from our door, she found a little clearing in our (small) yard beyond a ten-foot-wide-and-five-foot-high drift. Because children see beyond obstacles, she decided it was a good time to play in the clearing. So in the joy of escaping the house and with her snow clothes zippered from bottom to top, she marched down the stairs, aimed her little body at the clearing, and hopped into the snow bank. She got no further; she was stuck. She couldn't lift either boot, move forward, sideways, or backwards. Immobile, she turned to us on the steps as we cheered her on. Knowing she was incapable of mustering the strength to fight her way through the mounds of snow, I bundled up quickly, descended the stairs, scooped her up out of the snow, and placed her on the steps.

Then I shoveled a path through the snow (with considerable effort, I might add) to the clearing. Laura then was able to shuttle back and forth, between the warm living room and the chilly clearing, throughout the next few weeks.

Opening a path to a spiritual clearing is what Jesus does for us with his entire life.

JESUS LIVED FOR US

As Laura couldn't trudge through the snow on her own, so we are incapable of cutting a path to a spiritual clearing. As a father paves the way for a child through the snow, so Jesus trudged his way through the "human condition" to provide us with access to God.

Tucked inside this "trudging" of Jesus are three terms we need to understand. Using theological terms for what Jesus does for us is like looking at a map of our favorite place in the world after we've just visited it. The map is not quite the same as the place itself, even though it evokes the pleasures we've just experienced. So when we use theological terms to describe what Jesus has done for us, we use them the way we use a map: they point us to what Jesus has done for us, but we are not to equate the terms with what Jesus does.

To get these theological terms in focus, we need to remind ourselves of what God asks from us. Here's the mystery of the *Jesus Creed*: Jesus *both* loves God and loves others for us *and* he summons us to love God and to love others. Three theological terms clarify this. First, Jesus *substitutes* for us in loving God and others perfectly. The term "substitution" tends to be a little too clinical for what the Bible is getting at, so it is important to observe that, in substituting for us, Jesus also *represents* us before God in loving God and others. Further, by representing us he empowers us to *participate* with him in loving God and loving others.

Jesus does this for us in his entire life. Jesus loves God and others perfectly for us; this means that the spiritually formed person genuinely participates in Jesus' perfect life. But his loving for us does not make us spiritual couch potatoes watching the "show of Jesus for us" on the big screen. No, God calls *us* to love him and to love others. And Jesus loves for us not so we don't have to love, but so we *can* love. This is what it means to "participate" in the life of Jesus.

Jesus' life for us begins at the river Jordan, where John was baptizing Israelites in the water.

JOHN AND JESUS AT THE JORDAN

John tells everyone who will listen (and probably some who didn't want to listen) that his baptismal act of immersing in the Jordan was an act of *repentance*. "Repent," John says, "for the kingdom of heaven is near." John tells his listeners that they, too, are to "produce fruit in keeping with *repentance*," and he also says, "I baptize you with water for *repentance*." Repentance involves surrender to God, telling God the truth, and striking out in a new direction of sacred love. This is why people got down into the Jordan to be baptized by John: to repent and to find forgiveness. This is the first thing to keep in mind.

John's baptism is for repentance, but *Jesus is sinless*. So why was Jesus baptized? To begin with, we are no more baffled than John himself, for he does his prophet's best to keep Jesus from jumping into the Jordan with this jumble of sinners. "Then Jesus came from Galilee to the Jordan to be baptized by John. But John tried to deter him, saying, 'I need to be baptized by you, and do you come to me?'" According to John, never were two people more unequal: the sinful John and the sinless Jesus.

But Jesus is baptized anyway. John's baptism is for repentance, and Jesus doesn't need to repent. Clearly, then, if Jesus doesn't need to repent, then he must be repenting *for others*, for *us*. Why would he do that?

Because in so "repenting for us," Jesus begins *to unleash the power of the Holy Spirit* for his followers. John baptizes with "water," but Jesus will baptize "with the Holy Spirit and with fire." John is referring here to the great prophetic prediction of the coming of the Holy Spirit. That Spirit comes upon Jesus at his baptism when it comes down as a dove, and it comes on all his followers on the great day of Pentecost when they are flooded with the Spirit.

With these considerations, the baptism of Jesus becomes clear: *Jesus is baptized to repent perfectly so God can send the Spirit to empower us for our vocations.* As C. S. Lewis said, "Only a bad person needs to repent: only a good person can repent perfectly. . . . The only person who could do it perfectly would be a perfect person—and he would not need it."

Here's the big picture and how baptism fits into it: the spiritually formed person loves God (by following Jesus) and others. Jesus loves God and others perfectly. We don't love God perfectly, and we might as well admit it. We love God and others perfectly only when we follow Jesus through our piles of sin, which we do when we *participate* in Jesus' own life. This expression "following Jesus" that we've often used now gains full clarity: To follow Jesus means to participate in his life, to let his life be ours. By participating in Jesus' baptism, we participate in his life. By joining Jesus in the Jordan, we participate in his perfect repentance.

If Jesus is to bring the kingdom to earth, as Tom Wright says, "this is how he must do it: by humbly identifying himself with God's people, by taking their place, sharing their penitence, living their life and ultimately dying their death" and (I would add) being raised in their resurrection.

A CREED OF PERFECT REPENTANCE

There is only one reason for Jesus to repent for us: *We can't repent adequately*. An adequate repentance has four elements: a true perception of sin (conviction), telling the truth to God about sin (confession), the decision to change (commitment), and its demonstrable behaviors (consequences). Because we've already looked at the last two, we will look now at the first two.

We need Jesus' repentance because we don't know our hearts truly. But Jesus does: he sees into the hidden hearts of mistaken leaders and wayward people. The prophet Jeremiah once complained: "the heart is deceitful above all things and beyond cure. Who can understand it? [And the good news is that he continues with] 'I the LORD search the heart and examine the mind.'" Jesus understood the hearts of all people, what makes people tick. How? Perhaps a brief story will make clear what C. S. Lewis said, quoted above.

Alexis de Tocqueville was a French aristocrat who, in the nineteenth century, came to the United States to observe its social and political characteristics. His recorded observations became the classic *Democracy in America*, a tome studied by political thinkers today. Tocqueville was not an American. All today agree on this: it was Tocqueville's *foreignness* that gave him the ability to see the *distinctiveness* of America. Because what was going on here (particularly the separation of church and state) was not going on in France, his foreignness gave Tocqueville the ability to observe the value of this political doctrine for the democratic experiment in the United States. His *foreignness* permitted a clearer *perception*.

At a much deeper level than observing democratic institutions, it is Jesus' *foreignness to sin* that permits him to have a perfect conviction of the unique tragedy of our sinfulness. Since Jesus has perfectly clear eyes to see the tragedy of sin, his confession is utterly true. As the Truly Convicted Confessor, Jesus steps into the water and utters the world's first genuine confession—*for us*. This is why we *need* Jesus to step into the Jordan for us: We need him to confess *our* confession of sins for us.

But this doesn't mean that we don't have to get into the water ourselves. Nor does this mean that we don't have to repent. No, his repentance parts the water so that our (weak) repentance can stand up in that water. He clears away the waters of confusion so that we can utter, in our weakness, a genuine confession.

Our tentative convictions and our feeble confessions lead us to groan to God for help. I am a great fan of Paul's famous words about groaning prayer in Romans 8:26-27: Our weak prayers are strengthened by the Spirit's intercession for us. What Paul is speaking of here is analogous to Jesus' repentance for us. Even in our repentance, we are not completely clear—why we sinned and what our sin's implications were and will be. All we can offer is an incomplete repentance. But we know when Jesus waded into the deeps of the Jordan, he was there for us, uttering the true confession on our behalf.

REPENTANCE AND THE DOVE OF FORGIVENESS

John's baptism doesn't stop with repentance: it is also *for the forgiveness of sins*. Sometimes Christians are tortured into wondering if their sins are forgiven. In such a state of torture, they fear that their eternal destiny is with the grotesque, dark figures in Dante's *Inferno*. Such fears can be allayed knowing two truths that we see in Jesus' baptism for us: First, our conviction and our confession are each incomplete; this we must admit. *But*, second, Jesus has full perception and conviction and, therefore, makes the truthful confession. Through him our sins are dealt a knockout blow. Because of Jesus' conviction and confession, our fears about forgiveness can be released.

Even more: we need more than a true confession. What we seek is a clear conscience and (what Dallas Willard calls) a "renovation of the heart." So, let us return to the full story of Jesus' baptism: Jesus, with other Israelites, gets into the Jordan. Along with the others, Jesus utters the true confession—for us. And (here's the renovation part) the Spirit in the form of a dove descends upon Jesus. John promises that Jesus will send that same Spirit to us.

When we tell the truth to the Father, participating with Jesus in the water, we, too, are flooded with God's Spirit, who is the Spirit that forgives, and the Spirit empowers us to live out the *Jesus Creed*. A true confession triggers God's gift of renovation through the Spirit.

A REPENTANCE FOR WHICH
WE ARE TO BE THANKFUL

Jesus paved the way for us—with his entire life of active obedience. The baptism is one of those events where Jesus underwent an act for us. Unfortunately, we tend to limit Jesus' actions for us to his death and his resurrection. When we do, we fail to see what he has done for us, and we are not as grateful as we ought to be.

So unnoticing can we be of what Jesus has done for us in his entire life that it reminds me of the behavior of a duck that Kris and I recently encountered. In the middle of our community is Butler Lake. Kris and I walk briskly around Butler daily, almost compulsively. We chat, we think, we ponder, and we observe. One day, just beyond a small walking bridge, we noticed a Mallard female caught on something and struggling to escape. We hoped she might untangle herself from what we imagined was some fishing line.

After a few minutes, we knocked on Wally's (the neighbor's) door to see if we might use his canoe to free Mrs. Stuck Mallard. Wally said, "I'll do what I can." We perched ourselves on the bridge as Wally lumbered into the canoe, paddled himself over to the duck, and then dipped his oar into the water just below the wildly flapping duck. He poked and prodded, but with no success. Then, as if finding himself staring into the eyes of an oncoming freight train, he exclaimed, "Awesome! A huge snapper has the duck by the leg!" Snappers being what they are (slow), it was waiting until Mrs. Mallard succumbed. Wally kept poking, and suddenly the duck broke free and flew about thirty feet to a clearing.

To my amazement, like a proud teenage dweeb, Mrs. Mallard acted like nothing significant had happened for aeons. She swam around in a circle slowly and simply resumed her lifestyle of bobbing for underwater morsels. Not a word of thanksgiving, not a quick quack of "Thanks!" to Wally (or us, after all).

Sometimes we are a bit like that duck when it comes to the life of Jesus, in particular to the baptism of Jesus and to Jesus' repentance for us. Our insensitivity shows up in our inability to see just how needful Jesus' repentance is for us (at the levels of conviction and confession). We fail to see that we need to have Jesus repent for us so that we might experience the dove of the Spirit's forgiveness and power. In fact, we have experienced the descent of that Dove upon us, and we have failed to pause to thank Jesus that he made this happen.

Those who enter the river with Jesus and confess his perfect confession will also be flooded with the Holy Spirit, will find the same Father offering words of gentle approval, and (in faith) see the heavens break open in glory.

CHAPTER 26

In the Wilderness with Jesus

GOSPEL READINGS
Matthew 4:1–11; Mark 1:12–13

Every vocation is tested by God.

If the general vocation of all Christians is the *Jesus Creed*, then our love for God and love for others will be tested. Jesus' own vocation of loving God was tested severely. When the rest of those baptized by John cross the Jordan to enter the Land, Jesus turns around, faces the wind, and heads into it. He has just been declared Son of God in front of others, by none other than *Abba*. One would think he would charge up the road to Jerusalem to let the elites in on the revelation. But not Jesus. No, before Jesus crosses the Jordan and enters into the Land to offer the kingdom to his people, the Spirit of God *drives* him into the wilderness to test his vocation. Here he is prepared for what God has called him to do: offer the kingdom—the society in which the *Jesus Creed* transforms life—to his people.

When we think "vocation from God," we need also to think "test by God."

BUT FIRST A TEST

Our son, Lukas, senses that his vocation is to play baseball. One of the biggest days of our life was the day he was called by the Chicago Cubs to inform him they had chosen him in the professional baseball draft as a catcher. Talk about hopes coming to pass! We were not caught unaware and knew what such a call meant: The minor leagues are (among other things) a massive test of one's baseball vocation.

Some of our friends asked immediately if Lukas would be playing that summer at Wrigley Field. Countless times we have explained the system: players drafted begin climbing a ladder of seven rungs that only 7 percent of them complete. To get to Wrigley, a Cubs player must succeed at Mesa (Rookie), Boise (Short Season A), Lansing (Low A), Daytona (High A), Jackson (AA), and Des Moines (AAA). And then, possibly, the player can take the field in the Show—if there is a roster spot, and if the Cubs don't buy someone better for that roster spot.

Put simply, to be drafted means a young man *sets out on a series of severe tests*. For some, it takes as many as seven to ten years to make it. Success at every level (unless you were given bucketloads of dough) is necessary in order to move on. Most (93 percent) don't make it. But making it to the Show is a grueling ordeal: skills have to be splendid, the psyche has to be resilient, and a spot on a roster has to be open.

Vocations often involve severe tests. Jesus' vocation as God's Son is tested when he is tempted three times by Satan. The same is true for many others in the Bible. For instance, way back in time *YHWH* promised Abraham the world (and a little more), but he was tested before he got what was promised: among other things, Abraham had to surrender his son, Isaac, to the plan of God. We could add to this the examples of Moses or David, but enough has been said to see that Jesus' temptations fit into a divine pattern: *A vocation from God is tested by God.*

IN THE WILDERNESS FOR US

The test of Jesus' vocation comes in the *wilderness*. The Gospel of Matthew says that immediately after his baptism, "Jesus was led by the Spirit into the desert." In that wilderness, Jesus is tempted by Satan. Jesus quotes three passages from Deuteronomy, each of which is drawn from the nation of Israel's own *wilderness* experiences.

Under Moses' leadership, Israel was delivered from Pharaoh's brutal treatment, and God promised Israel that she could return to the Land. This was her vocation: to dwell in the Land and obey the *Torah* as God's people. But following the deliverance and before she entered the Land, she needed to be tested. *YHWH* tested Israel in three central issues of life: Would Israel trust God for provisions? Would Israel obey God patiently through trials? And, would Israel worship *YHWH* alone? Three tests for Israel. Israel failed each test.

Jesus, too, is tested along the same three lines and in the wilderness: Will he trust *Abba* to provide for his physical needs? Will he wait for *Abba*'s time to make him public? Will he worship *Abba* alone? Three tests for Jesus. Jesus passes each test. The coincidence of the three temptations, and the coincidence of both Israel's and Jesus' being in the wilderness, are not coincidences.

Jesus is tempted in the wilderness for a reason: He must *relive Israel's wilderness tests and pass those tests, so he can enter into the Land as the obedient Israelite—and do so for us.* Israel fails, and another generation enters the Land. Jesus succeeds, and he enters the Land with and for his own people.

That he does this for us illustrates again that Jesus operates by the *Jesus Creed*: he loves God and he loves others. He is tempted to offer to God a perfect obedience on our behalf, and as the one who represents us, he calls us to pass the testing of our own vocation.

IN THE WILDERNESS WITH JESUS

Why do we need to participate in his wilderness? To "enter the Land," or the kingdom, we must repent truthfully *and live obediently*. If an obedient life is God's expectation for us, our chances are worse than that of minor leaguers' making it to the Show. If our test is to live obediently—perfectly, mind you—then the odds are that we (with the ancient Israelites) won't make it either. Unless, of course, we catch someone else's perfect wave and ride that wave with that person. That is what the temptations of Jesus are all about.

What Jesus does for us can also be compared to baseball.

I won't tell you how many baseball books I've read in my life or how many games I've watched. But I know enough to say that the greatest catcher in the history of baseball is Johnny Bench (1967–1983), who was inducted into the Hall of Fame in 1989. He directed and pounded home runs for the Red Machine, the Cincinnati Reds, in their glory days of the late 1960s and 1970s. According to David Falkner, "With [Johnny's] low-to-the-ground build, quick reflexes, massive but soft hands, powerful throwing arm, and first-rate baseball mind to go with his best-ever bat, he was simply an ideal catcher." Simply the best.

What Jesus does for us in the wilderness would be like the greatest catcher in history (Johnny Bench) playing minor-league baseball for my son. Imagine Johnny Bench in his prime playing minor-league baseball. When the call to the Show for Johnny comes, instead of agreeing to the promotion, he hands his own bat and glove to my son and says, "I did this for you. You go up, kid."

Yes, this is like what Jesus has done for us. We are called to the *Jesus Creed*, to love God with all of our hearts, souls, minds, and strength. We are called to live this out perfectly, and we simply cannot do it. So Jesus does it for us.

Loving God, according to the Bible, means we are to trust him, wait on his timing, and worship him. We, too, will be tested in each of these areas of our vocation to love God.

IN THE WILDERNESS
WITH JESUS TODAY

Shawn, a student of mine, now happy in his life's dream vocation, called me about the pain of a ruptured relationship. He had explained a few things about his past to his girlfriend, and it harmed the relationship. He was depressed about it. She was struggling with his past. He encouraged her (as he should have done) to take all the time she needed.

His confession to me was that this was the biggest test of his life, and he was struggling with trusting God to work things out, and he was struggling to wait on God to work things out. His faith was being tested. Shawn had a plan for the relationship, didn't know what would happen, was a self-confessed "control freak," and was having a hard time waiting and trusting. Going to church to worship with other Christians was interrupting his worrying, so he

avoided that, too. He just wanted to "fix it." But he knew at a deep
level he was failing the test to trust the Lord. He knew the Lord's
will would come about, and he knew it would be the best thing for
him, but trusting was the hard part.

"It is good news," I said to him, "in these situations that we can
draw on the strength of Jesus who in the wilderness did trust the
Father perfectly." Then I added, "Jesus' own trust can empower
your struggle to trust."

Trusting is another one of those great ideas until we have to do
it. In fact, trusting God never gets easy. Why? It is easy, I told him,
to trust God to bring a woman into your life to love as long as you
have a woman in your life. When the prospects are dim, faith is
needed. We generally become aware of our need to trust only when
we've reached the edge of what is familiar. Looking over that edge
into uncharted wilderness, we wonder what will happen just over
the border. And we worry, as he was doing.

Jesus has been right where you are, I continued, and asks us to
join him: in the wilderness. When things were tough, *Jesus trusted
God* for what he didn't have. Jesus was hungry—Matthew tells us
he had fasted for forty days and nights and was (surprise, surprise)
hungry. Knowing his condition, Satan made an offer: "If [or, since]
you are the Son of God, tell these stones to become bread," which
was within Jesus' power to do. To do or not to do was answered
with "not to do." Though Son of God and though entitled to provisions, Jesus didn't let his physical desires dictate decisions. He
simply trusted God to provide. And I told Shawn that, when he was
struggling with his trust in God, he could join Jesus in the wilderness where Jesus would support his flagging faith as it was tested.
Think about him, I said, and it can give you strength. Ask him to

strengthen your faith with his faith. Open yourself to his faith and rely on his faith.

What is also obvious in Shawn's story is that he didn't want to wait for his girlfriend to make a decision. I pointed him again to the wilderness experience of Jesus who, when tempted not to wait for God's timing, did wait upon God. *YHWH* promised the Land to Israel, and *Abba* promised a kingdom to Jesus. A little display of Jesus' splendor at the temple just might have gotten Jerusalem's elites thinking about him as God's Messiah. So Satan offered Jesus the chance to jump to make the point, as Tom Wright puts it, to "go for it in one easy stride." But, if Jesus had done that to get what God surely had in store for him, it would have destroyed God's timing. And as Jesus chose to wait on God, I encouraged Shawn to turn to his experience for strength to wait.

Shawn's problem with worship was clear: He was so distracted by his worry and desire to fix things that he couldn't focus on life's central issue: "Love God with your whole being." He was trying, he said; he was praying, but he was also worrying. I encouraged him to think of Jesus in the wilderness. There Satan offered him the kingdom—which is what he wanted. But he could only have it for a price—if he would but worship Satan. So Jesus confessed what he learned from his father and mother, the *Shema*: there is but one God, and I will give only him my worship. He knew he was to love God only—in heart, soul, mind, and strength—and he knew that loving *Abba* properly meant to worship him alone.

When we struggle in faith, in waiting on God, and in centering on God in our worship, we need to remind ourselves that Jesus has done each of these for us. Our weak trust, our failure to wait on God, and our blurred worship are all swallowed up in his perfect trust, patience, and worship.

Christians can tap into the strength that comes from knowing that in the wilderness Jesus trusted *Abba* for us. Perhaps when tested in a matter of trust, we can learn to offer this brief prayer: "Jesus, you have trusted perfectly for me. I am struggling to trust *Abba*. Empower my weak faith with your perfect faith." The writer to the Hebrews knew this strength when he urged us to "approach the throne of grace with confidence, so that we may . . . find grace to help us in our time of need"—all because he knew Jesus had been tested.

Jesus is more than an example, though he is that. His very trust (and patience and worship) is ours, so let us join him in the wilderness and, by participating in his life, love God by following him. By joining him we learn the *Jesus Creed* in real life.

CHAPTER 27

On the Mountain
with Jesus

GOSPEL READING
Luke 9:28–36

Tragedies can change life dramatically.

After dinner and a walk around Butler Lake, Kris and I were sitting in the living room drinking tea and chatting about the day, when the phone rang. I answered it. "Scot," Pat Somers said, "have you heard about Tim Panther?" "No," I said. Knowing that Pat rarely calls me and sensing that this sort of question leads to tragedy, I braced myself for what was next: "Tim was hiking in Arizona and died. We don't know much more than that." I asked if Jim and Bonnie, Tim's parents and our good friends, were home, and Pat told us they were.

I sat down, stunned, and relayed the information to Kris. After a few minutes of soul searching and prayerful silence, we pulled ourselves together, got in the car, and drove the few blocks to their home. Another couple was consoling Bonnie and Jim. All we could say was: "We're sorry." We hugged them, we stood with them, and we listened to them pour out their hearts as they began to come to terms with the death of their only son at the age of twenty-three. Bonnie told us later that her heart physically hurt for a year, and that she knew what it meant (physically and literally) to have a broken heart.

Tim had been a student in Wyoming; he loved to trek into the mountains. He had learned to subsist on wild berries and plants. But this time he was in Arizona with a friend, and they had gone on a hike into mountains. They paused to eat some wild carrots along a stream of water, but Tim made a mistake in identification, and it cost him and his family a life. It was one mistaken moment. Instead of wild carrots, Tim had eaten wild hemlock. He was gone in minutes—in body. Not in memory.

When we got home later that night, I sat in the living room and I prayed for Jim, for Bonnie, and for Tami and Mandy (his two sisters), and I thanked God for Tim's life. The little card the funeral home handed out at the wake still sits on my desk, and it leads me to reflect on Tim, on tragedy, and also on eternal life.

This is an abiding reflection of mine: there are two trails. One trail is empty and it runs alongside us for those who have passed away. We are not sure where their trails would have gone; we can only wonder. At times we are lost in our "what if" wonderings. The second trail is for us, and we (the living) are asked to travel it together. Those who love Tim miss him. Nothing can bring him back. Those who love him remain on the trail of life, with only thoughts of wondering where his path might have gone.

Death bewilders all of us. Tragic deaths pound the core of our being, forcing upon us the deep question "Why?" Tragedies mock shallow answers, driving us deeper into the mysteries of life. We are led to one of two possible alternatives: either we face the wild winds of tragedy with our hearts anchored in hope, or we turn our backs to hope to be blown by the wild winds into the shoals of despair.

Jesus gives us something that helps us to face the wild winds of tragedy and the constant winds of death. He gives us a way to challenge death, to look tragedy in the eye, and to know that "all is elsewhere" —that there is more to life than what we presently sense. He helps us to know that there is more to life than this world and this mortal body, that there is an eternity with *Abba*. Knowing that "all is elsewhere" leads us not to minimize our pain, but to endure it, to embrace it, and to carry it with us as we walk on in hope.

ON THE MOUNT OF TRANSFIGURATION WITH JESUS

Jesus both explains and demonstrates that "all is elsewhere." Jesus *explains* to his closest followers that opposition to him is heating up and that he will be put to death. He also teaches them that "on the third day [he will] be raised to life." He then explains that his followers will experience the same—both death and resurrection.

Because they don't comprehend what he is saying, he takes a few of them onto a mountain to *demonstrate* that there is more, that there is an eternity. On the mountain, Jesus' body is transfigured before them. It is difficult to know what "transfigure" means, so we turn to the Gospel of Luke for its own words:

> As he [Jesus] was praying, the appearance of his face changed,
> and his clothes became as bright as a flash of lightning.

Jesus' explanation of his resurrection and his demonstration of it are a *response to tragic death*. The transfiguration of Jesus is surrounded by the aura of death. Jesus tells his followers that he will die at the hands of the rulers; he tells his disciples that they, too, will die. During the Transfiguration, Moses and Elijah, one representing the *Torah* and one representing the Prophets, speak "about his departure," or in Greek, his *"exodus."* That is, in the middle of an action that reveals that there is more to life, these two great prophets speak about Jesus' death! What they do is tantamount to delivering a funeral eulogy at a wedding! Prophets have less sensitivity than they do honesty, even in the face of death. The Transfiguration is a response to death.

But why is Jesus transfigured? Hear the following words from the Gospel of Luke: Jesus "took Peter, John and James with him and went up onto a mountain to pray." Here the question about "why" Jesus is transfigured is answered. Jesus does not need an "experience" with God to be assured that there is an eternity for himself. Jesus does not wander into the woods seeking a mystical experience. Jesus is transfigured *to reveal to Peter, John, and James life's deepest mystery.*

The transfiguration of Jesus is *for others*—for you and me. Jesus anticipates for his followers that he will pave a path through the valley of death, that he will bore a hole through the tragic, thick steel wall that we call death. It is a path for us to walk on and a hole through which we can enter the Great Beyond. In the Transfiguration, Jesus takes his disciples by the hand and lets them take a step or two on that path, to see that the path truly exists. He also leads them to the hole, lets them peer through it to the vast land of eternity. The disciples are like the Pevensie children of *The Lion, the Witch, and the Wardrobe*, for whom the wardrobe opens up before them into Narnia—and they feel the twigs and smell the faint air of a land beyond.

The Transfiguration is one of those moments when a full disclosure of life's mystery bursts open, brushes up against us, and reminds us that "all is elsewhere." Peter, John, and James do not glimpse what Jesus will be like *some* day so much as who he really is in the *here and now* for the eye of faith. The glory here is not just a "Jesus thing." Moses and Elijah are also all "gloried up." Even more, Jesus says on another occasion, *all disciples* will "shine like the sun." What the disciples see in Jesus, Moses, and Elijah on the mountain is something they have in common. In these three glorified bodies, the disciples are seeing themselves beyond the grave.

We need to join Jesus, his disciples, and both Moses and Elijah on the mountain and see that we, too, will someday shine in transfiguration glory. Standing there with Jesus can give us a trans-figuration perspective on life.

TRANSFIGURATION PERSPECTIVES TODAY

Others have joined Jesus on the mountain and peered into eter-nity. Of recent studies, I think of Margaret Kim Peterson. She tells the grim story of the death of her AIDS-infected and dying husband, Hyung Goo. She expresses a transfiguration perspective on humans when she writes about looking at the man she loved but who was dying by the minute:

> Maybe that was what I was seeing when Hyung Goo looked at me and all I could see was love. I was not succumbing to senti-mental imagination. I was living with an icon, with a person whose face had begun to shine like Moses' did when he came down from the mountain. [She adds . . .] Hyung Goo was more whole when he died than he had been at any other time in his life.

That same perspective can be seen in a little-known saint of the early church, St. Macrina, whose brother Gregory, Bishop of Nyssa, was considered the "Father of the Fathers." Macrina's discipline and devotion were legendary, as was also her influence on the churches. Someone referred to her as a "powerhouse of virtue." So influential was she that Gregory was compelled to write her biography for the encouragement of the church. In a revealing account, he offers a transfiguration perspective of her when she was on the verge of death: "Although the fever was devouring all her strength and driving her headlong to death, she refreshed her body as if with some kind of morning dew." And, "it was as if an angel had providentially assumed human form." In her last moments, she prayed, made the sign of the cross, and was taken to glory. This is a transfiguration perspective.

What we see in Jesus' transfiguration is not so much his deity, but the glorification of his humanity—what all humans really and potentially are. C. S. Lewis calls this the "weight of glory." He reminds us in a long sentence:

> It is a serious thing to live in a society of possible gods and goddesses, to remember that the dullest and most uninteresting person you talk to may one day be a creature which, if you saw it now, you would be strongly tempted to worship, or else a horror and a corruption such as you now meet, if at all, only in a nightmare.

There are (Lewis continues), consequently, "no *ordinary* people" even if our fallen framework for life prohibits us from seeing humans for what they really are.

It is because humans truly are wondrous beings destined to inhabit God's glorious presence that death is not the final word.

Death belongs to this "life," but death cannot ultimately lock down life's glory. Lewis continues:

> Next to the Blessed Sacrament itself, your neighbour is the holiest object presented to your senses. If he is your Christian neighbour he is holy in almost the same way, for in him also Christ *vere latitat*—the glorifier and the glorified, Glory Himself, is truly hidden.

Few can write as Lewis writes. Few also know the story of John and Ann Goldingay, who exemplify this transfiguration perspective.

WALK ON

As a doctoral student in my first semester at the University of Nottingham, I attended a "fortnightly" seminar with students and professors. In my first session, to my right, was a professor at St. John's Theological College, John Goldingay, a man in whom I was soon to discover a transfiguration perspective at work. John's wife, Ann, had multiple sclerosis (MS).

John and Ann's story is now available in the book *Walk On*, and it is surely one of the most heart-warming and faith-inspiring books I have read in the last decade. Stricken with MS as well as a fiery determination to "walk on," Ann became a doctor. A nurse presumptuously suggested she not marry. Ann was also told not to have children. She married John and had children, and then later shifted her medical interest to psychiatry. She and John walked on.

As Ann's body became progressively debilitated, John's faith was progressively activated. Theirs is a sad, sad story of an unfair twisting of life; it is also a glad, glad story of the unusual triumph of a transfiguration perspective on life.

John is an Old Testament professor, and so the stories of Job and Jeremiah figure prominently in the book. Like those tough Old Testament saints, John's faith is gritty and realistic and honest. So much so that one senses he at times bursts out of his home in heated passion with guns ablazin' and his fiery eyes alookin', and with everyone else aduckin' and awonderin'. Like the views of Job and Jeremiah, John's transfiguration perspective does not deny the painful realities of life in the here and now. It faces those moments of tragedy and walks on, right into the wild winds.

In a chapter on Job called "Calamity," John shows how he has learned to deal with tragedy. All of us, he says, search for meaning in tragedy, and "any inadequate answer to the problem of suffering is preferable to the honest and true answer, 'We do not know,' which is why people go around [like Job's friends] repeating inadequate answers." Is there an answer, though, to why Ann suffers with MS (or an answer to premature deaths like Tim Panther's)? To be sure, John writes, "there may sometimes be explanations for calamity that we do not know." "But," he says, sometimes "we have to live with God without knowing them."

We simply have to walk on in faith and in pain. His wisdom is found in this statement:

> We are invited to name our hopelessness and to let ourselves be soaked, enfolded, immersed in the counter-story of Jesus' life, death, and resurrection, because they are the basis for hope.

This, I believe, is what the disciples learn to do on the mountain. They see the glory beyond, but the glory, like Moses' face, fades. Soon they are shuffling down the mountain to realities more mundane and are asked to walk on in faith. From that moment on, the Transfiguration is both memory and hope. Their memory is our hope.

I know of no better way to grapple with premature deaths and with debilitating diseases than to reflect on the transfiguration of Jesus—for here we see that "all is elsewhere." That elsewhere is our hope. We need to stand among the disciples and the two prophets on the mountain, and cast our gaze at Jesus. As Thomas à Kempis says it, "Whoever shadows my every move won't lose me in the dark."

CHAPTER 28

At the Last Supper with Jesus

GOSPEL READING
Luke 22:7–38

Our memory awakens our past.

To keep its past as part of its present, God gives to Israel a series of rituals, routines, and rhythms. God bestows such gifts so Israel does not succumb to spiritual dementia, spiritual memory loss. When Israelites listen to the sacred speech of these rituals, routines, and rhythms, Israel detects the gentle beat of God's historic acts of love for her. If they listen, they hear of his creation, of his covenant, of his redemption, and of his promises. The daily repetition of the *Shema* serves to bring into the present the historic daily creed for every Israelite.

Sometimes, of course, rituals and routines can become "ruts." Kris and I tend to get into ruts when it comes to the restaurants we visit (Bobby's Barrel Inn) or the day and time to watch a movie (Friday matinees). Routines can become ruts; some people, no doubt, repeated the *Shema* mindlessly.

But there are rituals and routines that we all need, and when securely established, they become rhythms that create a beat, and they inspire in us a step and a dance. There are some gentle rhythms in nature, like seconds, minutes, hours, days, weeks, months, and years. Like spring rain, summer shadows, autumn leaves, and winter snow. We can't change the rhythms of nature, so wisdom teaches us to watch their beauty and trot along at their pace. There are spiritual rhythms, too.

God graces Israel with rhythm by establishing a series of Holy Days. They are to set the rhythm for Israel's spirituality by awakening the memory. They are to awaken Israel's past in her present. They are annually to remember God's great act of liberation from Egypt on Passover. The Israelite reenacts the original Passover and, in so doing, awakens the memory of what made Israel what she is: people liberated from bondage.

Passover is the decisive link between the rhythm of Israel and the rhythm of the church. Roughly speaking, Good Friday is to Christians what Passover is to Israel. In celebrating Good Friday, we find the rhythm of remembering the Lord's death. Even more, when we let the rhythm of remembering the Cross fill our hearts and minds, the day can become in the words of John Ortberg's daughter, Mallory, a "dee dah day." This is the kind of day when you dance in circles saying "dee dah, dee dah."

Recently Kris and I returned to our *alma mater* for an alumni day, and it, too, was a "dee dah day." I needed to kick-start my memory to remember the golden days of college life, but sure enough, some things starting coming back. We saw old friends, classmates, and teachers—many of whom we hadn't seen in nearly thirty years. We shared stories of our present and of our favorite events while in college. It dawned on both of us that four years of our life had gone to sleep, mostly because we had become involved in other schools and another life. Those days were not dead, but they were asleep. Just by returning, just by seeing faces, touching hands, giving hugs, and hearing voices, part of our life was resurrected. It was a "dee dah day." Our own past was awakened in our present.

God gives us sacred rhythms to keep all chapters of our lives awake.

SACRED RHYTHM AND THE *JESUS CREED*

Rituals and routines serve a variety of purposes. We go through a "morning routine" *to get us going*—spilling orange juice on the kitchen floor can create a day-lasting headache. In our family we solemnize Christmas by observing family-specific traditions *to keep family memories alive*. We attend Christmas services *to remind ourselves of what God has done for us*. Different routines have different purposes.

It is good to establish sacred rhythms to keep our spirits awake. Many of us have some sacred rhythms, like morning prayers and Bible reading, or a day of prayer, or a week at camp, or a weekend retreat with a spiritual director. Many of us also observe the church's calendar. There we discover Sacred Time (Advent, Christmas, and Epiphany along with Lent, Holy Week, Easter, and Pentecost) and Ordinary Time (from Pentecost to Advent). By observing the calendar, we evoke two seasons: redemption (Sacred Time) and response (Ordinary Time). The two seasons correspond to the premise and the response of the *Jesus Creed*: God's love for us (Sacred Time) and our love for God and others (Ordinary Time).

Even more, God grants us rhythms so they can become sacred theater in which the drama of faith is performed. The Passover meal, when Jews reenact the original last meal before escaping the clutches of Pharaoh, is sacred theater. As a family, Israelites proceed through the seder to remember Israel's first Passover. They eat lamb and bitter herbs; they drink a series of cups of wine. All of this is tied together in a story that is read to the family by the father. When this happens, the Israelite imagines himself or herself right back in the world of Moses in Egypt. They remember the night that differs from all other nights. It is the night when the avenging angel of death "passed over" the homes of Israelites so *YHWH* could liberate Israel.

To any casual onlooker at the time of Jesus, the Last Supper of Jesus looks like the official Passover meal. But the longer that onlooker observes, the more subtle differences appear. In fact, the onlooker can be excused for thinking that Jesus is setting *himself* in center stage much more than the Jewish father normally does. There is a reason for Jesus' becoming the center of the meal.

We've already observed that Jesus amended the sacred *Shema* to form the *Jesus Creed*; we've also seen that he amended the sacred *Kaddish* prayer to form the Lord's Prayer. Now we can see that he amends *Pesah** (Passover) to form the Last Supper. Jesus makes it clear that he is the Lamb of God, and he also makes it clear that the Last Supper anticipates his death, a death for others. That is, Passover becomes personal. Instead of an altar and a priest, Christians have a table and Jesus. Instead of sacrificing a lamb, Christians remember Jesus' death. Instead of eating a lamb, Christians drink the wine and eat the bread. Instead of slaying the firstborn of Egypt, *Abba* slays his own firstborn. And instead of protecting Israelite babies with blood-smeared doors, *Abba* protects those who drink from the Firstborn's cup.

These changes reflect the *Jesus Creed*: Because Jesus loves others (us), he offers himself for us to replace the lamb. Thus, the Lord's Supper is Passover morphed by the *Jesus Creed*. The Passover lamb becomes the Lamb of God, and the Lamb of God leaves us a rhythm by which to remember what he has done for us.

THE LAST SUPPER AS SIGN
AND SACRED RHYTHM

Humans need something tangible, something physical, something real. We are physical beings; we encounter life physically. We have wedding rings, Christmas presents, statues, memorials, and trophies.

At the bottom of Pearl Harbor, just off the northeast shore of Ford Island, lies a physical object, left alone as a memorial. It is a warship, the USS *Arizona*. An occasional oil bubble still rises eerily to the surface, sixty-plus years later. On December, 7, 1941, the Japanese stealthily flew over the sleepy borders of northern Oahu down the island to Pearl Harbor. Waves of missiles were met with shocks of confusion, leaving thousands dead and the American military humiliated. In the first wave of attacks, at 8:10 AM, the *Arizona* blew up and became the reluctant grave for 1,177 sailors.

Pearl Harbor Day, a "date which will live in infamy," was memorialized over the sunken *Arizona* when, in 1962, a 184-foot structure was dedicated. Its perpendicular location over the *Arizona* turns the site into a cross. The USS *Arizona* Memorial was built to mark the historic place physically so we can remember the tragic moment. Another aspect of remembering is the need to draw up an official account in a book so we can grip the story in our hands, and Walter Lord's *Day of Infamy* has served that purpose for nearly fifty years. When we enter the USS *Arizona* Memorial, when we read Walter Lord's book, we remember, and we participate in the event. The tangible evokes the memory.

From the beginning of time, and with a gentle tip of his divine cap to the empiricist in our hearts, God has shown his love physically so that we can see, touch, smell, and taste it. God creates; he establishes covenant ceremonies with Abraham and Moses and David; he forms a national body as his people (Israel); he gives this people a place to live (Israel), and in that Land he makes a temple for worship. Christians see the physical touch of God in the Incarnation, in baptism, in the Eucharist, in the physical act of worshipping together, in the physical expression of faith, in the church "building," and in the church itself—the one holy catholic church.

But only one of these is given as a sacred rhythm of remembrance.

We call it Eucharist or Holy Communion or the Lord's Supper. Jesus establishes for his followers a physical, sacred rhythm so they will never forget his gracious act of love for them. The bread and wine are his "tangible truth." As New Testament scholar Tom Wright observes, Jesus didn't give us a theory of the atonement but "an act to perform . . . a meal that speaks more volumes than any theory." Jesus' parting gift is bread and wine, a simple meal designed to create for his followers the rhythm of remembering him. These two little tangible truths need to be seen for what they are.

God is saying this: if you want to remember what I have done, look at Jesus. What makes God odd is that Jesus leaves two earthy bits as "mini-icons" of himself: a small chunk of bread and a short swig of wine. These two little tangible truths are physical elements designed to draw us into remembering Jesus so we can participate in his life for us. "Taste, see, and know my presence," he says.

COME, LET US TASTE AND SEE

The Lord's Supper is the Lord's gift of rhythm for us. He asks us to participate in the Last Supper with him. In the physical act of eating and drinking at the Lord's Supper, we remember Jesus physically, we express our trust in him—in his "body and blood"— and we physically proclaim liberation. In short, we *participate* in his life (and death) for us.

We participate in the life of Jesus by physically eating the meal

At the Last Supper, Jesus gave these directions: "Take and eat." Our calling at the table of the Lord is to *act*: we are to eat, and we are to drink. We are not called to "gloomify" the table with clouds of doom. We are called to *act*. By eating the bread and drinking the wine, we *physically remember* Jesus and participate in his life (and death). This is what Jesus meant by "do this in remembrance of me."

We sit together; we see the visible "elements" in front of us all; we see the leaders take the bread and the wine; we see them pass them out to us. Or, as is the case with others, we approach the elements and ingest them where the priest dispenses them. In some cases, the leaders say, "The body of the Lord" and "The blood of the Lord." Details of observance aside, what is important is that we participate by remembering.

We participate in the life of Jesus by trusting him physically

In John 6 Jesus feeds a multitude miraculously and then provides a discourse on the words "I am the bread of life." Those who eat this bread, Jesus says, will "not die." Why? Because, he says, "I am the living bread that came down from heaven. If anyone eats of this bread, he will live forever. This bread is my flesh, which I will give for the life of the world."

These statements of Jesus are not about the Lord's Supper. The Lord's Supper, in fact, makes physical what is said in these statements. What we remember at the Lord's Supper is that Jesus, the Bread of Life, offers his life to us so that we can be liberated. In eating the bread and drinking the wine, we express our faith in that Bread of Life. When we ingest these elements, we physically act out our faith in Jesus' sacred theater as he presents himself to us.

We participate in the life of Jesus by proclaiming him physically

All the sermons preached in the history of the church, all the dramas acted on the stages of churches, all the books written to expound the gospel, and all the instruction by teachers amount to merely this: they are attempts to explain what happens when the people of God gather round the table of the Lord to perform the sacred rhythm of sacred theater. Participation in the life of Jesus in the Eucharist is proclamation of the gospel.

The apostle Paul teaches this very thing: "For whenever you eat this bread and drink this cup, you *proclaim* the Lord's death until he comes." When we participate in the life of Jesus, we declare his death as our death and his death as the end of all deaths. This sacred rhythm of declaration characterizes and constitutes the community from the Last Supper until the Second Coming.

This last sentence may surprise some. What Paul is saying is that the Eucharist is fundamentally a *missionary action*. An Episcopal scholar, John Koenig, recently wrote a book on the Lord's Supper with the mission power of the Lord's Supper uppermost in his mind, and he titled his book *The Feast of the World's Redemption*. So it is, or as the early Aramaic-speaking Christians would have said, *Amen*. The Lord's Supper announces the gospel—and it is an offer of that gospel.

It is time for us to think what happens whenever Christians celebrate the Lord's Supper. They are performing the gospel itself in the sacred rhythm of a sacred theater. Just by participating in the life of Jesus, we proclaim the drama of the gospel, and this drama establishes the rhythm of spiritual formation in us. "Taste, see, and know his presence."

CHAPTER 29

At the Cross with Jesus

G O S P E L   R E A D I N G S
Luke 23:26–49; John 18–19

> ## "Many are wowed by his miracles; few are wooed by his cross."

Crucifixion is grotesque. It unleashes sadistic revenge. It hopes to deter crime. Its victims are "under God's curse." The victim is beaten and brutalized. The victim hangs before God and before gawkers: naked, bleeding, and gasping for air. Crucified victims are often not buried. Birds of prey pick flesh from the bones. Wild beasts tear loose what they can reach. The remains are tossed into a shallow grave for hungry dogs. Mercifully, Jesus' mangled body is removed by two Jewish council members for burial.

Beginning to end, the crucifixion of Jesus is a grotesque scene, one that is far from the mind of most persons who wear crosses around their necks. No one, to use a modern analogy, has the macabre affront to wear a necklace with a guillotine or a gallows or a noose or an electric chair, or cells on death row. If someone were to do so, there is a diagnosis for that person in the *Diagnostic and Statistical Manual of Mental Disorders* and people in white jackets waiting their appointment.

WHY CRUCIFIXION?

Why, then, did God choose this grotesque act of crucifixion to accomplish what otherwise could be done in a sanitized temple, or in running water, or in a simple act of personal contrition? Why resort to the grotesque?

We can explore this question by appealing to a story written by the Southern Christian writer, Flannery O'Connor. Her stories are so effective that fifty years after her (all too brief) life, they continue to transform readers around the globe. In addition, she opens a window on the transforming power of using grotesque images.

One of her stories, "Parker's Back," concerns a vulgar dropout named O. E. Parker, who, to cope with recurring moods of dissatisfaction, randomly adds tattoos of incompatible images to his grotesque body. He is "decorated" with animals and vulgarities, while his grotesque wife is a Bible-thumping, sin-sniffing hypocrite. In the crucial scene, Parker is blinded by the "sun" (Son), accidentally runs into a "tree," flips his boss's tractor, and everything goes up in flames.

Through this incident Parker discovers God and begins the process of conversion. To mark his newfound faith, he acquires a tattoo of a Byzantine Christ on the only part of his body without a tattoo: his back. Then, like the prodigal son, he returns home to his wife, but instead of receiving a welcome, he is beaten into tears with a broom by his "saved" wife. After she cleans the broom, she looks out the window to see O. E. "leaning against the tree, crying like a baby." O. E. are the initials of "Obadiah Elihue," "the servant of God, he is God." No reader can miss that Parker's life is turned upside down when he hits a "tree" or that the Servant is leaning against a "tree," and that the New Testament sometimes refers to the cross as a "tree." All Parker has now is a tree to lean on.

The scene is almost unbearable—the Servant of God is beaten by one who claims to speak for God. Like many who read the story, I find O'Connor's grotesque images repulsive. But the grotesque is necessary, she believes, because the modern reader's "sense of evil is diluted or lacking altogether and so he has forgotten the price of restoration." "There are ages," she says, "when it is possible too woo the reader; there are others when something more drastic is necessary."

O'Connor learns her method of appealing to the grotesque from the gospel itself. God gives the cross as his "drastic" measure, his "grotesque" image. That is the value of God's choice of the cross: In its grotesqueness it tells God's story, and when we participate in that story by joining Jesus at the cross, spiritual formation is advanced.

THE DIVINE DESIGNS OF THE GROTESQUE CROSS

We go through the process of being spiritually formed by participating in the life of Jesus, who lived the *Jesus Creed* perfectly. Jesus repents for us at the Jordan, he loves God faithfully in the wilderness when he is tempted, he transfigures earthly tragedy into eternal realities on the Mountain, and he transforms the Passover lamb into his own death for us at the Last Supper. Jesus' living out the *Creed* also explains the cross: his love for God and for others direct his path from the Galilee to Golgotha.

At Golgotha God invites each of us to hear his own story of love for us. What story do we hear? God erects a grotesque cross on Golgotha to reveal his physical sympathy with our earthly pain, his offer of spiritual freedom from our sin, and his graphic image for moral transformation.

A grotesque process designed for physical sympathy: Jesus with us

In the Garden of Gethsemane, Jesus anticipates Golgotha. From Gethsemane to Golgotha, one image that sticks with us, rendered starkly visible in Mel Gibson's *The Passion of the Christ*, is the physical suffering of Jesus. In fact, the writer of the Book of Hebrews explains something many Christians miss when it comes to the cross: Jesus sufferes *to sympathize* with our sufferings.

Jesus suffers immensely. In the Garden of Gethsemane, during a prayer of utter anguish, Jesus' sweat pours from his body like drops of blood. After a night of interrogation, Jesus is flogged and severely weakened by pain and loss of blood. Even though his nerves are firing themselves raw, some mocking soldiers jam a crown of thorns onto his head. The guards point him toward Golgotha. He is obligated by custom (if not law) to haul his own crossbeam. When he can carry the cross no longer, and with no disciples mustering the courage to support Jesus, Simon from Cyrene carries it the rest of the way. Jesus' wrists and ankles are punctured violently as he is nailed to the cross. The cross is then raised, and his wrists and ankles bear most of his weight, stretching and tearing in the process. When offered a sedative, he refuses. He does what he can to remain conscious to the end. To test that he is dead, soldiers puncture his side with a sword; water and blood gush out.

Yes, Jesus suffers immensely. These details are not told so that we participate like voyeurs in some sadistic torture. This grotesque suffering is God's loving communication of sympathy in our physical suffering. Jesus loves us, as his *Creed* teaches, and because he does, he suffers with us. In our pain, we are invited to join Jesus so he can share our pain.

Jesus is *with us*—in our pain, in our suffering, in our ghoulish encounters with abuse, and in our injustices. When we face debilitating diseases, when we see that our path leads into a dark valley, when we know that our days are running out, we can join Jesus—he's been there and he suffers *with us*.

A grotesque act designed for spiritual freedom: Jesus instead of us

Theological "interleckchuals" (as Flannery O'Connor dubs them) seek to explain the mechanics of the Cross by developing theories of the atonement. But the "central Christian belief is that Christ's death has somehow put us right with God and given us a fresh start. Theories as to how it did this are another matter." Before there were theories of the atonement, there was Jesus, and he had a few things to say about why he died. I suggest we begin with his own statements.

First, Jesus says his death is a "ransom for many." Second, at the Last Supper Jesus explains that the wine and bread are his own blood and body. And, third, though not a statement by Jesus but a comment by the Fourth Evangelist, Jesus dies at the time the Passover victims are being slain. These three texts open up Jesus' understanding of the Cross.

These texts swallow an old story with a new story. The old story is that blood from the Passover lamb was smeared on the door to protect the firstborn and liberate Israel from slavery. The old story is about blood that sets a people free. The new story is that

Jesus is the new Passover Lamb who is slain to ransom his people, to set them free. Instead of smearing blood on the door, Jesus' followers are asked to ingest the wine (his bloody death) and trust in his blood as a protection that will set them free.

Like the Passover lamb, Jesus claims that his death is vicarious as he represents us and substitutes for us. He experiences for us what we do not want but deserve (slavery and death), and provides for us what we do want but don't deserve (a life of freedom). By participating in his death, we are set free by his death.

All we have to do is drink "the cup of his death" as our own drink: what we do in the Lord's Supper is visibly express that his blood is our new Passover lamb and his blood takes away our sins. As John Stott explains, "Before we can begin to see the cross as something done *for* us (leading us to faith and worship), we have to see it as something done *by* us (leading us to repentance)." And: "As we face the cross, then, we can say to ourselves both '*I* did it, my sins sent him there' and '*he* did it, his love took him there.'"

At no place is love for others seen more than when someone gives his life for his friends, as Jesus says and does. Jesus gives his life as an act of love, not only to sympathize with our suffering but also to free us spiritually.

Opening our hearts to this grotesque image of the cross is also the ancient path of moral transformation, a path not easy to walk—as one of Jesus' friends, Peter, knows by experience.

A grotesque model designed for moral transformation: Jesus before us

Peter, our model of imperfection, rejects the Cross as a model for moral transformation. On Jesus' last night, he eats with his disciples, prays with them, is arrested, and then is taken away to be questioned. Peter, his closest follower, skirts the perimeter, ducks the authorities, and saves his skin. Had Peter found in the Cross a model for life, he would have denied himself and died with Jesus. He didn't. In this he fails, because the Cross is the model of moral transformation, the symbol of self-denial.

I have never been in the habit of making the sign of the cross on my forehead, chest, and shoulders, but recently I had lunch with a friend who did have the habit. This practice, so he explained, reminds him of the cross life we are to live. This custom of crossing ourselves is less comfortable for those in the evangelical communion than for those in liturgical traditions, but all should know that the practice is as early as the second century. Tertullian, one of our first theologians said this:

> At every forward step and movement, at every going in and out, when we put on our clothes and shoes, when we bathe, when we sit at table, when we light the lamps, on couch, on seat, in all the ordinary actions of daily life, we trace upon our forehead the sign.

A rhythm like this can offer gentle reminders throughout our day that the Cross is a model for moral transformation. As the biographer of John Bunyan, author of *The Pilgrim's Progress*, says, "There is no Christianity without the cross, the cross that carries us and the cross that we carry."

Indeed. It is the Cross that carries us (in giving us spiritual freedom) as well as the cross we are to carry (in giving us a model for moral transformation). One who found in the Cross the entire picture of the Christian life was a theology professor at Fordham University, Dietrich von Hildebrand.

A LIFE OF THE CROSS

Born into an aristocratic German family living in Florence, Italy, a cultured life was there for the taking for Dietrich von Hildebrand. But instead, he converted to the Christian faith and, in so doing, inscribed the grotesque image of the cross onto the face of his own life, and what's more, he did so under the scornful, suspicious glare of Adolf Hitler.

For von Hildebrand, who began his academic career as a theologian at the University of Munich, embracing the Cross meant living a cross life not just in confession but also in the details of life. For instance, he admitted to German authorities that a distant relative was Jewish when such an admission could have cost him his life. When his academic colleagues were writing scholarly pieces to establish their reputations, he wrote books on purity, marriage, and moral transformation. When scientific objectivity and personal distance (especially from faith) were the order of the day, von Hildebrand contended that it was the classical Christian faith that gave rise to true understanding.

And he knew that Jesus' own suffering was both divine sympathy and a personal call to suffer physically. As a very young professor of philosophy, Dietrich was one of the first to speak out against the evils of National Socialism and the demonic machinations of Hitler. Hitler's men had him in their crosshairs. Von Hildebrand fled with his family to Vienna, where he established himself as the editor of an anti-Hitler magazine, called *Der Christliche Ständestaat* (The Christian Corporative State). Quickly, Hitler pronounced Hildebrand Public Enemy Number One in Austria. Duly warned of the *Anschluss* (the annexation of Austria), von Hildebrand escaped to Spain in a series of events and providential protections that would make James Bond jealous.

When offered an escape from Spain to freedom without his wife (on a military transport), von Hildebrand, who had written on the sacredness of marriage and the Cross as the pattern for the moral life, asked: "Do you expect me to leave her all alone, exposed to the greatest dangers, just to save my own life? It is out of the question."

What is not out of the question is that what the world sees as a grotesque image, the cross, has become for Christians a place of grace—the spot where Jesus suffers to sympathize with us, where we are protected spiritually from the avenging angel of death, and where we find a model for moral transformation.

At the Tomb
with Jesus

G O S P E L   R E A D I N G S
Matthew 28:1–10; Luke 24:13–35; John 20–21

Jesus is dead and buried.

It is a total disaster as far as his followers are concerned. Jesus excited their hopes for the kingdom of God, he gave them reason to believe that what God had promised to his people through the prophets would come to pass. But now he is dead. Disasters abound—death, disappointment, and doubt.

Many of us face disasters: financial, relational, parental, marital, as well as physical and psychological diseases. Disasters rip rest from our sleep, hold us captive until the morning sun dawns, and make us wonder if we can possibly move on. And we all face the disaster of death.

Can we find new life on the other side of little disasters? And as for the big disaster we all face, what about it? Is there life beyond death? There are Christian "answers" to these questions, but it begins with the disaster of the death of Jesus.

LIFE BEYOND THE
DISASTER OF DEATH

According to the gospel records, everywhere we look on Easter Day there are little disasters—Jesus is dead and the disciples are full of doubt. Those at the tomb are afraid, bewildered, and speechless. The apostles don't believe the women when they claim that Jesus has been raised. Some leave the city in despair. Thomas makes a case for empirical evidence. We should give them the benefit of their doubts.

Jesus is the prophet from Galilee, a great miracle worker, and declares the arrival of the kingdom. It is risky for him to enter Jerusalem because the Romans are touchy about anyone's disturbing the peace. However, God has been with Jesus the whole time, and so he enters the city to the applause of a crowd of disciples. When he holds his own with the authorities of his day, things are looking very good for him and his followers.

Until the big kahuna of disasters: Jesus is arrested, tried, sentenced to death, and grotesquely crucified. The dream that Jesus excites among his followers, that the kingdom is near, is in ruins. The disciples see Jesus die, and at least some of them watch him (at a safe distance) placed by some Jewish council members in a tomb. The wheels of history turn and he is under them; they crush him and the disciples' hope.

What they need is some evidence that death and disaster are not the final words.

The Resurrection is the final word they need. We are, after all, rational beings, and we want things to make sense. Arguments work for us and sometimes generate a greater faith. In the history of the

Church the following arguments have been used to support the claim that Jesus was raised and that the Resurrection is the final word we all need:

- An empty tomb is found in a variety of gospel sources, and an empty tomb has to be explained: the body was either raised or stolen.
- Preaching the Resurrection in Jerusalem would have been well-nigh impossible had the tomb not been empty.
- Roman and Jewish leaders responded to early Christians but did not produce a body, because the tomb was empty.
- Women were used as the first witnesses of Jesus' resurrection—something indefensible were it not an unavoidable truth.
- Gospel records leave tantalizing questions about the order of events and who saw what and where and when—questions that would not remain unanswered had the early Christians simply gotten together to collude about a "pretend" resurrection.
- There were plenty of eyewitnesses who claimed to have seen Jesus.
- The best explanation for the rise of the church is its own explanation: it rose because Jesus arose.

We can't unpack, or even explain, each of these arguments. What we are more concerned with is the "so what?" question. What does his resurrection do for our own disasters? Christians make this claim: *If we participate in Jesus' resurrection by owning his story as our story, we find hope.*

The *Jesus Creed* is to love God by following Jesus and to love others. We follow Jesus when we enter his tomb with him and, in faith, cover ourselves with his empty grave clothes and walk out with him to a new life beyond our disasters. A good place to see what it means to join Jesus in the tomb is to look at the story of Margaret Kim Peterson and the death of her husband, Hyung Goo. We mentioned one small excerpt of her story before, but it is time now to look more carefully.

IS THE WHOLE WORLD LIKE THIS?

After a few years of discouragement with dating, Margaret Ault, whose story I mentioned before, was finally staring into the face of real love. On the verge of graduating from seminary and planning a Ph.D., Margaret went on a date with Hyung Goo Kim— dinner at a Thai place and a concert of modern music. Not much later, on New Year's Eve, they accidentally spent hours together waiting for someone else in the emergency room. That time together changed their relationship, and it nose-dived into serious, warm waters.

Hot water is what that water soon became. A few dates later Hyung Goo delicately but clearly informed Margaret that he was infected with HIV, the virus that causes AIDS. Here's how she expressed the disastrous revelation:

> I had never met anyone whom I liked half so much as I liked him. I had never met anyone who made me feel so whole, who was such good company, whose interests paralleled and complemented mine the way his did. He was a musician, he was a scientist, he was a thoughtful and committed Christian. He was

handsome, funny, considerate, creative. He owned a tuxedo, for goodness' sake. And he was going to die of AIDS. . . . Now I'd met someone I liked, and we were definitely not going to live happily ever after. I felt like I had been kicked in the gut by the biggest boot in the world.

Somewhat like Joseph marrying Mary, Margaret went ahead and married Hyung Goo, risking reputation (and health). What would make a person like Margaret marry a man like Hyung Goo? Why would anyone invite into the core of her being so much pain? How could a new reality emerge from this ruin? An answer unfolds in the rest of her story.

When Margaret was in graduate school at Duke, she and Hyung Goo loved to walk in the Duke gardens, and so knowledgeable did they become of its plants that they "supervised construction" of a new project. They walked through each part of the garden routinely and had names for some of the ducks. In their last spring together, the garden seemed especially beautiful "as if it were a gift just for us."

Hyung Goo died in the fall and Margaret returned to the gardens in the spring where a memorial garden of roses was being constructed in his honor. Her trip back led to these "new life" thoughts:

> Where peonies were promised, there were only the dead stumps of last year's stalks; where day lilies were promised, there were unprepossessing tufts of foliage; where hostas were promised, there was nothing at all. And yet I knew what lushness lay below the surface; those beds that were so brown and empty and, to the unknowing eye, so unpromising, would be full to bursting in a matter of months.

> *Is the whole world like this? Is this what it might be like to*
> *live in expectation, real expectation, of the resurrection?*
>
> Was not Hyung Goo's and my life together like this? Empty
> and sere, and yet a seedbed of fullness and life for both of us. He
> died, and I was widowed; yet in his dying, we both were made
> alive.

Where does she find strength to grip such faith and such hope?
What gives her the hope to ask for someone to "sing me to heaven"?
It is found in the italicized question: *Is the whole world like this?*

The answer, "Yes, the whole world is like this: the whole world
offers us tokens of new life beyond death and disasters." It offers the
promise of a new life beyond the grave, a life of renewed love in the
presence of God. Why? Because Jesus was raised from the dead.

Margaret's story of dealing with a tragic death is extraordinary
but reveals what the Resurrection provides us as we face tragic death.
But we would be unfair to the Gospels to think that the resurrection
of Jesus offers only life beyond the grave. In fact, the resurrection
of Jesus overturns a variety of disasters and gives to the followers
of Jesus a new life. This is seen in four of Jesus' followers, who
experience disasters of faith, abandonment, doubt, and confusion.

FROM DISASTERS TO NEW LIFE

Peter fails to love Jesus enough to own him as even a friend.
During Jesus' trial, Peter flat-out denies Jesus three times. If it
weren't so serious to deny Jesus, Peter's disaster could be a comedy.
Jesus predicted he would be killed and raised, and he predicted that
Peter would deny him. *And Peter still denies Jesus.* This is Peter's
disaster, and it is the Resurrection that addresses the disaster. Jesus

is raised from the dead, and he reinstates Peter to his vocation. Beyond *faith failure* is the new life of forgiveness.

Mary Magdalene, unlike other women, is defined only by her village. Not something like "Mary *bat Reuben*" (daughter of Reuben). Just, Mary "of Magdala" or "Mary *Magdalene*." She is exorcised of seven demons and is a traveling companion of Jesus; she is also at the cross when the disaster takes place, and she sees Jesus placed in the tomb. When she comes upon the tomb on Easter morning, she weeps bitterly when she discovers the tomb empty. Why? Jesus and his followers are her family. She's got nowhere to go; she's utterly alone. But Jesus appears to her. Beyond *abandonment* is the new life of God's presence.

Thomas, after hearing testimony from his fellow apostles that Jesus has in fact been raised from the dead, says, "Unless I see the nail marks in his hands and put my finger where the nails were, and put my hand into his side, I will not believe it." Jesus obliges him, and Thomas confesses: "My Lord and my God!" We know Thomas as the doubter; he is also Thomas the confessor. Beyond the disaster of intense doubt is a confident confession that shapes a Christian understanding of who Jesus is.

The eleven remaining apostles, now that Judas has deserted them, are confused—all of them. They are caught up in Jesus' kingdom mission. But the death of Jesus makes a disaster of their expectations. Jesus appears to them. Their response? "When they saw him, they worshiped him; *but some doubted*." What is Jesus' response? What we call the Great Commission—go make disciples in the whole world. Beyond the disaster of confusion is a mission.

Beyond death is the new life of resurrection. And beyond personal disasters there breathes the new life of Jesus' offer of forgiveness, Jesus' offer of presence, Jesus' offer of faith, and Jesus' offer of a mission.

Beyond personal disaster there is hope, as John Bunyan illustrates.

NEW LIFE BEYOND DISASTER: JOHN BUNYAN

The Englishman, John Bunyan, wrote the most successful popular book in the history of the Church, *The Pilgrim's Progress*. Most Christians today have been captured by other fictional dramas, but there was a time, and not long ago, when Christians were all conversant with Bunyan's sanctifying tale of Christian and his wife, Christiana. Samuel Coleridge, the great English poet, said:

> I know no book, the Bible excepted, as above all comparison, which I, according to my judgment and experience, could so safely recommend as teaching enforcing the whole saving truth, according to the mind that was in Christ Jesus, as *The Pilgrim's Progress*.

How that book came into print illustrates how God creates new life on the other side of disasters. Bunyan's own disasters included his education and his imprisonment, neither of which prevented his gifts from growing and glowing. Bunyan was a tinker—one who made and mended kettles. His was also an emotional, profane, blasphemous, and tormented soul, and he had little regard for education.

Because of his lack of the proper education, the establishment opposed and criticized his call to the pastorate at St. John's in

Bedford some years later. But the new life God granted him awakened in him yearnings to study, to ponder Scripture, to observe humans, and to hear what God was saying. In fact, along with many other saints, he saw his lack of a preparation as a supreme qualification for God's enabling power.

England itself was on the edge of disaster—there were fights between major political and religious parties, especially between those siding with a state church and those favoring religious freedom. Bunyan was caught on the wrong side and put in prison. Because he refused to stop preaching, there he remained (more or less) for some twelve years—with a threat hanging over his head that he "must stretch by the neck." He supported himself by making laces and worried constantly about his wife and blind daughter. He was released in 1672, but he was back soon for another bout with the dungeon. His biographer says, "Only those, like Bunyan, with a strong constitution had much chance of survival for any length of time."

The disaster of an imprisonment couldn't hold down the power of the resurrection life at work in Bunyan. In this second imprisonment he wrote *The Pilgrim's Progress*. Imagine separation from your family and your calling. For many of us, it would be the undoing of everything. But from Bunyan's disaster came forth a magnificent piece of practical theology that continues to stir Christians today. The secret to *The Pilgrim's Progress*, which most experts think created the modern novel, was his insight that, as life is a story, so also is spiritual formation a story—a journey from earth to heaven.

When you and I sit down to read Bunyan's book, we need to be aware of this: A disastrous personality is converted; a disastrous education is awakened; and a disastrous imprisonment is exploited to dream a journey. That journey was possible because of the journey of the Son from heaven to earth, and then—because of the Resurrection—back again.

Jesus' life, from front cover to back cover, including the dust jacket, is a life shaped by the *Jesus Creed*. He learned the *Shema* from his father and mother; he amended it for his followers in the shape of the *Jesus Creed*. Most importantly, he lived it. We are called to participate in that very life, for it is that resurrected life that can form our lives.

ACKNOWLEDGMENTS

I dedicate this book to Kris. Her wisdom, love, encouragement, and judgment can be found in every chapter And on every page. In simple terms, I am honored to live with someone who lives out the *Jesus Creed* daily.

Many friends and colleagues have read portions of this manuscript or have listened to me chat about them. John Ortberg has been a constant source of encouragement, both in word and book. I am grateful that he agreed to write the Foreword. Sonia Bodi has read and commented on every chapter. She always has the right word and expresses it with élan and compassion. Garry Poole interrupted his own busy schedule of ministry to read chapters, meet with me, and offer encouragement. Greg and Heather Clark, Doreen and Mark Olson, Kent Palmer, Steve Ratliff, Wes Olmstead, Kermit Zarley, Joe Modica, Bob Mulholland, and Rob Merola read the entire manuscript or portions of it, and I thank them for their suggestions. Mark Allan Powell, David Larsen, Akiva Cohen, and Greg Strand made extensive notes on various chapters; to them I give my heartfelt thanks.

Two other North Park colleagues deserve my thanks: David Nystrom has been my colleague for nine years, but is now returning to California to serve the Covenant Church. I will miss him as a brother, and our school will miss him as a leader. Jim Nelson, my golfing partner throughout the warmer months of the year, has walked many a fairway in silence listening to my ideas, many of which are in this book—and I thank him for his wise counsel and bibliographical expertise.

My daughter, Laura, and her husband, Mark Barringer, heard more than they cared to hear of what I was writing—usually in some restaurant—and their questions have settled into this book in some ways. My son, Lukas, when he was home during the off-season, read each chapter. As an English major, he had literary suggestions that made me proud; as a son, he encouraged his father (which also made me proud).

In the Spring semester of 2004 I read the entire manuscript of this book to my fourth-year practicum on spiritual formation, and I wish to record my gratitude to them. They relished the opportunity of turning the tables to make suggestions on my prose and ideas. Not a few of their ideas show up. Jacob Eisele, Chris Nelson, Jinny Chieu, Jessie Wuollet, and Andrew Kjer make teaching a holiday.

Finally, with perhaps the most enduring impact on the manuscript, I mention Lil Copan, my editor at Paraclete Press. She is the Melchizedek of editors, accepting my verbal offerings and turning them into a fragrance acceptable to God and others.

Holy Week 2004

Abba: the Aramaic term for "father"; the Hebrew term is *Ab* (or *Av*). While fatherhood is not the *emphasis* in Judaism for its understanding of God (*YHWH**), it is clear that Judaism understood God at times in terms of his fatherly relations to Israel. (Barbra Streisand sings a song by that name!). Christians are mistaken when they claim Jesus was the *first* to use the term for God, and they also fail to grasp the historical record when they claim Jesus was the first to understand God in loving, gracious terms. There is ample evidence for the gracious love of *YHWH** as *Ab* in the Old Testament (Pss. 68:5; 103:13-14; Jer. 3:19; 31:9, 20; Hos. 11:1–8; Mal. 2:10). Nor do Christians understand the term accurately when they think the language is simply baby talk and translate it "Daddy." The term *Abba* comprises the relationship of a child to a father from birth to death: hence, "Father" is surely the most accurate translation.

Almanah: Hebrew term for "widow." The *almanah* is stereotypically impoverished, destitute, and dismal (cf. Ruth 1:20-21). Although laws were enacted to protect widows (Deut. 14:28-29; 24:19–24), the laws were apparently neglected, because a theme arises in the Bible that God is the defender of the widow (Pss. 68:5; 146:9).

Am ha-aretz: Hebrew for "people of the Land." This term, which once meant "landed gentry in Judah," became a pejorative term for (1) those who were intentionally careless about following the specifics of the *Torah** and its interpretation, and (2) those who might be called today "country bumpkins." I consider highly likely that the colleagues of Joseph would have considered his decision to marry the unacceptably pregnant Mary unworthy of a person considered to be a *tsadiq**. In their perception, Joseph was no better than the intentionally careless of the Land. A good example of this attitude can be seen in Luke 15:1-2.

Anawim: Hebrew for "poor, humble." The "pious poor" of Judaism. After the Exile in Babylon (587 BC), a social class of Jews who returned were known as much for their commitment to the *Torah** and the temple as for their economic poverty. Their situation led them to trust in God and to pray for him to establish his justice in the Land. Accordingly, this group was one in which hopes for the Messiah flourished. Two other wonderful examples of the *Anawim* can be found in the accounts of Simeon (Lk. 2:25–35) and Anna (2:36–38). They seem to live in the cracks of society, they are near the temple, and their expectations for the Messiah strike the reader immediately. Some have suggested that the letter of James, which was written by the brother of Jesus, reflects the piety of the *Anawim*. A reading of the following passages from James confirms the suggestions: 1:9-10, 27; 2:1–13, 14–17; 4:13–17; 5:1–6.

God-fearer: a Gentile who partly converted to Judaism (without undergoing circumcision) and who participated in the Jewish life of the synagogue. See Acts 10:1–11:18; 13:16, 26, 43, 50; 17:4, 17; 18:7.

Impure: see Purity.

Mamzer: an illegitimate child. Because of Jesus' irregular conception through a virgin, he would have been considered by some in his world as (if truth be told) a *mamzer*. Such a social classification would have restricted Jesus' life in a variety of ways. *Sanhedrin* 67a).

Mechitza: a physical wall in an Orthodox synagogue, designed to prevent mixing of the sexes, to create a sense of order under YHWH*, to foster a sense of the sacred, and to discourage distraction.

Metsora': a leper. See Leviticus 13–14.

Mikveh: an underground "sacred Jacuzzi," or cistern, in which Jews performed water purification in order to restore unclean items (like pots, pans, chairs, etc.) to their ritual purity. The rule was that one side of the *mikveh* had to be lower than the other so that, if there was sufficient water, there would be a continuous stream of water (hence, "living water").

Pesah: Passover. Exodus 12.

Purity and impurity, clean and unclean: Purity is about the orderly classification of the temple. What is classified as irregular or abnormal is generally impure. Purity is not the same as morality but is about who or what is fit for the temple, and so classifications are made. Morality is about a heart that is right before God. Purity and morality get mixed up. A *niddah** may be [and often was] levitically impure and morally pure at the same time. Read Leviticus 11–16. Jesus broke down the purity system of Judaism and established a moral purity that transcended the temple's system. See Mark. 7:1–20; Acts 10–11; 15; 1 Corinthians 8–10; Galatians 3:28.

Quaker: or, Friends. At the origins of most Christian denominations and movements is a charismatic leader, and for the Quakers that person was George Fox. Other prominent leaders include William Penn (who founded Pennsylvania) and John Woolman. A modern well-known (evangelical) Quaker is Richard Foster. Quakers have always focused, to various degrees, on the Inner Light given by

God to all humans. Some think the Inner Light is constrained by Scripture, and such Quakers are more evangelical, while others find the Scriptures subject to the Inner Light, and these Quakers have at times wandered off into odd quarters. Quakers have exercised a significant influence in Christian mysticism. They were the first large social group to oppose slavery.

Samaritan: a society inhabiting the central hill country of Samaria, between Jerusalem and Galilee. They worshiped on Mount Gerizim (rather than Mount Zion) and followed a slightly revised *Torah**. By the first century, Samaritans were the stereotype enemy of Judaism, the embodiment of heretical faith, and the denier of Jerusalem-centered hope and faith. They still exist today at the same location.

Shema: Deuteronomy 6:4–9, where the first major term, "Hear," is *shema* in Hebrew. These verses were repeated two times daily in the first century by pious Jews—at the break of the morning and after sunset. Some added Deuteronomy 11:13–21 and Numbers 15:37–41 to Deuteronomy 6:4-9. A later rabbi called anyone who did not recite the *Shema* twice daily an *Am ha-aretz**.

Here is a full text of the Shema, with modern liturgical lines added (noted in italics).

Hear, O Israel: The LORD our God, the LORD is one. *Blessed is the name of His Glorious Majesty forever and ever.*

God, King forever. [This line is an acrostic: A-M-N. Thus, "Amen" became a line.]

Love the Lord your God with all your heart and with all your soul and with all your strength. These commandments that I give you today are to be upon your hearts. Impress them on your children. Talk about them when you sit at home and when you walk along the road, when you lie down and when you get up.

Tie them as symbols on your hands and bind them on your foreheads. Write them on the doorframes of your houses and on your gates. (Deut. 6:4-9)So if you faithfully obey the commands I am giving you today—to love the Lord your God and to serve him with all your heart and with all your soul—then I will send rain on your land in its season, both autumn and spring rains, so that you may gather in your grain, new wine and oil. I will provide grass in the fields for your cattle, and you will eat and be satisfied.

Be careful, or you will be enticed to turn away and worship other gods and bow down to them. Then the Lord's anger will burn against you, and he will shut the heavens so that it will not rain and the ground will yield no produce, and you will soon perish from the good land the Lord is giving you. Fix these words of mine in your hearts and minds; tie them as symbols on your hands and bind them on your foreheads. Teach them to your children, talking about them when you sit at home and when you walk along the road, when you lie down and when you get up. Write them on the doorframes of your houses and on your gates, so that your days and the days of your children may be many in the land that the Lord swore to give your forefathers, as many as the days that the heavens are above the earth. (Deut. 11:13–21)

The Lord said to Moses, "Speak to the Israelites and say to them: 'Throughout the generations to come you are to make tassels on the corners of your garments, with a blue cord on each tassel. You will have these tassels to look at and so you will remember all the commands of the Lord, that you may obey them and not prostitute yourselves by going after the lusts of your own hearts and eyes. Then you will remember to obey all my commands and will be consecrated to your God. I am the Lord your God, who brought you out of Egypt to be your God. I am the Lord your God.'" (Num. 15:37–41)

Shiva: literally, "seven." After burial in Judaism, the mourners return home and sit *shiva** for seven days. They sit on low stools to express that they are feeling low. There are many more customs connected to sitting *shiva*.

Torah: Hebrew for "instruction." The term *Torah** has been used for a number of items: (1) the entire Old Testament, (2) the first five books of the Old Testament, commonly called the Pentateuch, or (3) specific sections or laws within the Pentateuch—four are especially noteworthy: the Ten Commandments (Exod. 20:1–20), the Covenant Code (Exod. 20:21–23:19), the Holiness Code (Lev. 17–26), and Deuteronomy. For the Jews of Jesus' day, the *Torah** governed all of life (not just the spiritual) and was entirely from God (hence the sacredness of Scripture).

Tsadiq, tsadiqim: Hebrew for "righteous one, righteous ones." In Judaism the term described the person who observed the *Torah** faithfully and completely (Mt. 1:19) and also would apply to the person who treated others with full respect and love. More completely, the term refers to the person who is conformed to the will of God as taught in the *Torah*.* In much the same way that Jesus reshaped the will of God in his own teachings (e.g., Mt. 5:21–48; 7:12; 8:18–22), a *tsadiq* was a person who followed his interpretation of the will of God (cf. Mt. 5:17–20).

Tzitzit: the fringes at the bottom of Jewish clothing. The commandment to wear them comes from Numbers 15:38-39 and Deuteronomy 22:12. It represents obedience to the *Torah*.*

Unclean and clean: see Purity.

Virginal conception: Mary's supernatural conception is usually called a "virgin birth," which is short for "birth of a baby from a mother who was a virgin at conception." "Virginal conception" is a more accurate expression. The "immaculate conception," which is Roman Catholic dogma, does not refer to Mary's virginal conception, but instead to the special act of God on Mary to preserve her from the effects of original sin from the moment of her (own) conception. In this way, many think that Mary would not pass on the sinful nature to her Son, Jesus the Messiah. This dogma was declared by Pope Pius IX in 1854.

YHWH: the "Name" of God in the Old Testament; Hebrew was written only with consonants, and vowels were added later. Many Orthodox Jews today do not use vowels when they refer to God: e.g., "Lord" is spelled "L—rd" and "God" is "G—d." The name *YHWH* finds its origins in Exodus 3:14, and various interpretations have been given, including "I am who I am," or "I will be who I will be." As a result of Jewish reserve in pronouncing the name (often called the tetragrammaton—"four letters"); when Jews were reading the Bible aloud, they substituted *Adonai* ("Lord") for *YHWH*. Later, the vowels for *Adonai* were placed under the consonants for *YHWH,* and led to the hybrid (but nonexistent) word "*Yehovah,*" which in English has become standardized (however inaccurate) as "Jehovah."

Zealots: a Jewish movement in the first century AD that focused on the use of violence to restore the Land and establish the kingdom of God.

Zavah: a woman with a discharge of blood outside the rhythm of her monthly cycle. Such a woman is unclean; regulations for her are found in Leviticus 15:25–30. See also *niddah**.

CHAPTER ONE

5   *Thomas à Kempis knows . . .*
On these authors, see the Recommended Readings at p. 332 below

7   *According to a specialist of modern Jewish devotion . . .*
Rabbi Hayim Halevy Donin, *To Pray as a Jew: A Guide to the Prayer Book and the Synagogue Service* (New York: Basic Books, 1980), 144.

7   *And it is the "quintessential expression . . ."*
Jeffery H. Tigay, *Deuteronomy*, JPS *Abba* Commentary (Philadelphia: Jewish Publishing Society, 1996/5756), 441.

8   *"Of all the commandments, which is the most important?"*
Mark 12:28; the *Jesus Creed* is found at Mark 12:29–31.

8   *Jesus has "put a whole dictionary into just one dictum."*
The Imitation of Christ, trans. W. Griffin (San Francisco: HarperSanFrancisco, 2000), 160.

10   *"Lord," I want to love God . . .*
Luke 9:59. This discussion is based on the whole paragraph, 9:57–62.

10   *"One whose dead is lying before him [awaiting burial] is exempt from the recitation of the Shema."*
Mishnah *Berakot* 3:1.

10   *At the time of Jesus, burials took place in two stages.*
Mishnah Moed Qatan 1:5–7; Semahot 12.

11   *. . . applied the commandment to honor one's parents.*
see Exodus 20:12.

11   *As Rick Warren states, "Life minus love equals zero."*
The Purpose-Driven Life (Grand Rapids, Mich.: Zondervan, 2002), 125, 128.

13   *"let our life speak."*
Parker Palmer, *Let Your Life Speak* (San Francisco: Jossey-Bass, 2000).

CHAPTER TWO

14   *In the words of Richard Foster, prayer "catapults us . . . "*
      Celebration of Discipline: The Path to Spiritual Growth (New York:
      Harper & Row, 1978), 30.

14   *He was bluntly honest about his own perplexity with prayer.*
      Hal M. Helms, ed., *The Practice of the Presence of God* (Brewster,
      Mass: Paraclete, 1985).

15   *"Lord, teach us to pray."*
      Luke 11:1; the Lord's Prayer is in Luke 11:2–4.

15   *At the time of Jesus there was a Jewish prayer called the Kaddish*
      ("The Sanctification"). See Donin, *To Pray as a Jew*, 216.

18   *Dallas Willard relates how using the Lord's Prayer as a framework*
      strengthened his . . .
      The Divine Conspiracy (San Francisco: HarperSanFrancisco,
      1998), 268.

18   *As Richard Foster puts it, "In prayer, real prayer . . ."*
      Celebration of Discipline, 30.

18   *As Thomas à Kempis puts it: "O Lord . . ."*
      Imitation of Christ, 124.

18   *Lauren Winner, a convert from liturgical Judaism to liturgical*
      Christianity . . .
      Mudhouse Sabbath (Brewster, Mass.: Paraclete, 2003), 61.

18   *Again, Richard Foster tells how one of the most liberating experiences*
      of his life . . .
      Celebration of Discipline, 33.

19   *I am daily amazed at the truth of what Tertullian, an early Christian*
      leader . . .
      Tertullian, *On Prayer*, 1.

22   *. . . but no one has said this better than Frank Laubach:*
      "Meditation on the Lord's Prayer," in *Man of Prayer,* Karen R.
      Norton, ed. (Syracuse, N.Y.: Laubach Literacy International, 1990),
      325–326.

CHAPTER THREE

25 *"Abba, Father"*
Luke 11:2.

25 *"My God, My God, why have you forsaken me?"*
Mark 15:34.

26 *Wesley was an emotional . . .*
Crying for My Mother: The Intimate Life of a Minister, 2nd edition
(Chicago: Covenant Publications, 2003), 6, 50, 51.

27 *the Parable of the Prodigal Son . . .*
See Luke 15:11–32.

CHAPTER FOUR

34 *"Here is a glutton and a drunkard."*
Matthew 11:19, emphasis added.

35 *Matthew . . . once hosted an evening dinner for Jesus . . .*
See Mark 2:14–17.

35 *For his custom of including all at the table, Jesus was called . . .*
See Deuteronomy 21:18–21.

36 *"It is not the healthy who need a doctor, but the sick."*
Mark 2:17.

37 On Alec Guiness
Blessings in Disguise (New York: Alfred A. Knopf, 1986), 36.

39 *in the Age to Come Gentiles will sit at his table.*
See Matthew 8:11–12.

39 *At the Last Supper, Jesus tells his disciples . . .*
See Mark 14:25.

CHAPTER FIVE

42 *As Lewis Smedes says: . . .*
The Making and Keeping of Commitments, in *Seeking*
Understanding: The Stob Lectures 1986–1998 (Grand Rapids,
Mich.: Eerdmans, 2001), 7, 9.

43   *Laurie Hall's* An Affair of the Mind
        (Colorado Springs, Colo.: *Focus on the Family*, 1996), 49.

44   *"I am your God."*
        See Genesis 17:8; Leviticus 26:13; Jeremiah 7:23. I am drawing on
        Hosea, chapters 1–3.

44   *I am now going to allure her . . .*
        Hosea 2:14-15. The "Valley of Achor" refers back to Joshua 7,
        originally a bad memory for Israel: there Israel broke faith with
        God. Achan, of the tribe of Judah, stole sacred objects for his own
        use. Thus, the "Valley of Achor" evoked in Israel's memory a
        desecration. Hosea announces that this Valley will become a place
        that evokes hope, because it will be here that Israel once again
        returns to sacred love.

45   *"My husband."*
        Hosea 2:16.

46   *"do not call anyone on earth 'father,' for you have one Father, and
        he is in heaven."*
        Matthew 23:9.

46   *John Woolman, an early American Quaker . . .*
        I have relied in this paragraph on Phillips Moulton, ed., *The Journal
        and Major Essays of John Woolman* (New York: Oxford, 1971), and
        on David Sox, *John Woolman, Quintessential Quaker, 1720–1772:*
        (Richmond, Ind.: Friends United Press, 1999).

46   *Richard Foster, says that "no book outside the Bible has influenced
        me . . . "*
        Streams of Living Water (San Francisco: HarperSanFrancisco,
        1998), 144.

46   *What makes Woolman's love sacred was that this creed shaped his
        entire life . . .*
        Woolman, *The Journal and Major Essays of John Woolman*, 31.

48   *"Verbal" reserve begins with the command not to take the Name
        (YHWH) in vain.*
        See Exodus 20:7.

48   *. . . they "will see the Son of Man . . . "*
        Mark 14:62.

48   *"Our Father, hallowed be* your name," emphasis added.
Matthew 6:9.

49   *From the story Luke tells us about Zacchaeus . . .*
See Luke 19:1–10.

49   *that is why the gospel writers list them with sinners.*
For example, Mark 2:15.

50   *Luke tells us of Jesus' dining in the home of a Pharisee named
Simon.*
See Luke 7:36–50

CHAPTER SIX

53   *A good example is the Parable of the Good Samaritan.*
See Luke 10:25–37.

53   *One of Moses' books . . .*
See Numbers 19:11–22.

53   *In another of his books . . .*
See Leviticus 21:1–4.

55   *"Love doesn't sound so dangerous until you've tried it."*
Paul Wadell, *Becoming Friends* (Grand Rapids, Mich.: Brazos,
2002), 30, 32.

55   *Southeast Asia's Singapore Anglican churches . . .*
Michael Green, *Adventures of Faith* (London, England: Zondervan,
2001), 357–362.

56   *"Dear woman, here is your son" . . .*
John 19:26-27.

59   *"Do not judge, or you too will be judged."*
Matthew 7:1.

59   *"God has created a world in which we are the ones who care for
one another . . ."*
James Bryan Smith, *Embracing the Love of God: The Path and
Promise of Christian Life* (San Francisco: HarperSanFrancisco,
1995), 150.

59   *No book was more influential in the heady days of the late 1960s*
      and early 1970s among evangelicals than Francis Schaeffer's
      The Mark of a Christian (Downers Grove, Ill.: InterVarsity, 1970), 35.

CHAPTER SEVEN

65   *Now that I know the story of Vincent van Gogh . . .*
      See Kathleen Powers Erickson, *At Eternity's Gate* (Grand Rapids,
      Mich.: Eerdmans, 1998).

66   *First, when the children of Israel finally crossed that river . . .*
      See Joshua 3:1–4:18.

66   *Second, those who were baptized by John began life all over again.*
      See Luke 3:1–18.

67   *John sets up his baptismal stage on the far side of the Jordan.*
      See John 1:28.

68   *As Frederick Buechner puts it so memorably . . .*
      See Alan Jacobs, *A Visit to Vanity Fair* (Grand Rapids, Mich.:
      Brazos, 2001), 45.

68   *As America's essayist Joseph Epstein says . . .*
      Envy: The Seven Deadly Sins (New York Public Library; New York:
      Oxford, 2003), 15.

69   *Our "Yes" to God is, in the words of Dietrich von Hildebrand . . .*
      Transformation in Christ (San Francisco: Ignatius, 2001), 69.

69   *"Where are you?"*
      Genesis 3:9.

69   *As John Paul II has put it . . .*
      Joseph Durepos, ed., *Go in Peace: A Gift of Enduring Love*
      (Chicago: Loyola Press, 2003), 23.

69   *Mark Twain gave some advice to "good little boys" . . .*
      Collected Tales, Sketches, Speeches, and Essays, 1852–1890, 2
      vols. (New York: Library of America, 1992), 1.163 (from June 3, 1865).

69   *In the words of Henri Nouwen . . .*
      Robert A. Jonas, ed., *Henri Nouwen* (Maryknoll, N.Y.: Orbis,
      1998), 30-31.

70 *Henri Nouwen once confessed the following about truthtelling . . .*
Jonas, *Henri Nouwen,* 79.

70 *. . . Philip Yancey calls the cycle of ungrace.*
What's So Amazing About Grace? (Grand Rapids, Mich.: Zondervan, 1997), 83–93.

70 *Lewis Smedes, who has poured grace all over the discussion of forgiveness . . .*
Forgive and Forget (New York: Guideposts, 1984), 32.

71 *J. I. Packer . . .*
Hot Tub Religion (Wheaton, Ill.: Tyndale, 1987).

73 On William Booth's conversion
Hugh T. Kerr, John M. Mulder, *Conversions* (Grand Rapids, Mich.: Eerdmans, 1983), 140–143.

CHAPTER EIGHT

77 *The Gospel of Matthew tells us that Joseph is "righteous."*
Matthew 1:19.

78 *So he consults the Books of Moses to see what he is to do.*
See Deuteronomy 22:13–27; Numbers 5.

79 *With his reputation grasping . . .*
See Matthew 1:18–25.

79 *We learn, as Thomas à Kempis puts it, that when you surrender . . .*
Imitation of Christ, 184.

80 *John informed his father, Arnold, a physician.*
Timothy Dudley-Smith, *John Stott: A Biography, The Making of a Leader: The Early Years* (Downers Grove, Ill.: InterVarsity, 1999), 154.

80 *John later defined spiritual formation in terms of identity . . .*
Basic Christianity (Downers Grove, Ill.: InterVarsity, 1974), 112, 113, emphasis added.

81 *Another who followed the example of Joseph is St. Augustine . . .*
Confessions, 1.19.30; 10.40.65.

82   . . .*Dorothy Sayers observes* . . .
        Creed or Chaos? (Manchester, N.H.: Sophia Institute, 1999), 6.

CHAPTER NINE

83   *In the potent words of Dorothy Sayers* . . .
        Creed or Chaos? (Manchester, N.H.: Sophia Institute, 1995), 101,
        105, 107.

84   *Parker Palmer, after decades of wrestling to please others* . . .
        Let Your Life Speak , 3.

84   *Os Guinness echoes this wisdom* . . .
        The Call: Finding and Fulfilling the Central Purpose of Your Life
        (Nashville: Word, 1998), 47.

85   *One of the Bible's highlighted passages is the Song of Mary.*
        See Luke 1:46–55.

85   *As Tom Wright describes it, Mary's Song* . . .
        Luke for Everyone (London: SPCK, 2001), 14.

86   *Israelites instead sacrificed a lamb.*
        See Exodus 13:11–15.

86   *in the Torah for those who could not afford the lamb.*
        See Leviticus 12:6–8.

86   *[God] has scattered* . . .
        Luke 1:51–53, emphasis added.

87   *Roberta Bondi, in her account* . . .
        Memories of God: Theological Reflections on a Life (Nashville:
        Abingdon, 1995), 15, 78, 174.

89   *Frederica Mathewes-Green* . . .
        Facing East (San Francisco: HarperSanFrancisco, 1997), 38.

89   *As Mary blesses the holy Name of God* . . .
        See the following passages: Luke 1:49, 53 and Matthew 6:9–13
        with Luke 6:21; Luke 6:20; 14:21 and 7:11–17; 18:1–8; Luke 1:51-
        52 and 13:32-33; Luke 1:50, 53–55 and Matthew 9:36; Luke 1:54-
        55 and 13:34.

91   On Dorothy Sayers,
        Barbara Reynolds, *Dorothy L. Sayers: Her Life and Soul* (New York: St. Martin's Press, 1993), 293.

CHAPTER TEN
        This chapter is based on my (more academic) book *Turning to Jesus* (Louisville, Ky.: Westminster John Knox Press, 2002). The best academic study of conversion as an experience is Lewis R. Rambo, *Understanding Religious Conversion* (New Haven: Yale University Press, 1993).

94   *This friend's name is Shimeon Kepha, but we call him "Simon Peter."*
        "Shimeon" is often translated "Simon;" and *"Kepha"* (English, "Rock"), as "Cephas". "Peter" is the Greek translation of *Kepha.*

94   *In which of the five scenes below do you think Peter is converted?*
        The following account of Peter refers to John 1:35–42; Luke 5:1–11; Mark 8:27—9:1; 14:66–72; John 21:15–22; Acts 2; 10; and 1 Peter 2:18–25.

97   *Here are seven chapters in that development:*
        See the chapters and verses in the previous reference.

98   *Peter urged the Christians of Asia Minor . . .*
        See 1 Peter 2:11–17; 3:15.

99   *. . . the missionary with the most complete impact on the world was a man of much less fame . . .*
        On Frank Laubach, see the short (fact-oriented) biography by Karen R. Norton, *One Burning Heart,* Heritage Collection 4 (Syracuse, N.Y.: Laubach Literacy International, 1990). See also David E. Mason, *Apostle to the Illliterates* (Grand Rapids, Mich.: Zondervan, 1966).

99   *"What can I do for hateful people like these . . ."*
        Norton, *One Burning Heart,* 13.

99   *My lips began to move and it seemed to me . . .*
        Frank C. Laubach, *Forty Years with the Silent Billion* (Old Tappan, N.J.: Fleming H. Revell, 1970), 421.

100 *"I choose to look at people through God . . ."*
   Letters by a Modern Mystic, Heritage Collection 1 (Syracuse, N.Y.:
   Laubach Literacy International, 1990), 44 (from September 28,
   1931), also 20 (from January 26, 1930), 26 (from March 23, 1930),
   27, 29 (from May 14, 1930).

100 *"But the result of Laubach's prayer life . . ."*
   Norton, *One Burning Heart,* 12.

100 *It is as much our duty . . .*
   Letters by a Modern Mystic, 39 (from September 22, 1930).

101 *For mission groups "he developed an approach . . ."*
   Norton, *One Burning Heart,* 29. For Laubach's book about Jesus,
   see *The Autobiography of Jesus* (New York: Harper & Row, 1962).

CHAPTER ELEVEN

102 *Israel's once-famous King Saul is the Pete Rose of the Bible.*
   See 1 Samuel 8–15.

103 *the Christian leader and Old Testament scholar John Goldingay . . .*
   Walk On (Grand Rapids, Mich.: Baker, 2002), 75-76.

104 *Many scholars think John was a cousin of Jesus.*
   If you compare Matthew 27:56 and Mark 15:40-41 with John
   19:25, Salome appears to be the mother of John. Furthermore,
   Salome is Mary's sister. This would make John the cousin of Jesus.

104 *Jesus rocks the boat of all three when he calls James and John to
   "follow him."*
   See Mark 1:16–20.

104 *a "new" commandment . . .*
   John 13:34 and 1 John 4:21.

105 *In a moving, tender story of the love of a father and son, author
   Brian Doyle . . .*
   Two Voices: A Father and Son Discuss Family and Faith (Liguori,
   Mo.: Liguori, 1996), xiv.

105 *"Deeds, not words."*
   Aesop, *Aesop's Fables* (New York: Barnes & Noble, 2003), 60 (#49).

106   *First, John and James approach Jesus . . .*
      See Mark 10:35–45.

106   *Second, John's love for others is tested when he doesn't recognize*
      someone exorcising demons in Jesus' name.
      See Mark 9:38–41.

106   *Third, John hears that some Samaritans refuse hospitality . . .*
      See Luke 9:51–56.

106   *John was in the Thunderbolt Gang before he was an apostle of love.*
      See Mark 3:17.

107   *"Example is better than precept."*
      Aesop's Fables, 60 (#50).

107   *This is why Lewis Smedes . . .*
      My God and I: A Spiritual Memoir (Grand Rapids, Mich.:
      Eerdmans, 2003), 16, 22-23.

108   *Several incidents in the life of Jesus reveal how specially Jesus*
      treats John.
      See Mark 5:37–40; Matthew 17:1; 26:37.

109   *John refers to himself in his gospel as "the disciple whom Jesus loved."*
      John 13:23; 19:26; 20:2; 21:7, 20.

109   *He was "reclining next to him [Jesus]."*
      John 13:23 and 1:18.

110   *"this is his command," John says . . .*
      1 John 3:23.

CHAPTER TWELVE

111   *Jesus, oddly enough, seems "anxious to get them . . ."*
      Flannery O'Connor, *Collected Works* (New York: Library of
      America, 1988), 894.

112   *any effort to move "from hostility to hospitality" . . .*
      Henry Nouwen *Reaching Out: The Three Movements of the*
      Spiritual Life (New York: Image, 1986), 65, 71.

112 *When Jesus and his disciples enter Nain, a place for nobodies going nowhere, they encounter a funeral procession.*
See Luke 7:11–17.

113 *Jesus' Parable of the Widow Demanding Justice . . .*
See Luke 18:1–8.

113 *Sometimes the grief observed by Jesus is caused . . .*
See Mark 1:41; 6:34; 9:22; Matthew 20:34.

113 *A story is told of the famous Rebbe Wolfe of Zbaraj . . .*
See Elie Wiesel, *Souls on Fire* (New York: Random House, 1972), 51.

114 *"Abba of the abba-less"*
See Psalms 68:5; 146:9.

114 *In the home of Simon the Pharisee, Jesus encounters a prostitute . . .*
See Luke 7:36–50.

115 *In the words of Thomas Kelly . . .*
A Testament of Devotion (San Francisco: HarperSanFrancisco, 1992), 4; William Griffin's translation of Thomas à Kempis, *The Imitation of Christ*, 65; Nancy Mairs, *Ordinary Time: Cycles in Marriage, Faith, and Renewal* (Boston: Beacon, 1993), 91.

115 *Once again, a story of a compassionate rabbi, Abba Tachnah the Pious . . .*
Found in Eugene B. Borowitz, Frances W. Schwartz, *The Jewish Moral Virtues* (Philadelphia: Jewish Publishing Society, 1999), 78.

116 *In the words of Frederica Mathewes-Green, compassion without action . . .*
The Illumined Heart: The Ancient Christian Path of Transformation (Brewster, Mass.: Paraclete, 2001), 38.

116 *Notice how Jesus' compassion . . .*
See Luke 7:14-15, 48; 8:1–3.

116 *On other occasions, Jesus' compassion prompts other actions*
See Mark 1:41; 6:34; 9:22; Matthew 10:1–8; 20:34.

117 *It is these same women . . .*
See Mark 15:40-41; Luke 23:49.

118   *One of her biographers explains her single-minded focus on compassion . . .*
Kathryn Spink, "Mother Teresa of Calcutta," in *Great Spirits, 1000–2000: The Fifty-Two Chistians Who Most Influenced Their Millennium,* ed. Selina O'Grady and John Wilkins; foreword by K. Norris (New York: Paulist, 2002), 188-189.

119   *As an illustration of her empathy, an English volunteer once said of her . . .*
Mother Teresa: A Simple Path, compiled by Lucinda Vardey (New York: Ballantine, 1995), xxiv, 99.

CHAPTER THIRTEEN

127   *Jesus went throughout Galilee, teaching . . . ,* emphasis added.
Matthew 4:23.

128   *"The kingdom of God does not come visibly . . ."*
Luke 17:20-21.

129   *Whoever acknowledges* me *before men . . .*
Matthew 10:32-33, emphasis added.

129   *Isaiah's kingdom predictions were about him . . .*
See Luke 4:16–30.

129   *Most will remember the day Payne Stewart, a professional golfer . . .*
The story has been told in Tracey Stewart with Ken Abraham, *Payne Stewart: The Authorized Biography* (Nashville: Broadman & Holman, 2000).

130   *Jesus teaches that "Torah-style" needs a kingdom upgrade to "Jesus-style."*
See Matthew 5:17–48.

130   *Come to me, all you who are weary . . .*
Matthew 11:28–30.

131   *The apostle Peter complained . . .*
See Acts 15:10.

131   *G. K. Chesterton gets to the heart of how many felt . . .*
The Everlasting Man (San Francisco: Ignatius, 1993), 169.

132 *"Who are my mother and my brothers?"*
Mark 3:31–35.

132 *As a family they learn from Jesus about this new transforming . . .*
See Matthew 9:9–13; 18; Luke 4:18-19; 6:20; Matthew 23:8–12.

132 *. . . the upside-down nature of the kingdom itself.*
I borrow here the language of the Mennonite scholar Donald Kraybill, *The Upside-Down Kingdom* (Scottdale, Penn.: Herald Press, 1990).

132 *Instead of acting with power, his family serves . . .*
See Mark 10:35–45; John 13:34-35.

CHAPTER FOURTEEN

135 *Jesus' audience knows the great kingdom dream of the Bible . . .*
See Isaiah 2:4; 11:3–5; 11:6–9; 26:2; 45:22; 51:5; Jeremiah 3:17; 23:5-6; 31:33; Ezekiel 37:24; Zephaniah 3:9; Zechariah 9:9-10.

135 *The kingdom of heaven is like a mustard seed . . ."*
Matthew 13:31-32.

136 *As Thomas à Kempis has said, "humongous doesn't count" with Jesus . . .*
The Imitation of Christ, 25.

136 *June Sprigg . . .*
Simple Gifts: A Memoir of a Shaker Village (New York: Alfred A. Knopf, 1998), 90.

136 *Jesus chooses four unschooled fishermen . . .*
See Acts 4:13; Luke 19:1–10; 7:36–50; Matthew 9:9–13.

137 *Don't get me wrong, sometimes Jesus speaks to large crowds . . .*
See Matthew 5:1 and Mark 11–13.

138 *His Parable of the Wheat and Weeds explains his choice of peace.*
See Matthew 13:24–30, 36–43.

139 *But Bob Muzikowski . . . knew better.*
Bob Muzikowski with Gregg Lewis, *Safe at Home* (Grand Rapids, Mich.: Zondervan, 2001). This book corrects the screenplay version of Daniel Coyle, *Hardball: A Season in the Projects* (New York: HarperCollins, 1993), 42, 152, 187, 163, 237–244.

CHAPTER FIFTEEN

144 *We are learning, as Jim Wallis illustrates time and time again, that "faith works."*
Faith Works: Lessons from the Life of an Activist Preacher (New York: Random House, 2000).

146 *The follower of Jesus is to "hunger and thirst for righteousness [or justice . . .]"* Matthew 5:6.

146 *We can begin with Jesus' first public sermon . . .*
Luke 4:16–30; quotation is Luke 4:18-19, emphasis added.

146 *Blessed are you who are poor . . .*
Luke 6:20–23, emphasis added.

147 *At the end of his life, Jesus gives us a clear view of Judgment Day in the Parable of the Sheep and Goats.*
See Matthew 25:31–46.

147 *"For I was hungry and you gave me something to eat . . ."*
Matthew 25:35–40.

148 *Are we aware of the potential dangers of the growing, insidious cycle of hate . . .*
A brilliant, and altogether fair analysis of this can be found in Carol M. Swain, *The New White Nationalism in America: Its Challenge to Integration* (New York: Cambridge University Press, 2002).

148 *Is the gospel preached by established churches a subtle form of racism . . .*
Michael O. Emerson and Christian Smith, *Divided By Faith: Evangelical Religion and the Problem of Race in America* (New York: Oxford University Press, 2000).

149 *Virginia Stem Owens . . .*
Living Next Door to the Death House (Grand Rapids, Mich.: Eerdmans, 2003), 190-191.

CHAPTER SIXTEEN

152 *Frank Morison . . .*
Who Moved the Stone? (Grand Rapids, Mich.: Zondervan, n.d.), 12, 68, 192.

154 *"Rabbi, who sinned, this man or his parents, that he was born blind?"*
John 9:2-3, emphasis added.

155 *Jewish society at the time of Jesus . . .*
For this text, see The Rule of the Congregation, 1Qsa 2:3–9.

156 *A menstruating woman is classified as a* niddah *(nee-dah). A woman who bleeds beyond the normal cycle is classified as a* zavah.
See Leviticus 15.
Though concerned exclusively about modern Orthodox Jewish women's purity alone, the chapter on *mikvehs** in Sue Fishkoff's *The Rebbe's Army: Inside the World of Chabad-Lubavitch* (New York: Schocken, 2003), 148–159, provides interesting details of modern practice.

157 *Merrill Joan Gerber, a (not all that observant) Jewish woman . . .*
All quotations are from her *Botticelli Blue Skies: An American in Florence* (Madison, Wisc.: University of Wisconsin Press, 2002), 50–55.

158 *Lepers Come to the Table*
See Leviticus 13-14; Numbers 12:10–16; Luke 17:11–19.

CHAPTER SEVENTEEN

161 *Craig Barnes, in* Yearning, *observes . . .*
Yearning: Living Between How It Is and How It Ought to Be (Downers Grove, Ill.: InterVarsity, 1991), 31, 55, 56, 65, emphasis added.

163 *I can only wish I had attended the wedding in Cana of Galilee.*
See John 2:1–11.

167 *Lewis writes . . . in a letter to his good friend Arthur Greeves*
W. H. Lewis and Walter Hooper, eds., *Letters of C. S. Lewis,* rev. and enlarged ed. (New York: Harcourt Brace, 1993), 288-289. For a nice recent study of Lewis's conversion, see David C. Downing, *The Most Reluctant Convert: C. S. Lewis's Journey to Faith* (Downers Grove, Ill.: InterVarsity, 2002). Downing is especially insightful on the meaning of joy in Lewis's writings. Of course, Lewis tells his own story through the lens of joy; see his *Surprised by Joy: The Shape of My Early Life* (New York: Harcourt, Brace, 1956).

168   *As Lewis himself explains his quest, "But what, in conclusion, of Joy?*
    Surprised by Joy, 238.

CHAPTER EIGHTEEN

172   *I join hands with Alan Jacobs, who admits: "I'm not interested in any reconfiguration of the notion of eternal life . . ."*
    A Visit to Vanity Fair (Grand Rapids, Mich.: Brazos, 2001), 68. The resurrection body is discussed in the following passages: Matthew 17:1–13; 22:23–33; 28; Luke 24; John 20–21; 1 Corinthians 15; 2 Corinthians 5:1–10.

172   *the Son of Man . . . separates the "sheep" and "goats" . . .*
    Matthew 25:31-46.

172   *Eternal standing matters a great deal to Jesus, and he talks about it quite often.*
    See Matthew 13:36–43, 47–50; 24–25; Luke 22:28–30; 23:42.

172   *Jesus promises a resumption of fellowship with his disciples . . .*
    Mark 14:25; Matthew 8:11; 22:1–10.

173   *They will, he says, "sit on twelve thrones, judging the twelve tribes of Israel."*
    Matthew 19:28.

173   *So, in the words of Thomas à Kempis, "Practice now . . ."*
    The Imitation of Christ, 49.

174   *J. I. Packer, in his potent study of what the Bible teaches about God . . .*
    Knowing God (Downers Grove, Ill.: InterVarsity, 1993), 17–23.

174   *"It was the perpetual adoration . . ."*
    Kristin Ohlson, *Stalking the Divine: Contemplating Faith with the Poor Clares* (New York: Hyperion, 2003), 44.

175   *. . . from "information to formation" . . .*
    M. Robert Mulholland, *Shaped by the Word* (Nashville: Upper Room, 2000), 49–63

175   *"No sooner had I finished . . . than it was as if the light of steadfast trust poured into my heart."*
    Augustine, *Confessions* 8.12.29.

CHAPTER NINETEEN

183   *There is no better example of a person who confused relationship with perfection—and got ahead of himself—than Ben Franklin . . .*
See *The Autobiography of Benjamin Franklin* (New York: Barnes & Noble, 1994), 103–114. This book has been reprinted so many times, it is perhaps helpful to know that this account appears in chapter 6.

184   *. . . but of renovation, as Dallas Willard has explained so well.*
See his *Renovation of the Heart: Putting on the Character of Christ* (Colorado Springs, Colo.: Navpress, 2002).

184   *Or, in the words of John Ortberg, we are to "morph indeed."*
The Life You've Always Wanted (Grand Rapids, Mich.: Zondervan, 2000), 11–26.

184   *"Repent and believe the good news!"*
Mark 1:15, emphasis added.

184   *A good place to begin, therefore, is Jesus' encounter with . . .*
Mark 7:24–30.

187   *Hillel, a more merciful rabbi, converted the man by teaching him a summary creed:*
This may be found in *The Babylonian Talmud*, Shabbat 30b-31a. Jesus' Golden Rule is a positive version of this code, which has other echoes in the ancient world. Cf. Matthew 7:12.

189   *"Even the dogs . . .*
Matthew 15:27-28

190   *We cannot have a relationship . . .*
Mark Allen Powell, *Loving Jesus* (Minneapolis: Fortress, 2004), 53.

CHAPTER TWENTY

192   *Martha, Martha, you are worried . . .*
From Luke 10:38–42, emphasis added.

193   *The apostle Paul . . . sat at the feet of [the rabbi] Gamaliel.*
See Acts 22:3.

193   *Catherine Clark Kroeger* . . .
        Catherine C. Kroeger and Mary J. Evans, eds., *The IVP Women's Bible Commentary* (Downers Grove, Ill.: InterVarsity, 2002), 575.

195   *Robert Mulholland . . . calls attention to the distinction between "informational" and "formational"* . . .
        Shaped by the Word , 49–63.

197   *For where two or three come together in my name, there am I with them.*
        Matthew 18:20.

198   *I am the true vine, and my Father is the gardener.*
        John 15:1, 4. See the whole of John 15.

198   Brother Lawrence's quotations can be found in:
        The Practice of the Presence of God, 89, 93, 95, 99.

199   *"Now remain in my love . . ."*
        John 15:9-10.

200   *that love expresses itself as self-sacrifice* . . .
        See John 15:12-13.

CHAPTER TWENTY-ONE

201   *"May your will be done."*
        See Matthew 6:10.

202   *"If anyone would come after me . . . "*
        Mark 8:34.

203   *. . . as Dallas Willard says, "is the controlling principle of the renovated heart and the restored soul."*
        Renovation of the Heart, 74.

203   *But as John Stott observes, this life of surrender paradoxically is a life of blessing.*
        The Incomparable Christ (Downers Grove, Ill.: InterVarsity, 2001), 89.

203   *As Dale Allison puts it, "with every globule of one's being."*
        The Gospel According to Saint Matthew (Edinburgh: T & T Clark, 1997), 3.241.

203   *As Thomas Merton describes it . . .*
        The Inner Experience (San Francisco: HarperSanFrancisco, 2003), 6.

204   *For Alicia Chester, who was a ballet dancer . . .*
        See "Coincidence and Conversion," *First Things* 138 (December
        2003): 28–33; from p. 30.

205   *As Jesus says it, a disciple "must deny himself and take up his cross
        daily."*
        Luke 9:23, emphasis added.

205   *"Get behind me, Satan!" he says to Peter.*
        Mark 8:33, emphasis added.

205   *Wise Christians devote their lives to wisdom—a mind shaped to
        please God.*
        Willard, *Renovation of the Heart*, 95–139, who illustrates this section.

206   *Wise Christians also learn the history of the Church . . .*
        I recommend Bruce L. Shelley, *Church History in Plain Language*
        (Nashville: Nelson, 1996), and Timothy Dowley, ed., *Introduction
        to the History of Christianity* (Minneapolis: Fortress, 2002).

206   *After her conversion from her own brand of bohemian feminism,
        Frederica Mathewes-Green . . .*
        Facing East, 107.

207   *As Dallas Willard makes clear in several of his books . . .*
        Renovation of the Heart, 159. See also *The Spirit of the Disciplines:
        Understanding How God Changes Lives* (San Francisco:
        HarperSanFrancisco, 1988), 28–43.

207   *"Nothing outside a man can make him 'unclean' by going into him . . ."*
        Mark 7:15, 21.

208   Mark Twain, . . . *When I was younger I could remember anything . . .*
        The Autobiography of Mark Twain (New York: HarperCollins,
        1990), 4.

CHAPTER TWENTY-TWO

209   *"Be perfect as your heavenly Father is perfect . . ."*
        Matthew 5:48; Luke 6:36.

209   *Some dilute the acid . . .*
       Some understand "perfect" in Matthew 5:48 as meaning maturity in
       the sense of "loving all humans as God loves all humans," and this
       view makes eminent contextual sense.

210   *Michael Green . . . confesses that he and Rosemary, his wife, had
       serious marriage difficulties.*
       Adventure of Faith: Reflections on Fifty Years of Christian Service
       (Grand Rapids, Mich.: Zondervan, 2001), 66–71.

211   On the failure of the disciples. See the following list:
       Mark 4:10, 13, 33-34; 7:17–19; 8:16–21: failure to understand
       Jesus' teachings
       Mark 4:35–41: screaming fear in a storm
       Mark 6:35–37; 8:4: blindness about Jesus' ability to provide provisions
       Mark 7:24–30; 10:13–16: inability to accept Gentiles and children
       Mark 9:14–19: inability to trust God to heal
       Mark 10:32: fear of God's protection
       Mark 10:35–45: yearning for most valuable status among apostles
       Mark 14:37, 40, 54, 66–72: afraid to support Jesus in his Passion

212   *As for this final failure, when they fall asleep on Jesus in
       Gethsemane, Thomas à Kempis has it right . . .*
       The Imitation of Christ, 80.

212   *Peter's reputation is established*
       See Matthew 16:13–20; 10:2; Acts 2; 10; 15; Matthew 14:22–33;
       15:15; 26:36–46, 58, 74-75.

213   *If so, Phillip Yancey breaks the taboo as he describes his own racism.*
       What's So Amazing About Grace?, 129–38.

214   *Here are two examples from the Bible.*
       See John 16:8–11 and Galatians 2:11–14.

214   *After denying Jesus, Peter . . .*
       See Matthew 26:75; John 21:15–19.

216   *Lauren Winner . . . tells of the time she nervously wrote out her sins
       on a legal pad . . . .*
       Girl Meets God: On the Path to a Spiritual Life (Chapel Hill:
       Algonquin, 2002), 207–11.

CHAPTER TWENTY-THREE

218 *In the Old Testament, God's forgiveness is center stage, but we don't find a challenge for humans to forgive.*
See also Exodus 10:17; 1 Samuel 15:25, 28.

219 *"This is what you are to say to Joseph . . ."*
See Genesis 50:17, 19, 21.

219 *Israel sins, YHWH forgives.*
For example, 2 Chronicles 7:14.

220 *Schimmel observes a fundamental difference between Judaism and Christianity when it comes to forgiveness . . .*
Wounds Not Healed By Time: The Power of Repentance and Forgiveness (New York: Oxford University Press, 2002), 64, 69.

221 *Notice these statements by Jesus*:
Luke 11:4a; Matthew 6:14-15 (and see 18:21–35); Luke 17:3-4; John 20:23; Luke 23:34.

222 *The parade of forgiveness begins when Frederica's husband and her son . . .*
Facing East, 17–23.

224 *C. S. Lewis once said, "Every one says forgiveness is a lovely idea, until they have something to forgive."*
Mere Christianity (New York: Macmillan, 1960), 104.

224 *Simon Wiesenthal, for instance, is a Jew who was brought face-to-face with a young, dying Nazi officer who described an atrocity . . .*
The Sunflower: On the Possibilities and Limits of Forgiveness rev. and expd. ed. New York: Schocken, 1997. This book contains a string of responses by others on what they would have done.

CHAPTER TWENTY-FOUR

227 *In the Christian world today, 1.06 billion are Roman Catholic, 386 million are Independent-Pentecostal, 342 million are Protestant . . .*
See Philip Jenkins, *The Next Christendom* (New York: Oxford University Press, 2002), 2.

228 *"Come, follow me," Jesus said . . .*
Mark 1:17.

228 *Fishing "for others" then involves . . .*
     Matthew 16:13–19; 18:18; John 20:21, Matthew 10:14-15.

228 *Jesus regularly called his disciples to "fish for others."*
     Matthew 28:18–20; John 20:21; Acts 1:8.

228 *we need to examine several texts in the Gospel of Matthew*
     Matthew 4:23; 9:35; 10:1; and 10:5–10.

229 *Each of these instructions asks the disciples to do exactly as Jesus did.*
     Thus, see Matthew #1: 15:24; #2: 4:17; #3: 8–9; #4: 8:20.

232 *As Dorothy Sayers asks, "If this is dull, then what, in Heaven's
     name . . ."*
     Creed or Chaos? 9.

232 *Michael Green cuts through church cant . . .*
     Adventure of Faith, 29, 88.

232 *Most writers on spiritual formation tend to dwell on what happens
     in the inner life, . . . but Robert Mulholland gets it right:*
     Shaped by the Word, 25.

233 *The* Alpha *course, directed in England by Nicky Gumbel . . .*
     See Green, *Adventure of Faith*, 40–43, 184.

233 *Recently, Garry Poole published . . .*
     *Seeker Small Groups: Engaging Spiritual Seekers in Life-Changing
     Discussions* (Grand Rapids, Mich.: Zondervan, 2003), 13–19.

CHAPTER TWENTY-FIVE

241 *"Repent" . . .*
     Matthew 3:2, 8, 11, emphasis added.

242 *"Then Jesus came from Galilee to the Jordan to be baptized by
     John."*
     Matthew 3:13–17.

242 *John baptizes with "water" but Jesus will baptize "with the Holy
     Spirit and with fire."*
     Matthew 3:11.

242 *The Spirit . . . comes on all his followers on the great day of Pentecost
     . . .* Recorded in Acts 2.

242   *As C. S. Lewis said, "Only a bad person needs to repent . . ."*
       Mere Christianity (New York: Macmillan, 1960), 59.

243   *If Jesus is to bring the kingdom to earth, as Tom Wright says . . .*
       Matthew for Everyone (London: SPCK, 2002), 1.21-22.

243   *He sees into the hidden hearts of mistaken leaders . . .*
       Mark 2:8

243   *The prophet Jeremiah once complained . . .*
       Jeremiah 17:9-10.

243   *Alexis de Tocqueville was a French aristocrat . . .*
       Democracy in America, trans. Harvey C. Mansfield and Delba
       Winthrop (Chicago: University of Chicago Press, 2000).

245   *What we seek is a clear conscience and (what Dallas Willard calls)*
       a "renovation of the heart."
       Renovation of the Heart.

CHAPTER TWENTY-SIX

249   *YHWH promised Abraham the world (and a little more) . . .*
       See Genesis 22.

250   *"Jesus was led by the Spirit into the desert."*
       Matthew 4:1. The Temptation is found in 4:1–11 and in Luke
       4:1–12. A shorter account is found in Mark 1:12-13.

251   *According to David Falkner . . .*
       Nine Sides of the Diamond (New York: Fireside, 1990), 301.

254   *. . . "to go for it in one easy stride."*
       Tom Wright, *Luke for Everyone* (London: SPCK, 2001), 43.

255   *The writer to the Hebrews knew this strength . . .*
       See Hebrews 4:16.

CHAPTER TWENTY-SEVEN

258 *"All is elsewhere"* . . .
I take this expression from Julien Green, as found in Alexander
Schmemann, *The Journals of Father Alexander Schmemann*
(Crestwood, N.Y.: St. Vladimir's Seminary Press, 2000), 1 (and
throughout book).

258 *"on the third day [he will] be raised to life."*
Luke 9:22.

258 *As he [Jesus] was praying* . . .
Luke 9:29.

259 *"about his departure"*
Luke 9:31.

259 *Jesus "took Peter, John and James with him . . ."*
Luke 9:28.

260 *all disciples will "shine like the sun."*
Matthew 13:43.

260 *Margaret Kim Peterson . . . tells the grim story of the death of her
AIDS-infected . . .*
Sing Me to Heaven: The Story of a Marriage (Grand Rapids, Mich.:
Brazos, 2003), 134-35.

261 *. . . a little-known saint of the early church, St. Macrina . . .*
Gregory, *The Life of Saint Macrina,* trans. K. Corrigan (Toronto:
Peregrina Publishing, 2001), 52, 36, 40.

261 *C. S. Lewis calls this the "weight of glory"* . . .
The Weight of Glory and Other Addresses (Grand Rapids, Mich.:
Eerdmans, 1973), 14-15.

262 *John and Ann's story is now available in the book* . . .
Walk On, 33, 37, 83.

264 *As Thomas à Kempis says it, "Whoever shadows my every move
won't lose me in the dark."*
The Imitation of Christ, 3.

CHAPTER TWENTY-EIGHT

266   *. . . can become in the words of John Ortberg's daughter, Mallory,
a "dee dah day."*
The Life You've Always Wanted, 59–61.

267   *Passover meal, when Jews reenact the original last meal before
escaping the clutches of Pharaoh . . .*
See Exodus 12; Leviticus 23; Deuteronomy 16.

269   *Pearl Harbor Day, a "date which will live in infamy," . . .*
Walter Lord, *Day of Infamy* (New York: Henry Holt, 1957).

270   *The bread and wine are his "tangible truth."*
Tim Dearborn, *Taste and See: Awakening Our Spiritual Senses*
(Downers Grove, Ill.: InterVarsity, 1996).

270   *Jesus didn't give us a theory of the atonement but "an act to perform . . ."*
Tom Wright, *Luke for Everyone* (London: SPCK, 2001), 262.

271   *"Take and eat."*
Matthew 26:26.

272   *"do this in remembrance of me."*
Luke 22:19.

272   *"I am the bread of life."*
John 6:48, 50, 51.

272   *"For whenever you eat this bread . . ."*
1 Corinthians 11:26, emphasis added.

273   *An Episcopal scholar, John Koenig . . .*
*The Feast of the World's Redemption: Eucharistic Origins and
Christian Mission* (Harrisburg, Pa.: Trinity Press International,
2000).

CHAPTER TWENTY-NINE

274   *"Many are wowed by His miracles; few are wooed by His cross."*
à Kempis, *The Imitation of Christ*, 79.

274   *Its victims are "under God's curse."*
Deuteronomy 21:22-23.

275   . . . *the Southern Christian writer, Flannery O'Connor.*
        On her life, see Jean Cash, *Flannery O'Connor: A Life* (Knoxville:
        University of Tennessee Press, 2002).

275   *One of her stories . . . concerns a vulgar dropout named O. E.*
        Parker . . .
        "Parker's Back," in *Everything That Rises Must Converge,* in her
        Collected Works (New York: Library of America, 1988), 655–75. I
        use the term "grotesque" with a meaning similar to how O'Connor
        defines it; cf. "Some Aspects of the Grotesque in Southern
        Fiction," in *Collected Works,* 813–21. Grotesque: the "qualities
        lean away from typical social patterns, toward mystery and the
        unexpected" (815) and that which leads "into an experience of
        mystery itself" (816).

276   *the New Testament sometimes refers to the cross as a "tree."*
        So, for instance, at Galatians 3:13; Acts 5:30.

276   *But the grotesque is necessary, she believes, because the modern*
        reader's . . .
        "Some Aspects of the Grotesque in Southern Fiction," 820.

277   *In fact, the writer of the Book of Hebrews explains something . . .*
        See Hebrews 2:14–18.

277   *In the Garden of Gethsemane . . .*
        The following biblical passages are mentioned or alluded to: Luke
        22:44, 63-64; Mark 15:17, 21, 23; John 19:34.

278   *But the "central Christian belief is that Christ's death has somehow*
        put us right with God . . ."
        Lewis, *Mere Christianity,* 57.

278   *First, Jesus says his death is a "ransom . . ."*
        Mark 10:45; 14:12–26; and John 19:14 are the texts considered here.

278   *These three texts open up Jesus' understanding of the Cross.*
        I must add this: The darkness of Mark 15:33 is the outward symbol
        of the inner reality of the Son's separation from the Father as he
        absorbs sin on our behalf.

279   *As John Stott explains, "Before we can begin to . . ."*
        The Cross of Christ (Downers Grove, Ill.: InterVarsity, 1986), 59-
        60, 61.

279   *At no place is love for others seen more than when someone gives his life for his friends.*
See John 15:13.

280   *Tertullian, one of our first theologians, said this:*
The Chaplet, or De Corona, chap. 3.

280   *There is no Christianity without the cross, the cross that carries us and the cross that we carry.*
Gordon Wakefield, *Bunyan the Christian* (London: Harper Collins Religious, 1992), 79.

282   *von Hildebrand, who had written on the sacredness of marriage . . ., asked: "Do you expect me . . . "*
See Alice von Hildebrand, *The Soul of a Lion: Dietrich von Hildebrand* (San Francisco: Ignatius, 2000), 310-11.

CHAPTER THIRTY

284   *According to the gospel records, everywhere we look on Easter Day there are little disasters—Jesus is dead and the disciples are full of doubt . . .*
On this and the subsequent comments, see Matthew 28:5; Mark 16:8; Luke 24:11, 13–35; John 20:24–28.

284   *In the history of the Church the following . . .*
There are many good surveys of the evidence and arguments. My favorite remains Murray J. Harris, *Three Crucial Questions about Jesus* (Grand Rapids, Mich.: Baker, 1994), 31–64. A journalistic, very readable account can be read in Lee Strobel, *The Case for Easter* (Grand Rapids, Mich.: Zondervan, 2003). For a full, scholarly discussion of resurrection, see N. T. Wright, *The Resurrection of the Son of God* (Minneapolis: Fortress, 2003).

286   On Margaret Kim Peterson. *Here's how she expressed the disastrous revelation:*
Sing Me to Heaven, 11-12, 147–52.

289   *Peter fails to love Jesus enough to own him as even a friend.*
See Mark 9:31; 14:27–31; 14:66–72; John 21:15–19.

289   *Mary Magdalene, unlike other women . . .*
Luke 8:2; Matthew 27:56, 61; John 20:1–18.

289 *Thomas, after hearing testimony from his fellow apostles . . .*
John 20:25, 28.

289 *The eleven . . . are confused—all of them.*
Matthew 28:17, 18–20, emphasis added.

290 On John Bunyan: There are many editions. For the life of Bunyan,
I recommend Gordon S. Wakefield, *Bunyan the Christian* (San
Francisco: HarperSanFrancisco, 1992); also, I have used the
biographical note of Wilbur Smith in John Bunyan, *The Holy War*
(Chicago: Moody, 1948).

290 *The Englishman, John Bunyan . . .*
Gordon Wakefield, *Bunyan the Christian* (London: Harper Collins
Religious, 1992), 56-57.

290 I found Samuel Coleridge's quotation in:
Smith's introduction to *The Holy War*, 29.

JESUS AND THE GOSPELS

Green, Joel B., Scot McKnight, I. Howard Marshall, eds. *The Dictionary of Jesus and the Gospels.* Downers Grove, Ill.: InterVarsity, 1992. An advanced presentation of the major issues in Gospels studies.

Owens, Virginia Stem. *Looking for Jesus.* Louisville, Ky.: Westminster John Knox, 1998.

Wright, Tom. *Matthew for Everyone.* 2 vols. London: SPCK, 2002. With the next two entries, the finest popular commentaries on the Gospels.

____. *Luke for Everyone.* London: SPCK, 2001.

____. *John for Everyone.* 2 vols. London: SPCK. 2002.

Zarley, Kermit. *The Gospels Interwoven.* Eugene, Ore.: Wipf and Stock, 2002.

SPIRITUAL FORMATION

For the history of Christian thinking about spiritual formation, I recommend:

Alexander, Donald L. ed. *Christian Spirituality: Five Views of Sanctification.* Downers Grove, Ill.: InterVarsity, 1988.

Collins, Kenneth J. ed. *Exploring Christian Spirituality: An Ecumenical Reader.* Grand Rapids, Mich.: Baker, 2000.

Foster, Richard. *Streams of Living Water.* San Francisco: HarperSanFrancisco, 1998.

McGrath, Alister E. *Christian Spirituality: An Introduction.* Oxford: Blackwell, 1999.

For some of the leading thinkers in the modern-day discussion, I recommend:

Bonhoeffer, Dietrich. *Discipleship.* Translated by Barbara Green and Reinhard Krauss. Minneapolis: Fortress, 2001.

Foster, Richard. *Celebration of Discipline,* rev. ed. San Francisco: Harper & Row, 1988.

____. *Freedom of Simplicity.* San Francisco: Harper & Row, 1981.

____. *The Challenge of the Disciplined Life.* San Francisco: Harper & Row, 1985.

_____. *Prayer.* San Francisco: Harper & Row, 1992.

Larsen, David. *Biblical Spirituality.* Grand Rapids, Mich.: Kregel, 2001.

Lewis, C. S. *The Pilgrim's Regress.* Grand Rapids, Mich.: Eerdmans, 1981.

_____. *The Screwtape Letters.* San Francisco: HarperSanFrancisco, 2001.

_____. *Mere Christianity.* New York: Macmillan, 1960.

Mathewes-Green, Frederica. *The Illumined Heart.* Brewster, Mass.: Paraclete, 2001.

Merton, Thomas. *The Inner Experience: Notes on Contemplation.* San Francisco: HarperSanFrancisco, 2003.

Mulholland, M. Robert. *Shaped by the Word,* rev. ed. Nashville: Upper Room, 2000.

Ortberg, John. *The Life You've Always Wanted.* Grand Rapids, Mich.: Zondervan, 2002.

Schaeffer, Francis. *True Spirituality.* Wheaton, Ill.: Tyndale, 1971.

Schmemann, Father Alexander. *The Journals of Father Alexander Schmemann, 1973–1983.* Crestwood, N.Y.: St. Vladimir's Seminary Press, 2000.

Thomas, Gary. *Sacred Pathways.* Nashville: Nelson, 1996.

Vest, Norvene. *Gathered in the Word.* Nashville: Upper Room, 1996.

von Hildebrand, Donald. *Transformation in Christ.* San Francisco: Ignatius, 2001.

Warren, Rick. *The Purpose-Driven Life.* Grand Rapids, Mich.: Zondervan, 2002.

Willard, Dallas. *The Spirit of the Disciplines.* San Francisco: HarperSanFrancisco, 1988.

_____. *The Divine Conspiracy.* San Francisco: HarperSanFrancisco,1998.

_____. *The Renovation of the Heart.* Colorado Springs, Colo.: NavPress, 2002.

Here is a (very) partial listing of some classical studies of spiritual formation:

à Kempis, Thomas. *The Imitation of Christ: How Jesus Wants Us to Love.* Translated by William Griffin. San Francisco: HarperSanFrancisco, 2000. For those who would prefer a more sober translation, I recommend E. M. Blaiklock, trans., *The Imitation of Christ.* London: Hodder & Stoughton, 1979; or that of Hal M. Helms, *The Imitation of Christ.* Brewster, Mass.: Paraclete, 1982.

Augustine, *The Confessions*. Translated by Philip Burton; introduction by
    Robin L. Fox. New York: Knopf, 2001.

Bonaventure. *The Journey of the Mind to God*. Translated by Philotheus
    Boehner. Edited by Stephen Brown. Indianapolis: Hackett, 1993.

Brother Lawrence. *The Practice of the Presence of God*. Brewster, Mass.:
    Paraclete, 1985.

Bunyan, John. *Pilgrim's Progress in Modern English*. Edited by James H.
    Thomas. Chicago: Moody, 1964.

Eternal Wisdom from the Desert. Edited by Henry L. Carrigan Jr.
    Brewster, Mass.: Paraclete, 2001.

Fénelon, François de. *The Seeking Heart*. Jacksonville, Fla.: Christian
    Books, 1982.

____. *Talking with God*. Brewster, Mass.: Paraclete, 1997.

Gregory of Nyssa. *The Life of St. Macrina*. Translated by K. Corrigan.
    Toronto: Peregrina, 2001.

John of the Cross. *Selected Writings*. New York: Paulist, 1987.

Laubach, Frank. *Man of Prayer*. Syracuse, N.Y.: Laubach Literacy
    International, 1990. This includes various of his books: *Letters by
    a Modern Mystic, Learning the Vocabulary of God, You Are My
    Friends, Game with Minutes, Prayer: The Mightiest Force in the
    World, Channels of Spiritual Power, Two Articles on Prayer*.

Law, William. *A Serious Call to a Devout and Holy Life*. Grand Rapids,
    Mich.: Eerdmans, 1966.

____. *A Practical Treatise upon Christian Perfection*. Eugene, Ore.: Wipf
    and Stock, 2001.

The Philokalia. Compiled by St. Nikodimos of the Holy Mountain and
    St. Markarios of Corinth, 4 vols. Translated by G. E. H. Palmer,
    Philip Sherrard, and Kallistos Ware. London: Faber and Faber,
    1979-1984.

St. Benedict. *Preferring Christ: A Devotional Commentary and Workbook
    on the Rule of Saint Benedict*. Edited by Norvene Vest. Trabuco
    Canyon, Calif.: Source Books, 2001.

St. Francis. *The Little Flowers of St. Francis*. Garden City, N.Y.:
    Doubleday/Image, 1958.

St. Ignatius. *The Spiritual Exercises of St. Ignatius*. Translated by Louis
    J. Puhl. New York: Random/Vintage, 2000.

St. Teresa of Avila. *The Way of Perfection*. Brewster, Mass.: Paraclete,
    2000.

A few Jewish studies are:

Borowitz, Eugene and Frances W. Schwartz. *The Jewish Moral Virtues.*
    Philadelphia: Jewish Publication Society, 1999.
Buber, Martin. *Tales of the Hasidism,* 2 vols. New York: Schocken, 1947.
Heschel, Abraham. *Moral Grandeur and Spiritual Audacity: Essays.*
    Edited by Susannah Heschel. New York: Farrar, Straus and
    Giroux/Noonday, 1996.

Learn to live the *Jesus Creed*

A Companion Guide to
THE JESUS CREED
by Scot McKnight

ISBN: 1-55725-412-5
80 pages
USA $5.95

Designed for group or individual use, *A Companion Guide to The Jesus Creed* is perfect for Bible study groups, classes, or personal devotions. Each of the thirty sessions begins with reciting the *Jesus Creed* and ends with the Lord's Prayer. In between, Scot McKnight helps you follow the *Jesus Creed* in your life through:

• Reflections that summarize the theme of each chapter in *The Jesus Creed.*
• Prayers inspired by *The Jesus Creed.*
• Exercises to help you internalize the *Jesus Creed.*
• Scriptures that invite you to delve deeply into the Gospels to learn more about how the *Jesus Creed* shaped the lives of Jesus and his followers.

"As I worked through the daily exercises in *The Jesus Creed*, I found myself drawn to Jesus in obedience and worship. I am eager to recommend *The Jesus Creed* to others who want to pursue genuine, Christian spiritual formation."
—Steve Ratliff, Pastor
Faith Evangelical Free Church, Manhattan, KS

A Companion Guide to The Jesus Creed is available at your local bookstore and www.paracletepress.com.

The Jesus Creed and *A Companion Guide to The Jesus Creed* are available at special quantity discounts for bulk purchases for churches, hospitals, hospices, libraries, and schools. For more information, call Paraclete Press: 1-800-451-5006.